SOCIAL CONSTRUCTION AND THE LOGIC OF MONEY

SUNY series in Global Politics

James N. Rosenau, editor

A complete listing of books in this series can be found at the end of this volume.

Social Construction and the Logic of Money

Financial Predominance and International Economic Leadership

J. Samuel Barkin

State University of New York Press

Published by
STATE UNIVERSITY OF NEW YORK PRESS, ALBANY

Printed in the United States of America

For information, address State University of New York Press, 90 State Street, Suite 700, Albany, NY 12207

Production by Kelli Williams
Marketing by Michael Campochiaro

Library of Congress Cataloging-in-Publication Data

Barkin, J. Samuel, 1965–
Social construction and the logic of money : financial predominance and international economic leadership / J. Samuel Barkin.
p. cm. — (SUNY series in global politics)
Includes bibliographical references and index.
ISBN 0-7914-5581-5 (HC ACID FREE) — ISBN 0-7914-5582-3 (PB ACID FREE)
1. Finance–History. 2. International economic relations–History.
3. Money–History. 4. Leadership–History. I. Title. II. Series.

HG171.B37 2003
332'.042–dc21 2002002468

10 9 8 7 6 5 4 3 2 1

Contents

Acknowledgments

This book has had a long gestation. Its successes are due to the help of many people; its failures are, alas, mine alone. It began life as a doctoral thesis. At this stage it was shepherded along by a number of faculty at Columbia University, who provided constructive criticism and institutional guidance. These include David Baldwin, Robert Jervis, Edward Mansfield, William McNeil, Helen Milner, Jack Snyder, and Hendrik Spruyt.

It is often the case in graduate school that one can learn as much from one's fellow students as from one's professors. Kate McNamara and James McAllister read the entirety of an earlier version of this manuscript and provided invaluable commentary. For their help on this project more generally, including at times much needed moral support, I thank Bruce Cronin, Martin Malin, George Shambaugh, and Patricia Weitsman.

In this project's more recent incarnations, Eric Helleiner read the manuscript at two different stages, and contributed both thoughtful commentary and needed encouragement. Roger Haydon and, more recently, Peter Katzenstein, also provided welcome and useful comments, as have a number of anonymous reviewers.

A number of foundations and institutions have provided financial and administrative support for this project over the years. The MacArthur Foundation, through an Interdisciplinary Fellowship in International Conflict, Peace, and Security, and the Olin Institute at Harvard University's Center for International Affairs each supported a year of work on the project. The Social Sciences and Humanities Research Council of Canada supported two years' work. And unrequited administrative support was provided at various times by the Centre for International and Security Studies at York University, the Government Department of Colby College, and the Political Science Department at Wellesley College.

My greatest debt of thanks for help and support in this project goes to Beth DeSombre (pronounced dee-som-bree), who read and commented on the manuscript at several stages, and helped bring the project along through these stages. I owe her thanks for a wide range of other things as well, but that's outside the scope of these acknowledgments. Finally, a profound thanks to my parents for doing so well all those things that we count on parents to do.

1

Financial Predominance and International Economic Leadership

When crisis hits the international economy, the world looks to the United States for leadership. The American dollar remains the world's primary reserve and trading currency, and the preferred safe haven for wealth when there is trouble elsewhere. There are multilateral institutions designed specifically to take the politics out of the management of the international political economy, to make it a rule-based rather than a power-based system. But these institutions remain beholden to the United States, both for their financing and their decision-making. The United States in other words, whether by its intention, the intentions of others, or simply as a result of the structure of the global economy, is an international economic and monetary leader. But this leadership has raised questions. How committed is the United States to international leadership? How has its ability to lead been affected by the various changes in relative capabilities and institutional structure in the past quarter century? How has it been affected by the end of the Cold War?

The role of the United States as an economic leader is complicated by other political roles that it plays in the international arena. A country can lead militarily, ideologically, diplomatically. Leadership is sometimes seen by contemporary analysts as a general phenomenon, in which a country acts hegemonically with respect to all aspects of the international system.[1] But various aspects of international leadership need not correlate, and historically have not always done so. Moreover, there is no reason to expect that they will necessarily do so in the future. International economic leadership, as it is understood here, does not require military predominance, and does not require broad diplomatic leadership outside of the economic sphere. It requires only that a country be willing to provide a commercial infrastructure to the international economy of the sort that governments try to provide for their domestic economies.

One can thus make some generalizations about the role of international economic and monetary leaders. They all fulfill forms of the functions that, as we saw earlier, the United States is looked to for today. They supply international commerce with a core currency, they act as a focus for confidence in the economic systems that they lead, and they provide the source for the norms and rules through which the system operates.[2] But beyond these generalities, different leaders lead in different ways, and create very different international economic systems. Leaders do not lead purely for the good of the system; they act also (perhaps primarily) to pursue their own interests as they see them, and interests can vary substantially across time and place. These interests can be purely economic, but can also be driven by security concerns or ideology. To understand how the global economy got to where it is and to speculate on where it might be going, we must understand the role of the United States in leading it for the past half century, and have insight into what paths this leadership might take in the future. To understand this particular example of leadership, we must understand the broader phenomenon, the patterns that international economic and monetary leadership can take and the constraints on it.

International economic and monetary leadership is not a new phenomenon. From the beginning of the evolution of the contemporary global economy in medieval times, there have always been economic centers that were looked to for commercial and monetary leadership and that had overwhelming influence in the creation of the norms and rules that governed economic transactions across political units.[3] The banking centers of Northern Italy and the trading centers of the Hanseatic League in Northern Europe were the catalysts for processes of economic expansion that led directly to the evolution of the global market that we have today. Since that time, periods of sustained expansion of international economic activity have been associated with leadership by specific political units, originally cities and for the last several hundred years states.[4]

Similarly, the study of international economic leadership is not a particularly new one in the field of international political economy. It has been periodically going in and out of vogue for some three decades now.[5] Yet studies of this phenomenon have tended to be, in the end, unsatisfying; they have focused on either the generalities of leadership, or certain specific historical examples, but have not succeeded in integrating the two. One study might, for example, find general measures that predict when leadership might happen,[6] another might trace the particular trajectory of a leader's participation in the management of an international monetary system.[7] The former is of limited specific utility; international economic leadership is a broad category of behaviors, and thus predicting simply its presence or absence gets us only one small step along the path to understanding the phenomenon. Furthermore, finding predictors of economic policy that work across historical eras is a tricky proposition, as economic measures, the technologies of commerce, and even basic understandings of the nature of economics change.[8] The latter, the historically specific study, is a necessary precondition for the study of the broader category of international economic leadership, but without historical comparison, without analysis in a broader context, it does not by itself constitute such a study.

The phrase 'international economic and monetary leadership' is used here with a specific, and narrow, definition. It refers to the provision to the international political economy of a particular set of infrastructural public goods, to be discussed in the next chapter. This book makes no argument about broader patterns of leadership or hegemony in international politics. How does one center of economic decision-making come to be the source of this particular kind of leadership? What forms can this leadership take, and what is the relationship on the one hand between domestic politics and national interest in these leaders, and on the other hand between the expressed national interest and the structure and norms of the international economic system that the leader builds around it? The purpose of this book is to put the phenomenon of international economic leadership into this broader context. Doing so requires both a discussion of the phenomenon as a general form, and an exploration of patterns of leadership as specific historical events. The starting point for this exploration is the year 1600, when the city of Amsterdam first appeared at the focal point of the European trading system. This appearance marked, arguably for the first time, the emergence of a truly global economy, and of a truly global economic leader, as distinct from the pattern of overlapping regional systems that had been the case previously. Regional systems remain, but the past four centuries have been remarkable for the ultimate reliance of all these systems on one central focal point.

THE ARGUMENT

The two questions previously posed can be restated in their simplest form: When will a country become an international economic leader, and what will the content of its leadership be? These two questions are distinct, but related. The answer to each depends on a number of factors, both structural constraints delimiting the scope for action, and forms of political interaction that enable the expression of interests as state policy. The logic of international finance provides a basic structure by which both states and markets are constrained; prevailing commercial technologies and accepted understandings of how economies work provide the backdrop against which decisions are made; political structures supply the conduits through which various kinds of interests are expressed, mediated, even created. It is through the interactions of these various factors in their specific historical settings that the questions posed by this book can be addressed.

The answer to the first question, that of when countries become leaders, depends on two factors, which will be referred to here as capabilities and motivation. A country has the capabilities when it possesses the requisite resources for leadership, however those resources might be defined. Motivation refers to the desire to lead, and more specifically to the set of interests that policy-makers wish to see addressed. Most studies of leadership to date have focused on one or the other of these factors, either trying to create specific measures of when a country is likely to adopt a leadership role or discussing why a country might want to become a leader, and what sort of leader it is then likely to be.[9] The two factors cannot, though, be successfully isolated. A country without sufficient capabilities, it is true, will lack the economic wherewithal to lead effectively. It can try, but it is unlikely to succeed. Britain during the periods of reconstruction following both of the twentieth century's world wars, for example, would have liked to recreate its late-nineteenth-century leadership role, but did not have the financial wherewithal to do so.

But one cannot reasonably infer that countries that have the capabilities will then choose to lead, or assume that their leadership will be of a specific type; capabilities are necessary, but are not sufficient. By the same token, one cannot infer from arguments about the motivations of a specific leader, be it Britain in the nineteenth century or the United States more recently, what leadership in general entails. For example, British economic leadership in the second half of the nineteenth century was largely unilateralist, which is to say not particularly dependent on the policies of other countries. In contrast, American leadership in the second half of the twentieth century involved an important element of multilateralism, action taken only in concert with others. At the same time, British diplomatic policy was somewhat divorced from foreign economic policy whereas American diplomatic policy was intimately intertwined with foreign economic policy. Both were leaders, but their patterns and methods of leadership differed in fundamental ways.

In other words, discussion of international economic leadership as a general phenomenon can mask important, even fundamental, differences in the foreign economic policy of the leader, and in the shape of the system of global commercial exchange that the leader underwrites. What explains these differences? To a certain extent, as with all histories, the differences can be described as historical fluke, as the result of a set of individual decisions by individual decision-makers that cumulatively lead to a result that was never part of any grand design. And these decisions are affected by the broader global contexts, both physical and political, in which leaders find themselves. The institutions of international commerce, for example, are necessarily going to be different in a computerized world than they were before the discovery of electricity, and economic leadership in a bipolar world may well be a victim of very different geopolitical pressures than the equivalent in a multipolar world.[10]

But differences in patterns of leadership are generated not only by forces outside of the leader and accidents within it. They depend to an important degree on the reason that policy-makers within the country chose foreign economic policies that fulfill the functions of leadership in the first place. In other words, they stem from differences in motivation. Put simply, policies of international economic leadership entail certain costs to the country that undertakes them, the opportunity costs of benefits that might have been had from following other policies. It is therefore reasonable to expect that decision-makers will want to have good reasons for accepting these opportunity costs and engaging in leadership behavior.[11] Leadership policies, as we shall see, benefit some domestic groups, some sets of domestic economic interests, at the expense of others. The willingness of a country to act as an international economic leader depends to an important degree on the ability of those who benefit to affect national foreign economic policy-making. An important input into the form of leadership chosen is the relative domestic political strength of those who benefit from leadership, and the policy demands of other interest groups that would rather use the means of national foreign economic policy to pursue other goals.

In short, then, the two factors of capabilities and motivation must be addressed in tandem. It is only by combining the two that we can understand, for example, why at the onset of the Great Depression in 1929–1930 Great Britain tried to act as leader and failed, and the United States was looked to as a leader but failed to try.[12] Britain was motivated but not capable, the United States was capable but not motivated. A more nuanced reading of national capabilities can tell us much about the potential strength of leadership, and a more nuanced reading of patterns of national motivation, and the domestic politics underlying those motivations, can help to answer the question of what the content of international economic leadership will be under a given leader.

Which begs the question of what gives states the capabilities to act successfully as leaders, and what motivates them to want to do so. A variety of different answers have been given to this question, ranging from broad measures of aggregate size in general to export performance in particular.[13] The argument here is that it is one very specific activity that both empowers and motivates a country to act as leader: international finance, defined as investment in other countries and in the mechanisms of international trade and commerce. A country that is predominant in international finance will be capable of acting as a leader, whether or not it is dominant internationally in other fields, be they economic or military. Conversely, a country that is not financially predominant will not be able to act as an economic leader, even if it does predominate in other economic fields, or in military capability.

At the same time, the internationalist financial community, those who invest in the international economy, have a vested interest in providing leadership, because the provision of leadership to the international economy increases the profitability of investing in it. This logic applies to international financial interests whether or not they reside in financially predominant countries, but only when they do can they participate in a domestic political process that will generate leadership. They will not necessarily succeed in getting the foreign economic policies that they want; capabilities do not always generate motivation. The degree of success of the internationalist financial community in a country with the capabilities to lead the international economy will depend on a number of factors, including the importance of income earned internationally to the domestic economy, the structure of the domestic political system, the ideological and technological milieu in which policy is being made, and the particularities of personality and circumstance. The strength, and indeed the form, of leadership depend on their success.

The idea that financial motivations underlie foreign policy is not a new one. It was, for example, the subject of a debate among leading Marxist theorists of international economics early in the twentieth century. But these theorists argued that the concentration of international finance would lead either to world war or world government.[14] The argument here is that the concentration of international finance can lead a country to provide a financial infrastructure to the international economy, without necessarily leading to either military conflict or political confederation. And that the more diffuse international finance becomes, the less likely it is that this sort of leadership will be forthcoming. The next chapter will elaborate on this argument, and provide the logic that links finance and leadership. The bulk of this book will then examine the argument empirically, through the lens of four case studies of leadership or its failure.

THE METHODOLOGY

There is already a substantial body of literature on the subject of international economic leadership.[15] This literature encompasses a variety of different disputes, both empirical and theoretical. One of the disputes that threads its way through much of the literature concerns the effects of leadership; is a leader really necessary to stabilize the international economy? This question has been addressed both theoretically and empirically, yielding a range of answers. Some argue that leadership is necessary for stability, others that it has little effect. Some argue that the benefits of leadership accrue primarily to the leader itself, others that in the long run leadership benefits the leader relatively less than its followers.[16] Finally, some argue that an individual leader is required, others that collective action among states can be an effective substitute for the leadership of an individual state.[17] This study speaks to all of these questions, which in turn provide the topic of discussion for most of the concluding chapter.

Another of the differences among entrants in this literature is methodological. Different studies tend to adopt one of two distinct approaches to the analysis of international leadership, one focused on systemic comparisons and the other on specific case studies. Those in the former group argue that a state that displays a certain characteristic will behave in a certain way. Examples run from Leninist theory, in which large-scale exporters of capital inevitably come to act as aggressive imperialists, to more recent work of quantitative or formal bents, which posit that states of a given size will, out of economic self-interest, act in a given way. These quantitative and formal analyses span the various disputes concerning the necessity of leadership, but tend to display a preference for objective measures as indicators of the positions of states in the international system, generally some measure of power or of relative economic size.

This methodological preference for the objective tends also to extend to discussions of motivation. Systemic comparisons usually address questions of motivation, implicitly if not explicitly, but generally do so by ascribing to states preferences based on generalized assumptions of national interest that do not allow for variations either across states or across time. States are usually assumed to act in a way that maximizes rational utility, understood as the maximization of anything from aggregate national income to exports, either gross or net. Marxist theories suggest that the interest being maximized is that of a particular class, the financial elite, but assume that state policy is captive to the interests of this class, meaning that the state will still act to maximize a given rational utility, that of a class rather than that of the population as a whole. Thus the discussion of motivation in this branch of the study of international economic leadership focuses on explaining why a state with a given level of capabilities would act (or not act) as a particular kind of leader, but does not allow for variations in the type of leadership engaged in. States, in short, are categorized by size rather than by content.

In contrast, studies that focus on specific cases of leadership (or of the absence thereof) tend to incorporate the subjective, discussions of what policy-makers thought they were doing rather than objective measures to predict what they would do. In his classic study of the Great Depression, for example, Charles Kindleberger ascribes the set of decisions by the United States to undermine rather than lead the international economic system in the late 1920s and early 1930s to American irresponsibility as much as anything else.[18] One can certainly infer from this argument that in the future, when global depression looms, countries that are able to do so should try to act as leaders. However, one cannot reasonably infer from arguments about what states *should* do that they will do it. Similarly, P. J. Cain and A. G.

Hopkins discuss the evolution of British imperialism from the mercantilism of the eighteenth century to the liberalism of the nineteenth in terms of the social norms underlying British domestic politics.[19] This sort of empirical approach is invaluable in understanding specific national decisions about whether or not to adopt leadership policies, and necessary in explaining the specific patterns of and political choices reflected by those policies. By the same token, though, it is of much more limited value in understanding patterns of international economic leadership more broadly.

This distinction between a focus on objective, measurable data and on subjective or interpretive history mirrors a key contemporary methodological debate in international relations theory, between materialist and constructivist approaches. At its most extreme, a pure materialist approach would have it that only objectively measurable data are appropriate to the scientific study of international politics. Conversely, a pure social constructivist approach would deny any materialist base, arguing that the international system is a pure social construct, not guided by any inherent logic. Most theorists of international relations would likely locate themselves somewhere between these two extremes, but this still leaves a wide scope for methodological disagreement. Specifying the point on the materialist/constructivist spectrum that a particular study is starting from can be very useful as a shorthand for the methodological assumptions on which the study is based. The point of departure for this study is what has been called a thin constructivism.[20]

Constructivism is an epistemology of international relations that looks at both the structure of the international system and the identities and interests of actors within that system as social constructions, as sets of shared ideas and norms rather than as the result of brute material forces.[21] A thick constructivism is one that tends toward the post-positivist.[22] It questions any attempt to study international relations objectively, or "scientifically."[23] A thin constructivism is one that accepts a basic tenet of modern science, that one can proceed with research assuming a clear distinction between researcher and data, between the student and the studied. In other words, a thin constructivism argues that the data of international relations are intersubjective rather than material, based on social constructions rather than natural logic.

Most constructivists would accept that some natural logic comes into play in social science. At a minimum, people need to eat to survive. There is some debate as to how relevant these logics are to the actual structure and conduct of contemporary international politics; most constructivists would argue that they are not particularly relevant.[24] For a study of international economic leadership, however, choosing a single point on this spectrum of relevance can be unnecessarily limiting. A traditional materialist argument would be that there is an inherent logic to an international political economy, an inherent logic to a system of economic exchange among autonomous political entities without central authority. It is by specifying this logic that we can understand patterns of leadership. The constructivist response would be that the international political economy is a social construct, and is thus historically specific. To understand the content of a particular episode of international economic leadership, we must examine the particular social construction of that episode in its own historical context.

The contention of this book is that a full study of international economic leadership must encompass both the natural logic of economics and the social construction of international politics. The seminal question of whether or not there is an objective logic to international relations can, in this instance, be avoided by looking at only a particular subset of systems of political economy, those in which states with authority over their own legal and monetary systems interact on a market basis.[25] Looking at this subset of systems assumes a given set of intersubjective parameters. It assumes that a modern state system and patterns of market exchange have already been socially constructed. This limits the scope of the study, but still encompasses much of the international political economy over the past four hundred years, and its likely form through the foreseeable future.

Once this sort of system has been socially constructed, and to the extent that it defines actor interests, it does become constrained by its own internal inherent logic, the logic of systems of market/monetary exchange that is the basis of the study of economics. This logic allows us to do two things. We can draw the connection between predominance in international finance and the capabilities to lead. Successful leadership requires that a country, among other things, underwrite a currency for international exchange and provide liquidity to the international political economy, and both these activities, as argued in the next chapter, require of the leader a reserve of international assets that is secure from the speculations of others. The logic of systems of market/monetary exchange also allows us to draw a connection between investment in international finance and motivation to lead. A well-led system, as the next chapter also argues, maximizes returns to this sort of investment. This means that it is in the direct interest of the holders of this investment to promote international economic leadership.

But this logic is by itself insufficient either to predict or explain particular instances of leadership. It is insufficient to predict an outbreak of leadership because the motivations of the internationalist financial community within the country in question do not translate directly into national policy. They are mediated through the constructs of domestic politics, and are integrated with the policy demands of other interest groups. Both the constructs of and the conflicting interests within the domestic polity of the state in question are historically specific, are the expressions of the social context and intersubjective milieu of that polity. Whether a country will adopt leadership policies depends on the outcomes of these processes of mediation and integration. The logic inherent to market/monetary systems is insufficient to explain, or even to describe, particular instances of leadership because both the outcomes of these domestic processes and the norms of international contexts within which foreign economic policy operates are historically contingent.

For this reason, this study adopts a thin constructivist approach that is particularly cognizant of the limiting role of logics inherent in certain social constructs. These limitations mean that even though an international economic system based on market and monetary exchange is a social construct, within the bounds of this construct the logic of the system dictates that certain objectively measurable financial data both enable and constrain state foreign economic policy. The case studies examine both these international financial data, the objective distribution of investment across the international economy, and the contingent social constructs within which these investments are made. The former helps us to predict when leadership will be feasible, and gives us an indication of the relative strength of internationalist financial interests within the potential leader. The latter explain both the strength and the design of leadership policies. This methodology entails an examination of such objective measures as financial statistics and governmental types, and also of the intersubjective context within which policy is made. Elements of this context include such things as the normative structure of the practice of domestic politics, the existing consensus on economic theory and on the relationship between politics and economics, and the norms and practices of the international system for which the foreign economic policy is being made.

THE CASE STUDIES

Chapter 2 discusses the arguments made to this point in more detail. The following four chapters look at four historical cases, ordered chronologically and covering the majority of the past four centuries of international political economy. These cases are the role of Dutch leadership in the international political economy of the seventeenth century, the role of British leadership in the nineteenth, the failure of leadership in the period between the two world wars of the twentieth century, and the role of American leadership in the reconstruction of an international political economy following World War Two. Taken as a set, these four cases encompass a broad sweep of the history of the evolution of our contemporary international political economy. Individually, each case presents its own theoretical and empirical puzzles, making each both methodologically and historically intriguing in its own right.

The first case begins at the dawn of the seventeenth century, and looks at the role of the Netherlands and its various component political entities in the rapid expansion of international commerce at the time. The Dutch-led system marked a transition from the set of loosely connected regional political economies that were the norm beforehand to the more integrated and global pattern of international commerce that has been the norm since. As a comparative case in international economic leadership the Dutch case is particularly interesting, for three reasons. The first is the patterns of domestic politics within the United Provinces of the Netherlands. International economic policy was made at three different levels of government, the federal, provincial, and civic levels, each of which was authoritative in different issue areas. This allows for a comparative study of the relationship between finance and leadership within a single historical case. The second is the role that the United Provinces played on the broader stage of international politics of the time, a role much more circumscribed than the roles of the economic leaders that have followed. This allows us to look at economic leadership in isolation from political and military leadership. Finally, Dutch foreign economic policy was not embedded in a liberal ideology, which allows us a broader scope for comparative study of the role of ideology in leadership.

The second case, Great Britain from the middle of the nineteenth century to the eve of World War One, is often seen as the classic example of international economic leadership; no historical study of the phenomenon would be complete without it. But historical studies of British economic leadership often fail to illuminate both the question of what made Britain capable of acting as a leader, and the question of what motivated the British government to choose to do so. A link is often drawn between industrial exports, the role of Great Britain as the original home of the industrial revolution, and British foreign economic policy. But this link does not stand up well to historical scrutiny, not nearly as well as a link between the British position in international finance and its foreign economic policy. This case is a methodologically interesting one because it shows a clear and direct link between finance and leadership in an instance when the leader was economically predominant in several other ways as well.

The third case centers on a question that has often been asked: What went wrong in the Great Depression? Why was the depression in the business cycle that began in 1929 so bad, why did it last so long, and how was it allowed to undermine international commerce as thoroughly as it did? One answer to these questions is the absence of leadership; the internationalization of the Great Depression is often ascribed to "beggar-thy-neighbor" policies, in which countries act in their own short-term interests at the expense of the good of the system as a whole, and no one acts in the interests of the system. In other words, there was no effective international economic leader; this case allows us to study the failure of leadership, as well as its success.

Finally, the fourth case looks at the leadership role of the United States in the creation and management of the international economic system that came out of World War Two. The role of the United States in this period was in many ways broader than that of Great Britain a century earlier, in that its leadership encompassed both a more formal security role and a multilateral system of formal economic institutions and rules. It was in ways, however, shallower as well. The institutional structure excluded that part of the world that was on the other side of the Cold War; much of it failed to last much more than a quarter of a century; and the American commitment to maintaining its leadership wavered rather more than the British commitment had. Why would the United States choose to take on a broader international economic role than had Britain and yet be less committed to fulfilling that role? Looking at the postwar case through the lens of this question allows us to contrast the comparative roles of capabilities and motivations in the construction of forms of international economic leadership.

The conclusion summarizes and aggregates the findings of the case studies, and puts these in the perspective of the framework presented in Chapter 2. It also addresses the broader applicability of the methodology used here. It then asks what these findings, and this framework, suggest about international economic leadership in the near- to medium-term future. The answer is that they point to a role for constructive regionalism that is perhaps greater than at any time since the economy became global around 1600. At a time when the future of the international financial architecture is much under discussion, the dialectic of the logic of international economic leadership and the normative structure of the international political economy suggests the time may well be right for the architecture to be reconstructed regionally, rather than globally.

2

Social Construction and the Logic of Money

There are two key arguments in this book. The first is that the study of international economic and monetary leadership is best approached using a combination of rationalist and constructivist methodologies. In particular, the dialectics of the inherent logic of monetary systems and the social construction of historically specific political structures are synthesized in particular episodes of leadership. The second key argument is that, on the rationalist side of this equation, the logic of leadership is one specifically of international finance, in particular of what is called here financial predominance. On the constructivist side of the equation there is no generic logic, only historical contexts.

Within both the rationalist and constructivist arguments, states are affected in their policy-making choices by forces both external and internal. On the rationalist side, the argument made here involves both the capabilities of a country with respect to the rest of the international economic system in which it is located, and its motivation to lead, which is related to the importance of international finance to the broader national economy. On the constructivist side, leaders are constrained by the norms and practices of the international communities within which they find themselves. The sorts of leadership policies that financially predominant countries choose to lead with, given these constraints, are dependent on the social structure of the domestic polity. This chapter expands on these arguments in this order. A prior task, though, is to define that which is ultimately being explained by these arguments, international economic leadership.

INTERNATIONAL ECONOMIC LEADERSHIP

International economic and monetary leadership is used here with a very specific meaning. As employed here, it means the reliable provision by a country of infrastructural public goods to the international economy. These goods are infrastructural in that they provide a regularized and reliable financial and regulatory framework within which an economy can function with increased confidence. Before discussing this definition in more detail, it is worth stressing again what this book is *not* about. It is not about hegemony more broadly, however defined. Leaders as defined here may or may not engage in some form of predatory hegemony at the same time as providing infrastructural goods to the international economy; this argument does not speak to that issue one way or another.[1] This book is also not about leadership in the realm of ideology or security affairs. A final caveat is that leadership is judged here by the infrastructure provided, not by the apparent enthusiasm with which the leader provides it. For example, some analysts have noted that the British government played a fairly passive role in the late-nineteenth-century international political economy,[2] whereas the U.S. government was much more politically active after World War Two in attempting to manage that era's international political economy. From the perspective of the argument in this book, this observation is beside the point, because it does not address the quality of the infrastructure provided.

Examples of economic and monetary infrastructural goods include national currencies, countercyclical central bank interest rate policies, and an accepted body of contract law. A national currency makes commerce easier by providing a means of exchange that all parties to a transaction can have confidence in, and the value of which is transparent—that is, known to all. Central bank interest rate policies are often designed to ameliorate the business cycle, by dampening inflationary tendencies during expansion and stimulating growth during recession. Without such policies, business cycles would be more extreme and destabilizing. An accepted body of contract law, by making it clear who owns what and what rights and obligations such ownership entails, should make people more willing to use and invest in their property productively.

Such an economic infrastructure is an attribute, both in theory and in practice, of all advanced market economies, and is provided in domestic economies by national governments. The greater the reliability and consistency with which these goods are provided, the greater the stabilizing effect on the economy to which they are provided. This underlies the incentive toward consistency in domestic economic policy, and it is equally true internationally. An international economy may function without a conscious effort by a leader to maintain its infrastructure, but the more reliable and consistent the provision of a financial and regulatory framework to the international economy, the more efficiently the international market should work.[3] This economic infrastructure is what the neoliberal institutionalist literature refers to as market perfecting, and is one of the primary demands on governments at the domestic level. There should be a demand by the constituency of international economic actors for a similar economic infrastructure to perfect the international market.[4] There is, however, no sovereign body to provide infrastructure internationally.

The seminal work in the contemporary literature on international economic leadership is Charles Kindleberger's *The World in Depression, 1929–1939*. He defines leadership as the provision of public goods to the international economy, which is done by fulfilling the following five functions. A leader must: (1) maintain a relatively open market for distressed goods; (2) provide countercyclical, or at least stable, long-term lending; (3) oversee a relatively stable system of exchange rates; (4) ensure the coordination of macroeconomic policies; and (5) act as a lender of last resort by discounting or otherwise providing liquidity in financial crises.[5] These factors are stated in reference to the world economy at the time of the Great Depression, and are specific to that era. David Lake, in his general overview of hegemonic stability theory, reformulates these goods in simpler and more general terms. He reduces the public goods necessary to provide an international economic infrastructure to three: A medium of international exchange, and secondarily a store of value; the management of liquidity internationally in the long term to allow for economic growth, in the medium term to counter business cycles, and in the short term to manage panics; and a defined and protected set of basic property rights for assets engaged in the international economy.[6] This reformulation both encompasses and expands on Kindleberger's, and allows for a more generalized interpretation of these goods. An international economic leader is thus a country that successfully undertakes those foreign economic policies necessary to ensure the provision of these goods.

What does the provision of these public goods entail in an international context? A medium for international exchange fulfils a role in international commerce similar to the role played by a national currency in domestic commerce. It provides a common measure of value, so that various transactions can be compared against a common standard of economic measurement. It provides continuity in exchange, so that the values on which transactions are predicated remain relatively constant. This increases the extent to which economic actors can reliably commit themselves to commercial exchanges because it decreases the risk that the values involved will fluctuate unpredictably over the course of an economic relationship. And finally, it provides a store of value, which increases the ability of economic actors to plan and invest in the long term, by increasing confidence that the future values of their investments will be predictable.[7] In Coasian terms, these roles of a stable currency help to perfect the markets using it by increasing transparency, decreasing transaction costs, and improving property rights.[8]

National currencies have not always been the norm, and economic actors have used either subnational currencies or foreign currencies as their basic units of exchange.[9] But governments in most contemporary market economies try to provide a currency of exchange, and try for the most part to keep it as stable as possible. Similarly, the international economy can function without a currency for international exchange, but, other things being equal, should function more efficiently with one. In other words, a currency for international exchange should help to perfect international markets. Such a currency does not replace national currencies, but provides a standard for determining the values underlying international commercial exchange, sets a standard of value against which other currencies are valued and stabilized, and provides a reliable store of value for international economic actors when other currencies are threatened.

To a certain extent, the existence of a currency for international exchange is independent of the foreign economic policy of the government that issues and manages that currency. It is, after all, the decision of other actors, both national and economic, whether or not to use the currency as the yardstick of international commerce. But to an important degree policy choices do affect the viability of a currency as this yardstick. Macroeconomic policy affects the stability of a currency, and thus its appeal as a standard of value. Various aspects of economic policy affect the liquidity of a currency, its availability for use internationally, and the extent to which a currency holds its value, the degree to which it is useful as an international store of value.[10] Governments may be tempted for trade reasons, for example, to competitively devalue their currencies, but such a policy serves to make it less useful as a currency for international exchange. Thus the usefulness of a currency as a store of value and medium of exchange depends on a combination of government policy to support the role, and the willingness of users to adopt the currency for that role.[11] Similarly, the efficacy of a currency for international exchange depends both on the economy underlying the currency, which must be able to generate sufficient liquidity to provide enough of the currency to go around, and confidence in the currency, a much more tenuous phenomenon.

The second of the three functions of leadership is the management of liquidity internationally. As with the provision of a medium of exchange, this function mirrors the role played by the institutions of the state domestically. A number of state institutions participate in this function domestically. In the short term, central banks manage panics by acting as lenders of last resort, injecting liquidity into the financial system during financial crises. In the medium term, governments act through both central banks and treasuries to stabilize the liquidity in the system throughout the business cycle. Acting through both monetary and fiscal policy, they attempt to restrain the growth of liquidity in the system during periods of expansion and encouraging it during downturns in the cycle. In the long term, governments act to reduce impediments to commerce, to allow for the expansion of the economy. As was the case with currencies, not all governments will always succeed in managing liquidity effectively, but most governments will, to some extent at least, try.

An international economic leader will need to use a similar set of policy tools to ensure sufficient, and stable, liquidity to the international economy. In the short term, a leader, through its own institutions such as its treasury or central bank, or by encouraging cooperative or private lending, can manage panics by acting as a lender of last resort, lending to threatened institutions abroad.[12] The threatened institutions will in this case usually be other central banks or treasuries. In the medium term a leader can act to stabilize liquidity through the business cycle by using the traditional means of monetary policy; to the extent that the leader's currency is the primary medium for international exchange, the leader's interest rates will affect liquidity to the international system as a whole, as well as domestic liquidity.[13] Countercyclical stabilization can also be promoted through a stable flow of capital from the leader to the international economy, through lending or investment. Finally, in the long term a leader can ensure liquidity internationally by maintaining a core and open market to international trade, and by encouraging others to do the same, thus sustaining demand and encouraging the expansion of the international economy.

The third function of leadership is the definition and protection of a set of property rights for the international political economy.[14] This is perhaps the most basic economic function of governments, as almost all domestic law relevant to commerce (and much other law besides) is about the definition and enforcement of property rights. Without knowing what their rights are to property, to the means of production, and without knowing that those rights can be enforced, economic actors are unlikely to invest in the property, leaving no basis for growth in productivity and hence economic output. Some economic historians go so far as to argue that the history of economic growth in the West can be told entirely as a history of the development of more efficient property rights.[15] At its most straightforward, this third function of leadership entails that a government attempt to do for owners of property engaged in the international economy what they do for those engaged in the domestic economy, help to ensure that they know what their rights are to their property abroad, and to convince them that these rights will be protected.

This final function refers primarily to the act of defining and promoting through economic means a particular set of property rights internationally. It can also include, though, for want of a better term, an "enforcement" function, analogous to the function of police domestically. This involves either providing or arranging for a containment of such violence as would threaten the accepted set of property rights, and thus hinder international economic interactions. This does not mean imposing peace on the world—far from it, in fact. It is much more limited. It entails minimizing nonstate activities designed specifically to prey on international commerce. Fighting piracy is a common example of this sort of enforcement. It also can include minimizing economically damaging violence and wars involving those countries important to, and active in, the international economic system. Enforcement may mean working for general peace, but it may also mean peripheralizing interstate violence by staging proxy wars, or encouraging forms of warfare that do not cause widespread damage to economically productive assets. Finally, if nonacceptance of a set of property rights by parties to the international economy threatens that economy, the enforcement function may include forcing acceptance on those parties.[16]

In the discussion to this point property rights can be understood, as they usually are, as a formal set of rules and procedures delimiting rights and responsibilities. In other words, as law. Property rights can also, however, be understood in a much broader sense, as the general set of understandings of property and of economics that underpins commercial exchange.[17] In other words, property rights can be understood as an accepted set of popular ideas about how the economy, and its institutions, *should* work. For example, German law from the creation of the Bundesrepublik to the onset of EMU clearly gave the Bundesbank, the German central bank, the formal and legal right and responsibility to manage German interest rates so as to ensure domestic price stability.[18] During much of this period American law required the Federal Reserve Board to take both price stability and employment levels into account in the setting of interest rates.[19] Inasmuch as the national currency is the basic store of value in the economy, these laws affected property rights. The difference between these laws can best be explained by different historical experiences, the German with hyperinflation in the 1920s, the American with unemployment in the 1930s.[20] These different historical experiences created different sets of generally accepted understandings, what might be called intersubjective knowledge,[21] of what was most important in the management of that crucial expression of property, the national currency.

Another way of looking at this phenomenon is through the Gramscian concept of common sense. Antonio Gramsci argued that a primary way in which elites maintained their authority over subordinate classes is through common sense, the largely uncritical intellectual process of reacting to, rather than thinking through, situations.[22] To the extent that most people's common sense, their ingrained reaction, to a certain sort of event is similar, that common sense will usually provide either the reference point or the point of departure for policy decisions with respect to that event. The experience with hyperinflation led to a common sense in Germany that hyperinflation is to be avoided at all costs. In the United States, the absence of such an experience meant that this common sense never developed.

Property rights understood in this broader, intersubjective sense can be of great importance to the international political economy, as they serve to define the parameters, or the ground rules, of international cooperation. As suggested by the previous example, these sets of social norms as to what constitutes socioeconomic rectitude, justice, and even knowledge can differ across states.[23] They can differ, in fact, far more than was the case in this example. For instance, the American and Soviet postwar economies were based on fundamentally different sets of intersubjective understandings, on incompatible common senses. Yet for international macroeconomic cooperation to have a solid intersubjective basis, for everyone to have a compatible understanding of how to think about the international political economy, some understandings have to be reached as to which set of social norms is going to underpin the cooperation.[24] Thus a part of the third function of leadership is the internationalization of a common sense, a particular set of understandings as to how things are to be done in the international political economy, a normative structure on which international cooperation and coordination can happen.

FINANCIAL LOGIC AND SOCIAL INSTITUTIONS

The study of international economic leadership, as we saw in Chapter 1, has been approached using the methodological tools of both economics and sociology. The former looks for a logic that is inherent to the practice of international economics, and that as such can be applied to all international economic and monetary systems. The latter looks for the social rules that underpin particular instances of leadership. This distinction between on the one hand a set of clear and objective rules for participants in the international economy to follow, and on the other hand a set of undefined but generally accepted intersubjective understandings that underpin accepted rules in specific historical contexts, points to one of the key tensions that drive this study. The tension goes beyond the issue of international economic leadership; it has been the fundamental point of contention in the debate between rationalists and constructivists in international relations theory for over a decade. The rationalists, be they neorealist or neoliberal, argue that international relations can best be studied as objective science, as a logic that applies transhistorically, whenever a state system is the primary political construct on a regional or global scale.[25] The constructivists argue that there is no transhistorical logic in social science, that international relations are best understood as being based on social constructs that are intersubjective rather than objective and that are historically specific.[26] The argument here draws on both positions; it accepts that political and economic structures and behaviors are historically contingent, but also that given certain of these contingencies there are objective logics that can help us to understand the operation of both structures and behaviors.

Constructivists generally claim that most of what matters in international politics is socially constructed rather that inherent to human nature or to political structure. Alexander Wendt, for example, claims that "anarchy is what states make of it," and speaks of three logics of anarchy,[27] suggesting an indeterminate number of other logics of anarchy that are possible but have not yet been actualized. By implication, he is arguing that there is no inherent logic of anarchy.[28] This may well be the case, but it does not necessarily follow that other socially constructed systems have no inherent logic. The notion of Mutually Assured Destruction (MAD) that underpinned much of the process of nuclear competition and cooperation in the latter half of the Cold War, for example, was clearly a social construction. Yet, once constructed, it had a clear logic that led to the counterintuitive conclusion that ballistic missile defenses are destabilizing.[29] One can certainly imagine an anarchical world not subject to the logic of MAD, yet it is much more difficult to imagine a logic of MAD in which ABM systems add to stability.

The difference between anarchy and MAD is one of specificity of ends. Anarchy is (for want of a better word) a circumstance. It describes a situation, but not a goal. An anarchy in which all of the participants both were faced with a constraining set of circumstances and shared a goal may well turn out to have its own inherent logic. MAD is such an anarchy. The common circumstances were a mutual ideological hostility and the possession of large long-range nuclear arsenals. The common goal[30] was a desire to prevent the use of those arsenals and to constrain the process of nuclear arms racing, without undermining their positions as superpowers. Absent the common circumstances, such as the existence of nuclear weapons, and the inherent logic of MAD becomes irrelevant. The same is true of the absence of collective goals; if one or the other of the superpowers had been more enthusiastic about destroying the other than maintaining the nuclear peace, or about ending the nuclear arms race than maintaining its position as a superpower, the inherent logic of MAD would similarly have become irrelevant. But it would have been inherent nonetheless.

Shared goals will not necessarily impart inherent logics into political and economic systems. But they hold the potential to do so where circumstances would not otherwise dictate commonalities across social constructions. Systems constrain actors by mediating between action and outcome. If actors do not hold a common preference for a particular outcome, then there is no reason that systemic constraints should suggest compatible courses of action. If, however, actors hold a common preference, then systemic constraints should suggest compatible courses of action. The logic of a system does not of course determine the behavior of agents within it. But it can affect the extent to which actors can fulfill the preferences for which they are participating in the system in the first place. This is related to the phenomenon that Robert Jervis calls quasi-homeostasis, in which the interactions of system structure, actor goals, and negative feedback have a self-equilibrating effect on outcomes.[31] Such systems are socially constructed because their inherent logic is only relevant in situations of shared state identities and interests. But the logic is there nonetheless.

The argument here is that monetary systems are more like mutual assured destruction in particular than they are like anarchy in general. In other words, money is not just what states make of it. Note that I speak here of monetary systems in a fairly constrained way; a monetary system is an economic system in which money constitutes the primary means of exchange and the primary store of value.[32] An economic system in which control of the means of production is decided by political rather than market mechanisms, or in which the primary store of value is not money,[33] would not be considered by this definition to be a primarily monetary economic system. Monetary systems, unlike anarchy, share an inherent logic because they involve both common circumstances and collective goals. The common circumstances are economic interaction and a socially accepted definition of what constitutes money. The collective goal is a desire for increased efficiency in economic exchange. Without a socially accepted definition of what constitutes money, a monetary system cannot work, because something only serves as money if it is recognized as such by all parties to an exchange.[34] Without a desire for increased efficiency in economic exchange there is little point to participating in a monetary system in the first place.

Yet money, as any constructivist student of international political economy should insist, is a social construction.[35] A small piece of silver or gold, let alone a rectangle of printed paper, has little intrinsic value. The value of a coin or a monetary bill lies in the fact that we all agree that it has value, and therefore we are all willing to exchange other goods for it. If we did not agree, then it would not functionally be money.[36] The value of money not only is socially constructed, it can be socially deconstructed; the string of currency devaluations in East Asia and Russia in the late 1990s came about because the social consensus values of those currencies changed, even though the currencies themselves had not. Furthermore, social norms as to what can constitute money change over time, in response to new technologies, new ideas, or simply new social conventions. The ancient Romans did not use paper money, not because they did not have the technological capability for it, but simply because nobody had thought of it. The medieval Italians made little use of paper money even though they had been exposed to the idea because it lacked the solidity of gold and silver, and thus to their sensibilities simply did not feel like money should. Common sense in much of the nineteenth and twentieth centuries was that credible money had to be backed by gold, but that has gradually ceased to be the common sense of the contemporary world.[37] Money is thus not an objective phenomenon; it is a social category the full content of which can only be understood in historical context, with respect to a specific time and place.

And yet, at the same time, economists have built an elaborate science around claims of an objective understanding of the logic of money. These claims are based on the idea that there is something inherent in the nature of money that makes monetary systems behave in a certain way.[38] Thus economists can claim, for example, that printing money to cover a government budget deficit is more inflationary than borrowing it, or that having countries produce to their comparative advantages and then trade will maximize current benefit. Most of the contemporary literature on the international political economy (IPE) accepts that this logic governs much of what is going on (although there are numerous disagreements over what exactly the logic of economics entails). In other words, much of the contemporary study of the international political economy, be it from a liberal or mercantilist perspective, accepts that there are certain givens in the way economies work, and therefore that understanding IPE is, to a significant degree at least, an exercise in figuring out what those givens are.

These two approaches to understanding the role of money seem incompatible; one sees money as a historical artifact, the other views it as a transhistorical logic. Yet these two positions are not as irreconcilable as they might seem. One can accept that money is a historically specific artifact, and accept at the same time that societies in which money plays a central role in commercial exchange, in which it has been chosen as the primary unit of account and store of value, will be constrained by it in certain ways. Not all societies, nor all economic systems, allow money a central role in commercial exchange. Barter systems were the norm through much of human history, and systems of authoritative, rather than market-driven, allocations of resources have also been a common occurrence. For example, Soviet economics did not really depend on a logic of money, because in the end most basic productive resources were allocated by political authorities rather than by market mechanisms.[39] The reasons that money did not develop as the primary means of exchange in that part of the world at that time are historically specific and intersubjective. Yet once one accepts this, one can also accept that the means of exchange that, for those same historically specific reasons, did develop had an inherent logic by which Soviet economic practice was constrained.

This book concerns itself with those international economic systems in which money plays a central role as medium of exchange and store of value. It does not address those international systems based primarily on authoritative exchange, such as the international economics of the Soviet bloc during the Cold War, colonial relationships when these are based on the extraction of resources by force, trade among allies during wartime when such trade is governed by military rather than commercial logic, and so forth. It also does not address the question of why international economies develop monetarily in some cases and authoritatively in others. What it does is ask is, when money-based international economic systems develop, who leads them, how, and why.

Answering these questions requires investigation into both the logic inherent in economic systems in which money is the primary means of exchange and store of value, and the historically specific institutional structures that mediate and the set of intersubjective understandings[40] that develops around these logics. The former tells us whether or not a country can, and is likely to want to, be a leader. But it cannot tell us anything about how it will choose to lead. The latter, conversely, cannot tell us whether a country will be able to lead, but once a leader is identified, can go a long way toward telling us how it will choose to lead. In this sense, the relationship between constructivist and rationalist methodologies as they are used here is a three-step one. The first step is a constructivist one, in which one determines whether an international economic system is based on norms of monetary market-exchange, or not. If it is, the second step is the rationalist one, in which one determines whether there is a financially predominant country in the system. The third step is again constructivist, in which one gets at the content of leadership policies by looking at the social structures underlying the making of leadership policies domestically, and followership policies internationally.

FINANCIAL PREDOMINANCE

Financial predominance describes the middle step, the specific logic of international economic and monetary leadership. There are aspects of leadership that can be provided by a country incidentally to other policy choices, rather than intentionally. But to provide effective leadership, particularly in times of recession or crisis, requires conscious policy choice. These policy choices are not costless. They require the prioritization of the goal of leadership over other policy goals, be they macroeconomic or unrelated to economic issues altogether. When, and why, might this happen? The previous chapter discussed a number of answers that have been proposed to this question, ranging from predominance in global trade, to a sense of international responsibility.[41] But these answers succeed neither theoretically nor empirically. Theoretically, the internal logics of the arguments fail to explain the outcome. The internal logics also tend to address either the question of what constitutes the capabilities for leadership or that of what motivates countries to lead, but not both. The trade argument, for example, cannot explain why hegemons would prefer an open international system to one in which they can use their market power to achieve national goals, ranging from improved terms of trade to influence in high politics.[42] Empirically, existing theories of leadership either work only for one case, or fail to explain processes of leadership across cases.[43]

It is the contention here that the answer to why certain countries become leaders is to be found specifically in international finance.[44] A central part of the argument of this book is that international financial predominance, a situation in which a country's investment in the international economy is crucial to both domestic and international prosperity, is what both enables and drives a country to act as an international economic leader. The internal logic of the financial argument can thus explain both the capabilities and the motivations of leadership at the same time. This section develops the logic of international financial predominance, of what happens when one country predominates in the market for investment in the international economy. The next four chapters look at the historical fit.

The logic of international financial predominance is an inherent one—if the argument holds, then it should affect behavior across social constructs, as long as they are embedded in a historical context of a money-based international economic system. There are two key aspects to this logic, an external and an internal one. The external is the capabilities that allow a country to effectively play a role as international economic leader. The internal is the motivational effect of this financial predominance, the interest that it generates within the country's international financial community in an international economy with a well-managed financial infrastructure. This is, in the terminology used earlier, an inherent logic; it does not determine the behavior of actors, but it does constrain them. Financial predominance thus suggests that a country will, other things being equal, have a strong incentive to act as a leader. To understand the extent to which it does so, we have to look at the ways in which other things are not equal.

The capabilities aspect of this logic requires that a country be the preponderant investor in the international economy. A country must control a sufficient proportion of investment in the international economy to be able to provide international economic leadership in a stable and convincing fashion. Preponderance in investment gives a country both the physical and reputational resources to be able to fulfill the functions of leadership as previously discussed. For example, the income from abroad generated through such a high level of international investment can serve to offset the demands on a country's balance of payments caused by the maintenance of a relatively open market and a highly valued currency. The denomination of a majority of the investment in the international economy in a country's currency will help to give that country the resources and liquidity to underwrite central banks in crises without critical strain on the currency. And, as a final example, the reputation generated by such a predominant position in international finance will help to generate the confidence in a country's currency necessary for it to be used as a currency for international exchange.[45]

It should be noted at this point that investment in this context refers primarily to long-term capital. In other words, it refers to a financial commitment to the international economy that is not liquid in the short term, that cannot be repatriated hastily in times of crisis or in response to short- and medium-term economic fluctuations. For example, portfolio investments such as foreign stocks can often be sold quickly in response to changing economic conditions, and thus will not necessarily give the holder of those stocks a strong long-term interest in the economic stability of the country in which the stocks were purchased. Direct investment in such things as production or commercial facilities, on the other hand, cannot be so easily or quickly transferred or disposed of, and should therefore lead to a stronger commitment to the stability of the country and region in which the investment is located. As such, in looking at degrees of financial predominance the case studies will focus on long-term capital flows, and on stocks of fixed investment.[46]

The capabilities aspect of financial predominance is measured in the case studies by comparing the stock of investment in the international economy held by a particular country with the total stock of such investments at that point in time. There is, alas, no clear point at which it can be said that this or that country now has the necessary capabilities. It depends, among other things, on the eagerness of the country to lead, and on the willingness of others to be led. The willingness of others to be led in turn depends on such factors as the concentration of financial power in the international economy, in other words whether there are other countries with the potential to lead, and the compatibility of economic norms across the international system. When the ratio of a country's holdings to the systemic total passes half, it has clearly become predominant in international finance; since only one country can have over half the total, that country has clearly achieved financial predominance. Below that threshold, however, it becomes a historically contextual question whether a country will attempt to be, and will be accepted as, an international economic and monetary leader.

The second aspect of the logic of international financial predominance that is central to the story is motivation. A state may indeed have the capabilities to act as an international economic leader, but it only makes sense to expect that state to do so if it has some reason to be motivated to act that way. The traditional discourse of international relations theory would suggest that it is only reasonable to expect a country to act as a leader if it is in its national interest to do so.[47] The logic of financial predominance provides such a motivation, by suggesting that, given the inherent logic of international financial systems, foreign investment creates an economic interest in the internationalist financial community as a domestic constituency in providing leadership.

Following this logic allows us to assign policy preferences to various domestic economic interest groups, as is the practice in most rational choice approaches to domestic foreign policy formation.[48] This is, as discussed later in this chapter, somewhat simplistic; preferences cannot be objectively assumed, and certain elements of foreign economic policy are often accepted as conventional wisdoms, and provide a common ground for rather than a topic of policy debate. As such, the logic of financial predominance should not be taken to be determinist. It does not mean that the domestic constituency will necessarily act on its economic interests, that these interests will automatically become the national interest, or that even if it does the country will then necessarily create competent leadership policies. Nonetheless, some economic interests do logically suggest particular policy preferences. This does not mean that those preferences will always predominate; among other things, people do not always make decisions on the basis of economic interests. But it does mean that there will be a domestic constituency that defines its interests as including the health of the international political economy, and that this constituency will be in a good position to influence government policy.

There is, in the discussion in the last couple of paragraphs, an apparent tension between a discourse of "national interests" and one of "domestic preferences." The former suggests that the state is a unitary actor, the latter that it is not. But both can be true simultaneously. The state can at the same time be a set of people, institutions, and expectations that interact in complex ways to produce and reproduce the activities of government, and an actor, with its own identity and interests, on the international scene.[49] The national interest looked at in this way is not an objectively obvious category, but rather the outcome of the interactions of various particular interests mediated through a set of institutions and intersubjective understandings that constitute national politics.[50] But, as an outcome, it becomes a thing in itself. So in order to address national policy outputs, the national interest, with respect to international economic leadership, we must first look at the relevant set of particular interests that affect foreign economic policymaking and then at the political and economic institutions through which these interests are mediated.

International economic leadership is dependent on a particular set of economic policy outputs, which have the effect of doing things like ensuring international liquidity, coordinating macroeconomic policy, and so forth. As with all policy choices, the various policies that can result in leadership have opportunity costs, the cost of policy choices foregone. Leadership in maintaining an open international trading system, for example, is not compatible with a policy of using tariffs to protect domestic industry. The former will help certain domestic interests, the latter will help others.[51] This suggests that most policy choices will, to some extent or other, be contested by those interests that will lose as a result.[52]

The relevant interests here are those associated with international finance, or more specifically with the collectivity of owners of investment in the international economy. Put simply, the logic of international financial predominance suggests that members of this group, to the extent that they see their primary interest as the security of and maximization of return on their capital, should demand of their government that it act as international economic leader. In other words, when in a country with financially predominant capabilities, this group should endeavor to define international economic leadership as being the national interest of their country.

Two forms of investment in the international economy can lead to financial predominance: foreign investment and investment in international commerce. Foreign investment is investment in the assets and production of other countries, whether direct or portfolio. Investment in commerce is investment in the processes of and assets required for international trade and commerce, such as shipping, insurance, and financial services. Countries may become financially predominant through either or both. The two are mutually compatible and to a certain extent mutually reinforcing, but need not coexist. These two kinds of investment work through somewhat different logics to generate a policy demand by the international financial community in a country with the capabilities for financial predominance for international economic leadership. The effects of these two kinds of investment on policy preferences, though, is quite similar. To promote the profitability of investments in either case, the logic of economic theory suggests that a leader should attempt to maintain three primary sets of conditions in the international economy. Both types of investment require an element of each of these sets of conditions.

To maintain the profitability of investment in international commerce over the long term, a country must ensure its ability to service substantial amounts of profitable commerce over the long term. This refers to all commerce, not simply the export of goods, as it is the processes of financing and trading themselves, not production of any sort, that is the source of wealth for the financial interests in question. Profit may be made in a number of ways, including direct financing, that is, buying goods at a low price and selling them higher, the provision of financial services for trade and commerce, such as insurance or debt financing, or investment in trading services, such as shipping or warehousing. The leader need not be the primary exporter or importer in this trade; it need only service the trade.[53]

The three conditions that investors should demand in order to promote international trade, and thus the profitability of investment in such trade, are as follows. The first is the maintenance of international financial stability, and the focus of that stability on the leader. In other words, international traders and financiers must have confidence in the currency and financial stability of the leader. This stability, by reducing uncertainties, will promote commerce, and the focus of the stability on the leader will encourage traders and financiers to use its services. This is necessary to attract traders to the trade services of the leader, at the expense of other potential servicers. The second is the presence in world markets of relatively productive sellers and reasonably affluent buyers. Without these there would be either little to trade or no one to trade it with. A corollary of this is the promotion of the growth of both this productivity and this affluence to encourage the growth of the profitability of financing the resulting increase in trade. The third condition is a relatively peaceful system, and relatively secure trade routes. The potential for violence in the process of trading increases costs and thus decreases both volume and profitability.[54]

Foreign investment benefits from three similar conditions that help to ensure the value of investments abroad and the liquidity of profits. The first is the maintenance of the value of the currency in which the investments are made and denominated, and the convertibility of local currencies, without which the perceived values of the investments will fluctuate unpredictably and profits will be difficult to repatriate. The second is the maintenance and creation of profitable investment opportunities abroad. This will enhance the potential for growth and the promotion of conditions in which existing investments can remain productive and therefore profitable. The third condition is the limitation of direct threats to the value of foreign investments that can eliminate the value of these investments entirely, such as war or expropriation by local governments.[55]

The logic of financial predominance suggests that international investors in financially capable countries should demand of their governments that they promote these conditions by acting as international economic leaders. Motivation is a shorthand for their likelihood of success. While they stem from slightly different concerns, these three sets of conditions have very similar practical implications. The first set of conditions, the maintenance of financial stability for investors in trade and the maintenance of currency-of-investment values and convertibility for foreign investors, can be addressed by the first of the functions of international economic leadership, the provision of a medium of exchange. This requires that the leader establish its currency as the primary international currency of exchange, and create a banking structure capable of stabilizing the currency and maintaining international confidence in it. This course of action is further recommended by the benefits of seigneurage, the profit that accrues to a sovereign from the issuance of a currency.[56] Because the use of a leader's currency as a standard for international exchange expands its circulation, it should expand the profitability of seigneurage as well.

The second set of conditions is the presence of sufficient buyers and sellers and their continued growth for investors in trade, and the maintenance and creation of profitable opportunities abroad for foreign investors. These conditions can be addressed by the second function of leadership, ensuring sufficient liquidity to the international economy. In the long term this function allows an outlet for growth in production elsewhere by opening the presumably most affluent market in the system to international trade. This opening encourages growth in both trade and further investment opportunities. In the medium term the leader acts to help insure against unnecessary contraction of the international economy during recurrent and apparently inevitable downturns in the business cycle, by providing liquidity countercyclically. In the short term, the leader helps to prevent withdrawals from the international economy precipitated by panics, primarily monetary, that can be alleviated through the leader's role as international underwriter of distressed currencies.[57]

The third set of conditions, relatively peaceful trade routes and limited international conflict for investors in trade and the limitation of direct threats to foreign investment, can be addressed by the third of the functions of leadership. The coordination of macroeconomic policies will mitigate much international conflict over economic issues. By providing an agreed, or at least mutually recognized, set of property rights, rules of interaction, and norms of behavior common to all states, it will alleviate the threat posed to foreign investments by host governments. The "enforcement" element of this function helps to control threats to both trade and investment by nonstate actors and to protect both from threats by those countries not acquiescing to the leadership. This may entail global military domination and the imposition of peace, but can also be much more limited, involving perhaps an explicit mutual nonbelligerence in which belligerent states agree not to interfere with the trade serviced by the leader. It should be noted that both the macroeconomic policy coordination and the boundary of those protected by the policing function need not be universal. There can be a group of 'follower' countries to which the leadership functions apply, and an outside group, of nonparticipating countries, to which the logic of relative gains applies.[58]

DOMESTIC POLITICS

All of this suggests that, to the extent to which they define their interests in investment terms, international financiers as an interest group in financially predominant countries should, logically, prefer leadership policies, other things being equal. As such, they should attempt to create an understanding of the national interest, at least with respect to foreign economic policy, that focuses on, or at minimum includes, international economic and monetary leadership. But do they succeed? Traditional realist international relations theory suggests that they should not; leadership, after all, means the provision of public goods to one's rivals at one's own expense, not a good idea in a competitive self-help system.[59] Traditional Marxist theories of imperialism suggest that the state will invariably become captive to its financiers.[60] History lies on various points on a continuum between these two theoretical extremes.

How do states make foreign economic policy? The answer depends on the state in question, on the structure of its political institutions and its traditions of political practice. The process by which, and the degree to which, international financial interests impact state policy is historically and contextually contingent; examples of these processes are discussed in the next four chapters. There are, though, several aspects of this interest group that lend themselves well to a disproportionate ability to influence policy-making in financially predominant states, both by capturing state policy-making apparati within their own areas of interest and by influencing the dominant conception of the national good.

International financiers generally constitute a very small percentage of a national population, yet they usually are a disproportionately powerful one.[61] A major reason for this is that, quite simply, they are rich. Investors in general tend to be wealthier than the popular average. Because of the complications and uncertainties of international investment and the resulting barriers to entry, it can be expected to attract the most substantial from among the investors. Wealth, cliché though the phrase is, generates power. More specifically, concentrated wealth allows for such means as are necessary in almost all societies for access to government.[62] These means can range from the purchase of lobbyists, to the more direct method of bribery, to various forms of oligarchy. At the same time, this concentration helps to avoid the constraints of collective action problems.[63] Furthermore, to the extent that leadership policies succeed in encouraging international commercial activity, this should in turn empower international financiers in their domestic political sphere.[64] Leadership policies can thus have a self-reinforcing effect; the more successful they are, the more able their proponents are to lobby successfully for them.

This privileged access is perhaps most pronounced with respect to issues of monetary policy, a key component of international leadership.[65] Monetary policy, more than most other forms of policy, tends to be managed by a small group of specialists, and insulated from outside pressures, be they popular or executive.[66] Central banks are usually the branch of the national executive most independent of direct political management and pressures, especially in highly capitalized economies.[67] The bankers who manage these central banks are often the same ones who manage international investments. Thus the institutional structure of the monetary policy process often favors the ability of financiers to convert their interests into national policies. With respect to the lender of last resort function of international monetary leadership, this privileged role is reinforced by the absence of natural direct domestic policy antagonists, as this function of leadership does not come at the direct expense of any other direct domestic economic interest. It is also privileged by the nonexcludability of monetary policy. Whereas tariffs can differ across industries, and so affect various sectors of the economy differentially, there can only be one national monetary policy.[68] This makes monetary policy more susceptible to strong central coordination than other forms of foreign economic policy.

These two factors, the relative wealth of international investors and the insularity of monetary policy-making, point to two routes through which international financiers can affect their state's foreign economic policy-making. These factors provide a causal link between the logic of financial predominance and state economic and monetary leadership behavior. There is also another route through which financial predominance may affect the propensity for a state's understanding of its national interest to include international economic leadership. This route involves a constitutive rather than a causal logic. In the three-step methodology discussed earlier, this route is part of the constructivist first step rather than the rationalist middle step.

For a country to become financially predominant in the first place, it is likely to have an established economic ideology and culture, or cultural hegemony in Gramscian terms,[69] that is at minimum compatible with and at maximum strongly supportive of international commerce. The capital export that underpins financial predominance requires a supportive domestic as well as international economic infrastructure, the latter of which must have preceded financial predominance both temporally and ideologically. In other words, national economic policy must have favored international economic activity for the internationalist financial community to develop in the first place. This domestic economic infrastructure suggests an intersubjective understanding of the national interest, at least among policy elites, that includes domestic financial stability and international financial penetration. It is but a very small step from that to an understanding of the national interest that stresses international financial stability. This phenomenon will, once again, be discussed in more detail, and become clearer, in the case studies.

None of this should be interpreted as meaning that international financial interests will determine state foreign economic policy in financially predominant countries. International financiers will have varying degrees of influence in different countries and in different contexts. Institutional influence will be stronger in some countries that in others. For example, internationalist economic interests directly controlled the Dutch government in the seventeenth century, which was not the case in the United States of the second half of the twentieth. Ideological/cultural influence will similarly vary across historical contexts. Whether or not the influence, institutional and ideological, of international finance will be sufficient in a particular case can only be established on a case-by-case basis.

FORMS OF LEADERSHIP

All of this suggests that financial predominance should motivate rational internationalist financial interests to move their country's foreign economic policy toward the requirements of international economic leadership, and that they should have some significant ability to do so. But while financially predominant countries can be expected to play some sort of international leadership role, the specifics of these roles in policy terms, and even the general thrusts of different leaderships, can vary widely. The rationalist logic, for example, can tell us that both the Dutch in the seventeenth century and the British in the nineteenth should have been disposed toward leadership. It cannot tell us, however, why the former tended toward the pragmatic and mercantilist, while the latter tended toward the ideological and the liberal. Getting at these differences requires looking at contextual social structures. This brings us to the third step of the constructivist/rationalist/constructivist methodological sequence.

Leadership requires that a country fulfill a set of infrastructural functions in the international economy, but these functions can be fulfilled in a variety of ways, and to a range of degrees. There are two general sets of reasons for this variance, one internal and one external, mirroring the internal and external components of the logic of financial predominance. Internally, different kinds of domestic political structures and practices affect the degree of success with which financial elites will be able to penetrate state policy-making, and different degrees and kinds of internationalist common senses affect what the leader will want to do. Externally, the different international settings in which financially predominant countries find themselves affect what leaders can do.

The internal set of reasons begins with different degrees of success by internationalist financial elites in penetrating state policy-making. This process can affect the nature of a country's leadership as a straightforward matter of scale; the more effectively these elites influence or capture the state policy-making process, the stronger that country's commitment to international economic leadership will be. The domestic politics of foreign economic policy-making can also, however, affect the form and content, as well as the strength, of a country's attempts to lead. Foreign economic policy, and foreign policy more generally, can represent various sorts of compromises among competing visions of the national interest, and the nuances of these compromises can affect the fundamental direction of attempts to lead. For example, Dutch foreign policy in the seventeenth century often reflected both the financial demand for economic leadership, and the ideological demand for a Calvinist foreign policy. Similarly, American postwar foreign policy often reflected various compromises among financial interests, isolationist interests, and the ideological demands of the Cold War.

Underlying this political interaction is another layer of discursive structure that affects policy output in subtle but very real ways, the layer of intersubjective understanding, of social identity, of Gramsci's common sense.[70] This represents all those assumptions that the major participants in the policy-making process share in common, be these assumptions about the appropriate nature of the political process, the proper form of property rights, or the functioning of economic systems. For example, there is a general consensus in contemporary American politics that social security is part of the role of the state, although there is disagreement over how much should be spent on it and how it should work. This affects the way in which the American government makes foreign economic policy, because it is popularly accepted that the government must take into account the effects of policy change on social security. In nineteenth-century Britain there was no such consensus on the role of the state in social welfare. Nineteenth-century British financial orthodoxy prioritized stable exchange rates and balanced budgets over price stability and demand stimulation, whereas contemporary financial orthodoxy, as argued by such institutions as the IMF and World Bank and practiced by most OECD governments, is more concerned with price stability and allows for the need for demand stimulation in parts of the business cycle.[71] One can argue that the difference stems from advances in economic science (Keynesianism and the economics of expectations) or from different social priorities or intersubjective understandings, but either way the difference will have a significant impact on the form of international economic leadership that a financially predominant country is willing to provide.

Intersubjective understandings that affect policy decisions need not even, however, be directly related to broader notions about politics or economics. They can be contextually specific historical quirks that do not have direct analogies elsewhere. A straightforward example of such a quirk is the British attachment to a particular value of sterling, the British currency. Throughout the period from the Napoleonic Wars to World War One the pound sterling maintained the same value in terms of gold, called its par value. But convertibility to gold was suspended at the onset of the war. Following the war there was an extensive policy debate in Britain over whether to return to a system of convertibility to gold, but there was never any thought given to returning to convertibility at a different exchange value; it was either return at the prewar rate, or not return at all.[72] There was no real economic reason for framing the question in these terms. Rather, sterling had fit into the gold standard system at a particular value for so long that it was simply accepted that within the system, that was its value. It had become common sense. In other words, this was a social reality that affected perceived policy choices simply because people accepted it as such.

The external reasons for variance in the form and content of international economic leadership are the different international settings in which financially dominant countries find themselves. Both the patterns of and the success of leadership depend, among other things, on the willingness of others to be led in general and, more specifically, on the forms of leadership that followers are willing to accept. As with domestic sources of variance, these differences in international settings can be both causal and constitutive. Differences in the structure of international politics—what realists would call the balance of power,[73]—constrain the choices that financially predominant countries have in attempting to lead, while different sets of intersubjective understandings on the conduct of international relations, different international belief structures, define the sets of policy choices that leaders are likely to consider, and that followers are likely to accept.[74]

As with domestic political structures and norms, the structural and the intersubjective can be very difficult, as both an empirical and conceptual matter, to separate. A good example here would be the Washington Consensus, the widespread agreement among both governments and the international organizational structure of the international political economy at the turn of the twenty-first century on what might be called neoclassical economic orthodoxy, the international economics of open markets.[75] This new orthodoxy on the one hand represents a monopolar world, one in which the one remaining superpower is also the leading ideologue of the market. It also represented a genuine broad acceptance among policy-makers worldwide of the idea that markets are more efficient than central planning, and therefore more conducive to economic growth. In other words, it represents a Gramscian common sense. The role of the new orthodoxy in the international political economy of the mid-1990s cannot be fully appreciated without taking into account both the structural and the intersubjective environments within which it arose.

The skeptical reader might look at this example and see the makings of a tautology; the United States can provide leadership by way of property rights to the international economic system because those property rights are already there. This raises a chicken-and-egg problem: Which comes first, the leadership or the system? This question is relevant to a number of issues discussed in this chapter. For example, the capabilities required for leadership depend on the strength of motivations, but the effectiveness of motivations in turn depends on the level of capabilities. This is, however, a case of what can be referred to as recursive causality or positive feedback loops, rather than a tautology.[76] In other words, I am not continually changing my mind about what is causing what. Rather the argument is that these things are causing each other. A weakly accepted set of international property rights that becomes effectively supported by a leader will become more strongly accepted. The increasing acceptance of that set of property rights will in turn strengthen the leadership. Through this process of mutual reinforcement, both become stronger simultaneously. This will not necessarily happen; leadership may be ineffective because it does not build on the existing normative structure of the international system. For leadership to be effective, however, requires recursive causality; a positive feedback loop must be created.

The logic of financial predominance, then, suggests that a country with both the requisite capabilities and motivations is likely to act to some degree as an international economic and monetary leader. It is likely to undertake foreign economic policies that provide a medium of exchange, manage liquidity, and help to define property rights internationally. To understand both the form and the strength of this leadership, however, the contextual social structures within which leadership policy is made are key. Among other things, the form of leadership depends on both the country's domestic political system and the international system in which it finds itself; patterns of leadership are historically and contextually specific. In other words, the argument here is that the logic that leads to international economic leadership is one of international finance specifically, rather than one of trade, economics, or hegemony more broadly. But the leadership that this logic leads to is only a framework, and in order to understand the leadership policies, and the resultant international economic systems, that are hung on this framework, we must use a constructivist rather than a rationalist methodology. The next four chapters discuss four specific historical contexts, and the patterns of leadership (or absence thereof) that developed within them.

3

The Seventeenth Century and Dutch Leadership

The empirical section of this book begins in Amsterdam at around the beginning of the seventeenth century. The seventeenth century was, for the international political economy, a period of marked transition. It saw the beginning of the first truly global patterns of economic interaction, rather than the overlapping regional patterns that had predominated earlier. It also saw the transition from the city-based economies that had marked the late Middle Ages to the national economies that have predominated since.[1] This makes it an appropriate starting point for a discussion of leadership of the international political economy and monetary system.

The story of Dutch international financial leadership in the seventeenth century serves to illustrate two other aspects of the logic of financial predominance as well. The first is that leadership need not be embedded in any particular normative structure. The predominant economic wisdom of the seventeenth century was mercantilist rather than liberal. This allows us a perspective on the relationship between the logic of money and the social construction of financial leadership quite different from those provided by later cases more deeply embedded in a liberal worldview. Many theories of international economic leadership are placed quite self-consciously within the context of such a liberal worldview; some go so far as to speak explicitly of "liberal leadership."[2] To do so is to make the assumption that any economic logics driving a country to leadership are subordinate to the social construction of a liberal worldview. In other words, it makes the assumption that a liberal ideological hegemony is necessarily historically prior to decisions by national policy-makers to provide infrastructural public goods to the international economy. But if money has its own logic, then there is no inherent reason to make this assumption. It should simply be the use of money as the primary means of exchange and store of value, rather than laissez-faire liberal ideology, that is necessarily historically prior to such decisions. Dutch international economic practices in the seventeenth century provide an opportunity to explore how an international economic leader can develop in the absence of liberal economic ideology, as will be discussed explicitly later in the chapter.

The other aspect of the argument that this case serves well to illustrate is the distinction between financial predominance and other power resources in international relations. The Dutch were not hegemonic in the traditional sense in which the term is used in international relations theory, as arguably later the British and then the Americans were.[3] Dutch leadership was much more exclusively financial than more recent leaderships, enabling us to look at financial leadership in isolation from broader political hegemony. While for historians of the international economy the seventeenth century was the Dutch century, for diplomatic historians it was the French century. Some, for example, speak of "France's clear military superiority and her predominance in the European states system";[4] others refer to it as the "age of Louis XIV."[5] France also at the time not only had a larger economy and industrial base, but was a larger exporter than the United Provinces of the Netherlands.[6] The French thus ranked higher than the Dutch in the seventeenth century in most traditional measures of hegemony in international relations. A comparative history of the two should therefore be able to help to illuminate the relationship between predominance in international commerce and predominance in the politics of diplomacy and war. As such, some explicit comparisons between the two countries are made throughout this chapter.

THE DEMAND FOR LEADERSHIP

The European economy at the end of the sixteenth century was marked by a high degree of segmentation and regionalization. The city-states of Northern Italy dominated the commerce and finance of the Mediterranean basin, while those of the Hanseatic League dominated that of the Baltic region. In both cases, these cities acted as locations of entrepôt trade, a pattern of trade in which goods are imported to a central clearinghouse, and then re-exported to a final destination. The original importer need have no final destination for the goods; a final purchaser can be found for the goods at the entrepôt. This is in contrast to direct trade, in which goods are shipped directly from the producer country to the consumer country. The Iberian countries, meanwhile, dominated Europe's commerce with the rest of the world.[7] Antwerp appeared for a short time as a predominant center for European entrepôt trade, but lacked the domestic institutions or the political autonomy to play a major, long-term role in the international economy.[8] Thus it is more realistic in this period to speak of several overlapping regional economies than of one general European economy.

The same could be said of the economies of the large European states. In France and Spain, and to a lesser extent in Eastern Europe, large political units were not matched by national economies. These countries were marked by numerous barriers to internal trade and commerce, and small regions tended strongly toward economic autarchy. Such economic interactions as these regions had, beyond the payment of taxes to the central government, were often directly with the international economy. There was a pattern of small regions within countries interacting economically with port cities and foreign trade representatives without interacting much at all with each other. The only "national" pattern of capital accumulation was thus through taxation; regional barriers to commerce prevented the accumulation of commercial capital on a scale commensurate with the size of the political units.

The entrepôt pattern of long-distance trade was to a great degree dictated by the slow speed of communication at the time, and irregularities in the supply of and the demand for the most heavily traded commodities. Most of these were either primary agricultural products, the supply of which depended on such things as the quality of the annual harvest, or luxury goods, the demand for which depended on the health of the economy in the primary market for the good in any given year. This meant that direct trade was impractical, because traders could not know from year to year (and the speed of seventeenth century ships was such that often only one annual shipment was possible) either how much of the good was available, or how much was needed. Entrepôt trade overcame this difficulty by bringing all the sellers and buyers of a good together in the same place at the same time.

A final feature of the European economy at the end of the sixteenth century that is fundamental to this story is the nature of money at the time. The predominant form of exchange was a specie system, in which the value of money was determined by its metallic content, primarily its silver content. The ratio of silver to base metals in the alloys from which the coins were minted varied greatly amongst currencies, and even within currencies, as they were regularly devalued by decreasing their silver content. This meant that an accurate measurement of the exchange value of a currency entailed both a process of careful weighing, and the melting down of samples of the coinage to determine its silver content, a time-consuming and expensive process. The process was complicated by the fact that there were a large number of issuers of currency in Europe at the time, meaning that transactions could involve several different currencies, each of which might have to be valuated separately.

This combination of entrepôt trading and specie currency led to two particular demands for infrastructural goods in the international economy of the time, demands that needed to some extent to be supplied for long-distance trade to become efficient enough for a truly global pattern of commerce to emerge. The first was for more efficient entrepôts, where as great as possible a variety and volume of goods could be traded for, at as little expense as possible. The second was for a more efficient way to trade currency, one that did not require a full process of individual currency valuation for each set of commercial transactions.

INTERNATIONAL FINANCE

The city of Amsterdam appeared on the scene right around the turn of the century as the center of Europe's, and of the world's, shipping and entrepôt trade. Although the antecedents to Amsterdam's rapid rise to primacy in European commerce in the first decade of the seventeenth century can be seen in hindsight, to many contemporary observers it seemed that the city had just appeared suddenly at the center of the world's economy, with no warning. "Suddenly, as it seemed, the city was there."[9]

Amsterdam had been a growing trading center for a century, but one of only regional importance. Its large herring fishery, the backbone of the economy until the seventeenth century, provided a large stock of ships, shipbuilding expertise, and a strong port infrastructure and maritime tradition on which to base a trading fleet. It was well located for a European entrepôt, and had a highly urbanized and defensible hinterland, well suited for the accumulation of commercial capital. Finally, it displayed a religious and cultural tolerance that was less constraining to commercial enterprise than many European societies of the time. For example, restrictions against usury and various other commercial practices were milder than elsewhere in Europe, and members of minority religious groups, while excluded from direct participation in government, faced few restrictions on their ability to do business.[10]

Although it built on this base, the remarkably sudden rise of Amsterdam to prominence was a result of the Dutch war of independence from Spain. This gave the Dutch political autonomy from Hapsburg rule. At the same time it created a large refugee population from the Spanish Netherlands, particularly Antwerp. These refugees brought to Amsterdam the commercial and industrial skills that allowed it to dominate international commerce so suddenly.[11]

Dutch investment in international commerce throughout most of the seventeenth century was primarily in the form of investment in the mechanisms of international commerce. This included investment in shipping, in the infrastructure required for entrepôt trade, such as warehousing and port facilities, and in the financial services that helped attract this trade to Amsterdam. The international economy, in turn, soon became critically dependent on Dutch financing of trade services.[12]

The value of many of these services is difficult to quantify precisely, as aggregate records were not kept. Fairly accurate measures of shipping exist, though, and these show an overwhelming Dutch dominance. "In 1670 the volume of Dutch-owned shipping—some 568,000 tons—considerably exceeded that of Spanish, Portuguese, French, English, Scottish, and German combined; and the preponderance of Dutch-built shipping was even greater. It is true that at that date the remarkable late seventeenth-century increase in English shipping was already under way; but even at the end of the century the volume of English-owned shipping was still only one-third to one-half that of Dutch-owned, and probably more than a quarter of English-owned ships were Dutch-built."[13] Taking shipping as an indicator of financial investment in the servicing of trade generally, Dutch dominance was pronounced.

Most of this investment in shipping and in the infrastructure required for entrepôt trade was only useful for international commerce, and required a healthy international economy to remain profitable. Unlike others at the time, much of the Dutch fleet consisted of very specialized ships, such as bulk cargo carriers, that possessed no military capabilities and were useless outside of the specific role they were designed for, international shipping.[14] The infrastructure required for entrepôt trade, such as a high-capacity port, large warehousing capabilities, and the like, is also not particularly useful for other economic pursuits. And the financial services developed to service this trade, such as insurance and the brokering of bills of exchange, were far in excess of anything that could be absorbed by the domestic market. Thus while the growth of international commerce in this period depended on Dutch investment in international commerce, that investment in turn, on which the wealth of Holland was based, depended on the continuing profitability of the international economy.

France, in contrast, had very little investment in the international market economy. The French exported and imported a fair amount, by the standards of the time. By the middle of the seventeenth century they were in fact quite dependent on international commerce, through both the development of export-oriented industries and the need for imports that could not be substituted domestically. There was, however, little financial commitment abroad, except in the French colonial possessions—in other words, in those areas over which France had direct political control. Most French trade was carried on foreign, primarily Dutch, ships,[15] and was often organized and financed by Dutch commercial representatives in residence in French ports.[16] Thus not only did the French not have much involvement in the international commerce of other countries, they were often excluded from the management of their own. Such capital accumulation as occurred in France tended to go toward government finance and, by the eighteenth century, domestic agricultural improvement, rather than investment in commerce and industry generally. It rarely went to international commerce.

DOMESTIC POLITICS

The European pattern of government, as it had developed by 1600, had two primary forms. In predominantly rural areas political powers tended to be vested in feudal authorities. In different polities relations among various levels of feudal authorities differed, varying from a strong monarchy and weak nobility in France to strong nobilities under little centralized control in East Central Europe. In predominantly urban areas, such as the city-states of Northern Italy and the Hanseatic

League, power tended more often to be in the hands of an urban patriciate, a commercial oligopoly. France was an almost pure example of the former model, an absolutist state with few avenues for nonfeudal participation in government. The United Provinces of the Netherlands were a fragmented mix of the two models; local merchant oligopolies controlled the towns, and vied for control of national policy with the feudal authorities in control of the rural hinterland.

France was the archetypal absolutist state. The nobility had substantial economic privilege, but no real input into the political process. The monarchy was largely unfettered in its ability to make policy to suit its aims.[17] These aims were usually focused on the maintenance of social order and the raising of revenue.[18] Merchants were of little importance to either of these two aims. Because they were outside the feudal economic order and were often from minority religious or ethnic groups, merchants and their interests had particular difficulty penetrating a political elite based on land and titles. Merchant interests were also not particularly important for purposes of raising revenue. Most of the crown's revenue came from land and agricultural taxes, and from the selling of offices.[19] Under Colbert, France did create a mercantilist industrial policy. This was intended, though, primarily to promote industrial production rather than commerce, and the motives behind industrialization were the creation of a larger tax base and increased potential military production. The only financiers in France substantial enough to make important loans to the government were those who had become rich in government service, such as fiscal management and tax collecting.[20] These financiers had no particular reason to want to support the international economy. French internationalist financial interests, such as they were, therefore had no means of access to government foreign economic policy-making, reflecting their marginal importance to the national economy and the national interest.

The Dutch system of government was in some ways the opposite of the French, and is difficult to characterize because it was so decentralized. The United Provinces consisted of seven individual provinces, each of which enjoyed a large degree of political autonomy. Five of these were coastal and predominantly urban. The other two were inland and predominantly rural.[21] Each province, and within the coastal provinces each individual city and town, enjoyed a high degree of autonomy. These cities and towns were ruled by their burghers, the elite of the merchant and industrial bourgeoisie. The countryside was under the ultimate rule of the Prince of Orange, the hereditary feudal lord.[22] The Prince of Orange was called *Stadtholder*, an office similar to hereditary constitutional monarchy. It commanded the army and was nominally head of state. Overall control of national policy, such as it was, was the object of a constant tug of war between the urban elites and the House of Orange.

The general form of government in the cities and towns of the United Provinces was a civic council on which sat the local aldermen. These were drawn from a class of wealthy, well-established merchants and merchant bankers (industrialists in predominantly industrial towns such as Delft) who constituted a fairly small and cohesive elite. This council had extensive powers, far greater than any city governments today. It controlled both legislation and the judiciary, and had broad powers of taxation and oversight of the local economy. The key attribute of these elites was wealth. They tended to be fairly stable and generational, but allowed for some social mobility as new wealth was created and new families established themselves as being suitably substantial. The one caveat to this pattern of oligopoly was Calvinism. Although there was considerable religious tolerance, particularly in Amsterdam, political elites were usually restricted to those of Calvinist backgrounds. The very wealthy of other religious denominations had little direct access to government.

The sources of wealth for these elites was urban commerce. There was little prestige in rural estates, and thus the urban elites remained in the cities and continued their traditional businesses. This is in marked contrast to patterns elsewhere in Europe. In England at the time, for example, the most successful of urban businessmen usually invested their fortunes in rural estates and became members of the rural nobility. Their children thus tended not to continue in whatever business had created the wealth in the first place. In Amsterdam, where the primary source of wealth was international commerce, the ruling patriciate continued to participate actively in this commerce, as governmental tasks were not particularly remunerative.[23] Thus the access of internationalist financiers to the government of Amsterdam was direct—they themselves, and they only, constituted the civic government, and as such they had broad discretionary powers over economic policy.

In the rural areas, particularly in the two inland provinces, government had a more feudal structure. There was a hereditary landed nobility, but it had been weakened and impoverished by the war of independence from Spain, and played little political role. The peasantry, in contrast, was fully free, and among the most affluent of European peasantries of the time. It was also by far the most innovative European peasantry of the seventeenth century, which may well be related to its freedom and affluence.[24] Given the relative weakness of the nobility with respect to the peasantry, most of the real political power in these areas was in the hands of the Prince of Orange, who was in function, if not in name, a hereditary monarch.[25]

Provincial governments were made up of parliaments of the various estates contained within them, be these city or town corporations, or rural noble estates. Within the province of Holland, the city of Amsterdam was such an overwhelming economic presence that its government dominated the provincial government. The Prince of Orange had thorough control of the governments of the two inland provinces, but very little in the two most urbanized provinces, Holland and Zeeland. The government of the United Provinces in turn was made up of representatives of the provinces. Because of the central role in the Dutch economy played by Amsterdam and the political base of the Prince of Orange, in practice either Amsterdam's representative or the Prince was head of state at any given time.[26] Although this position had, by itself, limited power, variations in Dutch policy can be traced to which of these two forces predominated at the time. An interesting feature of the Dutch government was that, in the execution of policy, it often acted more as a coordinating committee than as a single actor. For example, when the Dutch navy went to war, it was as an inadequately organized set of provincial navies rather than as a unified force.[27] This allowed for considerable variation in the degree of provincial input into, and often collective action problems with, the execution of national policy.

One of the results of this diffuse power and decision-making structure was the lack of any clear, generally recognized concept of a national political and security interest, beyond the basic defense of the country's borders from invasion.[28] The House of Orange, and the more traditionally feudal political elements it represented, perceived a national interest that was similar to that perceived by other monarchs of the time. This centered on maintaining the social status quo domestically, the expansion of political influence abroad, territorial aggrandizement, and the defense and expansion of religion, in this case Calvinism.[29] This notion of national interest was often at odds with the commercial interests of the coastal cities. Social conservatism worked to the benefit of the entrenched plutocracy, and political influence could be used to secure commercial advantage. However, the associated military expenditures could be ruinous, and continental territorial aggrandizement gained international financial interests nothing. Furthermore, the puritan Calvinism associated with the House of Orange could be quite hostile to commercial interests and certain commercial activity. "Extreme Calvinism, which had some grip on the government between 1619 and 1650, and again briefly after 1672, was narrowly bigoted, attached to medieval ideas about merchants, prices, profits, usury, and monopoly; it was potentially a force wholly unfavorable to economic enterprise."[30]

Against these monarchical interests, though, the urban elites and the civic governments, led by Amsterdam, had no real sense of a national interest separate from economic interest. "Profits? Yes. Power? Only so far as it might be necessary to protect private trade and provide the minimum apparatus for trade in a world of war."[31] There was only immediate commercial interest. It was seen as valid for the state to actively support these, but not to interfere with them. "In this politically atomized society where *raison d'état* was generally subordinated to the private interests of trade, national policy was reduced to something residual, not positive."[32] An extreme example of this sort of view of government is provided by the absence of any enforced rules concerning trading with the enemy. Even when the Dutch government went to war with another power to support commercial interests, it did not prevent Dutch merchants from trading with, and thereby supporting, that power. The state could use its resources to aid the interests of economic internationalists, but could not in any real way regulate them to support any separate state interest.

In France, then, the domestic political process as it was then constituted allowed international finance little access to policy-making processes, and there was little notion of international economic infrastructure as a core national interest. The situation in the Netherlands was more complicated, but allowed much more access to international financiers. At the civic level, where much of this policy was created and put into effect, merchant interests had direct control of the government, and thus of policy. The absence of any real conception of a separate political national interest, though, often led to a peculiar shortsightedness, a lack of any long-term vision of the goals of government. The state was seen as a tool for addressing immediate economic concerns, but not one for creating any long-term national planning or development.[33] At the national or federal level, where diplomatic and military policy was created and where some economic policy was coordinated, the degree to which these interests predominated varied, and to a significant degree depended on who was head of state at the time. When Amsterdam's representatives filled this position, international financial motivations went unchecked as the source of policy, and policy priorities conformed to those at the municipal level. When the Prince of Orange was acting head of state, two very different sets of priorities, commerce and Calvinism, interacted in the making of national policy.

MERCANTILISM AND LEADERSHIP

The task at this stage in the chapter is to look at economic policies and their relationship to the financial situations and political processes discussed earlier. It is important to remember at this point that these policies were embedded in a mercantilist ideological setting or worldview. The idea of international economic leadership, often associated with economic liberalism, seems at first blush to be incompatible with classical mercantilism, a set of ideas that has as its common themes the capturing of economic rent through the application of political power, and the national accumulation of specie.[34] This apparent incompatibility is exacerbated by a tendency in contemporary discourse to think of "leadership" as progressive while regarding mercantilism as a primitive and shortsighted set of ideas.[35] Classical economists have tended to use mercantilist ideas as straw men in the presentation of their own ideas, a trend that began with Adam Smith, whose *Wealth of Nations* was presented as a critique of mercantilism.

It is in a way unreasonable to speak of mercantilism as an economic worldview in the same way that we speak of liberalism. Both mercantilism and liberalism are, in Gramscian terms, economic "common senses," in the sense that they provide a template through which people react to their economic surroundings without having to think through their actions from first principles every time. But they are different kinds of common senses, in that mercantilism, being the less ideological of the two, contains within it less a sense of the "ought" than liberalism. It is thus less likely to drive, as well as just inform, the making of policy. It has only been presented as economic theory in hindsight; what we now call mercantilism was in the seventeenth century a set of specific policy ideas and preferences that were not necessarily viewed as having a coherent theoretical logic. Mercantilism was, in short, a set of practices rather than ideology. As such, we should not expect it to inform policy as a matter of principle, but rather as a matter of expediency. In other words, it was a tool of other policy goals, be these goals focused on commercial profit as in Amsterdam or political control as in France.

For example, liberal economic historians often point to the mercantilist fixation on the accumulation of specie as irrational. One must remember, though, that at the time specie metal constituted all of the money in circulation. Given that coins wear out, that some forms of trade with Asia required a consant outflow of silver from Europe, that the use of military force had to be paid for in coin, and that most Western European countries had little in the way of domestic sources of supply of these metals, there was a constant downward pressure on the money supply. To the extent that monetary contraction can cause real economic contraction, and could undermine the national defense as well, policies intended to increase domestic supplies of specie made good economic and political sense.[36] But this was a matter of sound political practice, not a matter of principle. As such, any practice that ensured the domestic supply of specie was acceptable, be it the traditional mercantilist preference for exports over imports, or the creation of extractive monopolies in Asia or the Americas. The creation of an entrepôt also supported the domestic money supply, by bringing in exchange profits and fees for services rather than by restricting domestic consumption. Few polities could do so successfully, but those that could were not hindered from doing so by any inherent logic of relative gains.

INTERNATIONAL ECONOMIC POLICY

France throughout the seventeenth century was the quintessentially mercantilist state. French policy took the international economy as something from which to generate specie, not something to which to provide infrastructure. Tariffs were kept relatively high both to generate revenue and to protect and encourage domestic industry and exports, at the expense of imports and the entrepôt trade. No action was undertaken to create a currency suitable for the role of international exchange. France at the time had a number of different issuers of currency, and such efforts that were made to centralize the monetary system were done to allow the crown to capture more of the rents from seigneurage rather than to make it more appealing for international use. Economic policy in general focused on integrating and developing the domestic economy, and there was little if any effort made to provide infrastructure to the international economy.[37]

Dutch decision-making often reflected the logic of mercantilism as well. Yet Dutch policy in issues relating to the international economy, as practiced, was substantially different from French policy. Dutch policy, as previously discussed, was based largely on commercial expedient, rather than ideology or any other long-term worldview. The major exception to this rule, particularly when the House of Orange was able to predominate over the government of Amsterdam in the making of foreign policy, was Calvinism. For example, the House of Orange pressed for a continuation of the war of independence with Catholic Spain long after de facto independence was achieved, for religious reasons. The end of this war coincided with a decline in the *Stadholder*'s power (or, more precisely, the death of William II and his replacement by an infant). In the third quarter of the seventeenth century the Dutch fought a series of wars with Protestant England over the issue of freedom of navigation, in support of Dutch mariners and merchants. Not long after a resurgence of the power of the House of Orange in 1672 the Prince set out on a military expedition in support of England, to protect the established Protestantism against a Catholic threat. By and large, though, commercial expedient predominated in the making of foreign policy.

Dutch foreign economic policy can be divided into two quite distinct categories, depending on the demands of commercial expedience. To simplify somewhat, Amsterdam acted as a mercantilist power in those areas in which it could establish exclusive political control, and as an economic leader where it could not. In practice, this meant a mercantilist support for some export industries and government chartered trading companies to manage trade outside of Europe, and leadership policies with respect to European trade. By far the most successful and most important of the trading companies was the Dutch East India Company. This was similar to, but more profitable than, the trading companies set up by most of the Atlantic countries during the seventeenth century.[38] It adopted policies that, to put it charitably, established predatory, exploitative monopolies.[39] The basis of the company's profitability was its ability to militarily subdue and politically control its primary producers, securing artificially low costs, and to monopolize the products, securing artificially high returns. This type of policy only worked, though, when the entire source area of the product could be controlled both militarily and politically.[40] This was not the case in Europe and the Mediterranean, where the bulk of Dutch trade was conducted. As such, Dutch policy with respect to its European trade was very different. It showed a clear and unmistakable bias toward international economic leadership, all the more pronounced when seen in contrast to the practices of the mercantile companies.

The first of the functions of leadership as discussed in Chapter 2 is the maintenance and underwriting of a currency for international exchange. This requires three things of a currency. First, that its value fluctuate little enough that people develop long-term confidence in its stability. Second, that it be valued highly enough that people prefer it to other currencies as a store of value. Third, that it be available in a large enough supply internationally that people can make general use of it for international commerce. The government of Holland fulfilled the first and second functions through its minting policy. The government of Amsterdam fulfilled all three functions through the creation of the Bank of Amsterdam.

Very soon after taking control of the currency from the Netherlands (part of the decentralization that was both a goal and a result of the achievement by the United Provinces of de facto independence from Spain in 1581) the government of Holland stabilized the value of the guilder.[41] It allowed a few minor devaluations of the currency against silver over the course of the seventeenth century, but these totaled some 10% while the European norm was to devalue currencies by over half over the course of the century.[42] In other words, the guilder appreciated over the course of the century by a factor of almost two against the average of European currencies. The guilder also retained a high silver content, at the time the sign of a desirable currency. This desirability was so pronounced that there was a constant outward flow of Dutch coin, and the currency base was maintained only through the inflow of some 50 million ounces of new silver from the Americas, via Spain.[43]

The twin problems of a shortage of local coin and the expense involved in converting among a multitude of constantly changing specie currency exchange rates led the government of Amsterdam to create the Bank of Amsterdam in 1609. This was strictly an exchange bank; it accepted deposits and dealt in currency exchanges, but did not lend money, except later in its history to the government of Amsterdam.[44] The Bank created a fixed money of account, the *florin banco*, and published and continually updated exchange rates of other currencies against this. Since the Bank did not print notes and derived its income from service charges, it never had any reason to devalue its currency of account.[45]

Anyone could open an account and thus have access to the largest and most efficient exchange market in the world. As such, the Bank's florins, even though they were really an accounting unit rather than real money, had the same effect as a currency of international exchange; they lowered exchange costs by creating confidence in exchange stability, and they functioned efficiently as a store of value. And finally, because they were an accounting unit rather than a specie currency, the inherent limit on the supply of coinage that hindered commerce at the time did not affect them.

The second function of leadership is the provision of liquidity to the international system, in the long term by maintaining a relatively open market at the core of the international economy for trade goods and services, in the medium term through the provision of countercyclical liquidity, and in the short term by acting as an international lender of last resort. There is no evidence that Holland acted in this last capacity, as lender of last resort. There is in fact no indication that this role was played at all until late in the eighteenth century.[46] With respect to the medium term aspect of the liquidity function, the Dutch government took little direct or legislative action to further this goal. It did, however, help to maintain a steady flow of Dutch capital abroad both diplomatically and by acts of omission.

Diplomatically, it acted in support of Dutch trade representatives abroad in such a way as to stabilize international commerce. In the first half of the seventeenth century the primary form of Dutch foreign direct investment was human capital rather than financial capital. Dutch trade representatives, or commercial factors as they are often referred to, established themselves in all of the major, and most of the minor, ports in Europe.[47] The factors had two main roles; to contract for products in off-seasons and to lend money for bridge financing and capital improvements. The contracts helped to ensure sources of supply and prices from their own points of view, but also guaranteed a market from the producers' point of view. The loans allowed for increased production that might otherwise not have occurred. This proved a very stable form of investment, as these factors tended to stay in the same place for long periods of time, often generationally, and provide steady dividends.[48] The position of the Dutch government was that these factors at the same time remained under Dutch protection but were not to be considered as Dutch political partisans. This helped to secure them in place over long terms, and thus to stabilize this form of foreign investment.

The Dutch government also refrained almost entirely from interfering with the commerce of its citizens with belligerents, a restraint shown by few governments either at the time or since. The seventeenth century featured frequent warfare, with a pattern of constantly changing belligerents and alliances. The Dutch were often involved in these wars, as belligerent, mediator, or financier. Dutch merchants were under no real obligation to support Dutch war efforts (except insofar as they paid for them through their taxes), and were free to trade with, and on occasion even finance, the enemy. In wars in which the United Provinces were nonbelligerent, the Dutch traded with, and often financed, both sides.[49] This break from common practice in not allowing wars to affect commercial and financial flows helped to prevent recurring international violence from interfering with international economic health too substantially.

The long-term aspect of the provision of international liquidity is the maintenance of an open market for the promotion of commerce. It was in this aspect of the provision of liquidity that Dutch government, primarily the city government of Amsterdam, was most active, in two ways. The first was by keeping the domestic market relatively open to foreign goods. The second was by maintaining through public funds the infrastructure necessary for the entrepôt trade, which, through re-exporting, created markets for international goods that would otherwise not have been found.

In the mercantilist era the bulk of revenue raised through taxation in Europe came from some form of land or agricultural tax, and through customs and excise taxes. The urban jurisdictions of the United Provinces, particularly Holland, were the most notable exception. Although it was, by contemporary standards, a very heavily taxed society,[50] customs and excise taxes were infrequent, and where they were to be found they were very low. Revenue was raised through sales taxes, which do not favor domestic products over imports, and through an income tax, a rarity at the time.[51] The accepted rationale for maintaining these forms of taxation was that they were the least likely of possible taxes to be deleterious to foreign trade and commerce. Although the Dutch market itself was relatively small, this absence of tariff barriers allowed easy access to the warehousing and entrepôt facilities that formed for over a century the center of Europe's international commerce.

These entrepôt facilities, at which all major European international buyers were represented, served the function of a market for distressed goods even better than a large domestic market would have, because they allowed access to most of the markets of Europe. Cyclical downturns have, among other things, the effect of lowering confidence of sellers that they will be able to find buyers. This in turn may lead to a decrease in quantities produced. The larger and more liquid the markets in which sellers sell, the less the decrease in confidence. Investment in entrepôt facilities has the effect of creating larger and more liquid markets. Dutch civic governments, particularly the government of Amsterdam, used public funds to help underwrite this entrepôt by maintaining its infrastructure. This included its port facilities, canals, docks, and warehouse facilities,[52] and also included the public regulation of such financial services as insurance, in order to maintain reliability and accepted standards.[53] Although it was not unusual for governments of the time to invest in physical infrastructure to support the local economy, Amsterdam's efforts were unusual both for their focus on international commerce, and for their scale.

The third of the functions of international economic leadership is the definition and protection of a set of basic property rights internationally. The main barriers to trade at the time were technological, organizational, and financial. The Dutch did provide leadership in defining new property rights by diffusing and popularizing new commercial and financial technologies and organizations. This is a form of property rights coordination, as it got everyone using the same forms of monetary and commercial organization. They also introduced some new innovations to the European monetary system, primarily the idea of exchange banking, that by creating new forms of financial property aided the international flow of commerce. Finally, they helped through the innovation of the quasi-public trading company and the example of the East India Company to introduce the idea of non-European territories as commercial, rather than sovereign, territory, or in other words the idea that it was mercantile companies rather than sovereign governments that should occupy and administer colonial/imperial territory.[54]

The Dutch could also provide substantial military force with which to protect their economic prerogatives and with them their conception of international property rights. The confederal political structure meant that this force was often used inefficiently, but that is a different matter.

The Dutch, although possessing a fairly small country, had at their disposal one of Europe's largest navies and the ability to expand it on fairly short notice. They showed a willingness on several occasions to use this navy to fight against other large naval powers in support of commercial principles, and to control piracy on the high seas. For example, they fought two wars with the English, in 1652–1654 and 1664–1667, over (among other things) the principle of freedom of navigation. For a variety of reasons, both organizational and technological, the Dutch navy often lost many of its battles.[55] This was, though, an era of debt-financed wars. Because of the ability of the Dutch governments to raise more capital domestically at better rates than anyone else, they usually outlasted their opponents in wars.[56]

DENOUEMENT

By the end of the seventeenth century the unique Dutch dominance of the servicing of Europe's international trade had begun to fade, a process that continued throughout the eighteenth century. Amsterdam remained a major center of entrepôt trade, but the importance of this trade declined as transportation and financial technologies improved, allowing for more direct trade, and as commercial skills diffused throughout Western Europe. A century of concerted efforts by the English and French governments to develop their shipping industries reduced the need for Dutch shipping, as did the decline of trade in Amsterdam's single most important commodity trade, Baltic grain.[57] The financial capital that had been amassed through this dominance, though, remained, and could not be absorbed domestically. The Dutch gradually went from being the world's traders to being the world's financiers.

Dutch involvement in the direct financing of world trade continued to grow, but the involvement of Amsterdam in other aspects of the servicing of international trade declined continuously. It was replaced by Dutch foreign investment, particularly in government bonds. This investment was scattered across Europe, but the greatest part of it went to England and, to a lesser extent, France. By the late eighteenth century, over a third of total Dutch capital was absorbed by loans abroad, of which some four-fifths was in England.[58] The investments in England included a greater element of commercial paper than was the case elsewhere, but did included a significant portion of the British national debt.[59]

As this transition occurred, the position of Amsterdam in the world economy, and its commercial and financial capabilities with respect to the international economy, declined. Amsterdam ceased being the necessary financial intermediary in international transactions. It continued to be important, and the resources of Amsterdam's financial community continued to increase in absolute terms, but at a rate slower than the rate of growth of the international economy. This meant that Dutch financial resources got smaller relative to the total of financial transactions that affected them, which in turn meant that the Amsterdam financial market was less able to withstand shocks from outside. Dutch financial predominance declined slowly in this fashion for roughly half a century. In the third quarter of the eighteenth century it disappeared completely, undermined both by financial crises and domestic social unrest.

As Amsterdam's financiers removed themselves increasingly from direct involvement in commerce and trade, the city's financial markets became increasingly speculative. Given a shortage of real outlets for investment and very low domestic rates of interest, paper assets became increasingly overvalued.[60] This, in turn, led to the occasional panic, as the assets, the value of which was based primarily on investors' faith in them, crashed in value. Three particularly bad financial crises were sparked by such panics between 1763 and 1783. These involved some of the most substantial and respected firms in Amsterdam, and eliminated a significant portion of both the city's financial resources and its prestige.[61] During the same period the Dutch East India Company, which was by far the largest company in the Netherlands and was almost a country unto itself, collapsed after a century and a half of high profitability.

To complement the disappearance of wealth caused by this series of collapses and crises, the Dutch political structure was paralyzed by domestic civil unrest in the 1780s, by a revolution that heralded the social changes that were soon to affect all of Europe.[62] The Dutch pattern of government that had remained relatively constant throughout the seventeenth century began to change in the eighteenth. The Prince of Orange became King of England, and focused less of his attention on the United Provinces as a result.[63] The gradual decline of the Netherlands from Great Power status made decisions of the national council less important internationally. The greatest part of this decline coincided with, and was to some extent caused by, the war with France in 1702–1713, motivated by religious and dynastic more than commercial concerns, in which the Dutch overreached themselves. The resultant debt load prevented them from being able to engage in major wars or naval activity for the rest of the century.[64] These two factors led to a decline of the national government with respect to the urban governments, particularly that of Amsterdam. At the urban level the plutocracy began to ossify and with it social mobility.[65] At the same time the income base of the plutocracy began to shift from merchant banking, a pursuit requiring active participation in the urban economy, to *rentier* finance, which did not.[66] While the elite retained its control over government, its interests began to diverge from those of Amsterdam generally. These two trends created a degree of class conflict that increased steadily throughout the eighteenth century, and culminated in the revolution of 1784–1788 that effectively put an end to independent government and policy in Amsterdam.[67]

Mirroring the decline in Dutch financial predominance, the Dutch leadership role in the international economy declined gradually throughout the course of the eighteenth century. The Amsterdam entrepôt became less viable as a market for distressed international trade goods as the Dutch role in the financing and organizing of international trade waned. With the decline in the entrepôt trade came a decline in the international role of the Bank of Amsterdam, as its services were available only to those traders physically present in Amsterdam. The institution had in any case failed to keep pace with the modernization of financial technologies, and was being increasingly seen by the government of Amsterdam primarily as a source of loans rather than as a service to commerce. The decline in the importance of Dutch capital to the international economy also limited the extent to which they were able to promote liquidity countercyclically; they lost the capability to do so effectively. Finally, the decline of Dutch financial predominance contributed to the political marginalization of the United Provinces in Europe, further limiting their already circumscribed role as macroeconomic policy coordinators, and as creators and protectors of property rights.

CONCLUSIONS

The seventeenth century began with a pattern of long-distance trade in Europe that was based on a system of monetary exchange, but did not have a central government capable of authoritatively providing economic infrastructure. Expansion of the European economy was, at the turn of that century, being hindered by limitations inherent in the logic of monetary systems of exchange, limitations that could only be overcome by the provision of financial infrastructure that increased liquidity and decreased the costs of commerce. In other words, a money-based system was in place, and it created a demand for international economic leadership. Global trade more broadly, on the other hand, cannot really be characterized in the same way. In particular, the trade between Europe and much of the rest of the world was based on coercive exchange, on the use of force, rather than market exchange.

It was the Dutch who were most capable of supplying the demand for leadership, because they had the investment in international commerce in place that generated both the liquidity and the confidence necessary for successful leadership. For example, the liquidity in the Amsterdam entrepôt generated by the dominant Dutch investment in maritime commerce made a central exchange bank such as the Bank of Amsterdam feasible, by both bringing sufficient numbers of traders together in one place for the bank to work efficiently, and creating confidence among them that the bank would remain liquid in the future. Similarly, the confidence generated by this predominant level of investment generated the confidence necessary to attract the customers that infrastructure needs in order to have effect.

At the same time, the community of Dutch investors in international commerce, primarily the merchants and merchant bankers of Amsterdam, had a strong interest in providing this infrastructure, insofar as they were interested in protecting the value of their investments. International financial infrastructure had the effects both of making easier for them to invest efficiently by decreasing transaction costs, and of increasing the potential profitability of international commerce by generating growth in the international economy that that commerce serviced. This combination of the ability of Dutch governmental authorities to provide international economic leadership and the interest of a key political community within the Dutch polity in doing so suggests a strong likelihood that some form of international commercial infrastructure would be provided by the United Provinces.

Meanwhile, France had neither the ability nor the interest. This in itself is not remarkable; few countries have the ability to act as international economic leaders, nor is it common for an economically and politically central community within a country to have such a strong interest in doing so. What makes the comparison of France with the United Provinces interesting in this case is the central role that France played both in European politics and in European production and trade at the time. By most traditional measures, France was hegemonic. Yet there was never any possibility of it providing a basic financial infrastructure to the European international economy. This is both because one of the few measures in which it was not hegemonic is the one that matters in this context, and because leadership requires of a country not only the requisite power resources, but also a decision-making elite motivated to lead. France had neither.

So the Dutch acted to some degree as leaders. They did not, it is true, address the full range of demands of leadership in the way that, for example, the British did two centuries later. One has to some extent to take Dutch leadership in the context of its time and compare it with the behavior of its contemporaries, rather than the behavior of future leaders. In this context, it shows a far more pronounced and consistent tendency to lead than anyone else. But the content of this leadership was heavily influenced by, and significantly hindered by, the social construction of seventeenth-century economics and politics. In particular, two historically specific contexts of Dutch leadership mark the most distinct contrasts with more recent patterns of international economic leadership, ideology and the system of government in the United Provinces at the time. The most notable aspect of the ideology of Dutch leadership, from our current perspective looking backward, is its absence. In contrast to the variants of liberalism that have informed both British and American foreign economic policy in the past two centuries, the only hegemonic social construction to inform Dutch policies of economic leadership involved those of immediate commercial expedient. Ideology, specifically Calvinism, did inform aspects of, or more precisely some makers of, Dutch security policy: Much of the history of Dutch military endeavor in the seventeenth and into the eighteenth century can be read as a tug-of-war between commercial expedient and Calvinism for control of this policy. But in most aspects of specifically economic foreign policy, commercial expedient predominated. This point is made clear by the overt and predatory mercantilism of Dutch commercial practice whenever such an approach proved profitable, and the provision of market infrastructure only where commerce could not be controlled by force. As a result, Dutch leadership tended to be somewhat ad hoc, providing specific solutions to immediate demands for commercial infrastructure, but without embedding these solutions in a broader institutional framework.

This tendency to the ad hoc was exacerbated by the Dutch system of government. Broad economic and juridical powers were vested in civic governments, and by far the most important of these governments, Amsterdam's, was controlled by a patriciate, a commercial oligarchy with a strong and direct economic interest in an international financial infrastructure. In other words, those most interested in international economic leadership did not have to compete with other interest groups to sway policy-makers; they *were* the policy-makers. As such, policy in Amsterdam in the seventeenth century often did not reflect the sort of compromises among interests often seen in the making of foreign economic policy, but rather catered directly to the specific demands of the entrepôt trade, and thus to the infrastructural needs of the international economy. But again, it did so in the service of immediate commercial expedient, in a way not particularly colored by any broader worldview. Furthermore, the norm of commercial expedient as justification for policy went largely unchallenged within Amsterdam, and to a lesser extent within Holland more generally. And as the commercial oligarchy became a *rentier* oligarchy over the course of the eighteenth century, the same commercial expedient led to a gradual withdrawal from the leadership role.

This direct institutional link between finance and government characterized the policy of the city government of Amsterdam, and to a significant degree the provincial government of Holland that it dominated politically, but not that of the United Provinces. Even when policy at the national level was made in support of leadership policies, as was to an extent the case with the Anglo-Dutch wars, it was left up to Amsterdam to actually implement the policy. Thus the specifics of Dutch seventeenth-century international economic leadership were colored not only by the ideological milieu in which they were constructed, but also by the quirks of the system of government; in those areas in which city governments had primary jurisdiction, Amsterdam led. In those areas where the national government had primary jurisdiction, the United Provinces for the most part did not.

In short, this case illustrates all three stages of the methodological argument being made here. In the first stage, it separates economic systems based on money/market exchange from those based on authoritative exchange. Dutch trade within Europe was of the former kind, while Dutch trade with most of the rest of the world was of the latter. Within the former, the logic of financial predominance applies; within the latter, it does not. The logic of the European market economy at the beginning of the seventeenth century suggested both that there was a demand for international economic leadership, and that the Dutch, having both the capabilities and motivations of financial predominance, were well placed to supply it. At the third stage, the specific mechanisms, and the limitations of the mechanisms, designed to provide that leadership reflected the historical social context in which Dutch policy was made. The focus on physical infrastructure such as port facilities and banks over social infrastructure, such as macroeconomic policy coordination, reflected both the ideological milieu of the policy process and the political/institutional norms that governed policy-making. The ad-hoc style of leadership policies, the focus of those policies only on those areas where they would maximize Amsterdam's commercial profit, without any real policy overflow onto other areas of Dutch international relations, suggest that social contexts not only affect leadership policies, but can constrain them as well.

4

The Nineteenth Century and British Leadership

From roughly 1860 to 1914, Britain was the financial center of the world. The City of London, as the square-mile area of downtown London just west of the Tower of London is known, generated most of the world's foreign investment, managed most of the world's international trade services, and was looked to as the center of the global economy. The majority of international trade was carried on British ships. The economic well-being of Great Britain was critically dependent on the expansion of the international economy, and its government recognized this and made conscious efforts to act accordingly. Britain was in many ways the classic example of international economic and monetary leadership. This chapter picks up the story as the Dutch were leaving the spotlight of the international financial stage and as the British were entering it.

If Dutch policy in the seventeenth century is an interesting case in the study of international economic leadership because of the absence both of a liberal ideology as context and of a broader Dutch hegemony, Great Britain in the latter half of the nineteenth century is the flip side of the coin. The *Pax Britannica* was a world order that seemed dominated by the British both politically and ideologically, as well as economically. The story of Dutch leadership allows us to focus on finance because the Dutch predominated in little else. The British story is methodologically interesting for the opposite reason; the connection between finance and leadership becomes even more compelling when the link is clear and is embedded in a case where the international predominance of the leader was far more widespread. The contrast between Dutch and British leaderships also provides an interesting contrast in social contexts and leadership policies. The story often told of the British economic role at that time is not a convincing portrayal of British foreign economic policy and international economic leadership in the period from the middle of the nineteenth century to the outbreak of World War One. The history of British policy in this period, particularly as it is used by theorists of hegemony and leadership in international relations, is often told as one of industrial predominance and export promotion.[1] It suggests that Britain was motivated by its industrial strength to maintain an open international trade system. There are two primary historical problems with this story. First, most of the period of openness in the late nineteenth and early twentieth century coincided with a relative British industrial decline. Declining industries often perceived that their interests lay with increased tariffs; these industrial interests did not, however, become the national interest. British industrial predominance, which peaked in the early nineteenth century, simply does not coincide with the period of British international economic and monetary leadership, which lasted from the 1850s until 1914. The second problem is that Britain, with few exceptions, did little to open markets abroad; its own free trade policy was unaffected by the tariff policies of its trading partners. If exports were the factor motivating British policy, they should have been more interested in opening the markets of other countries and less adamant about keeping their own open. The story told here, informed by a logic of money rather than one of trade, runs into neither of these difficulties.

ANTECEDENTS

The roots of the predominant position of Great Britain in the late nineteenth century international economy can be traced well back into the eighteenth century. By the end of that century, at the outbreak of the Napoleonic Wars, Britain was already one of the world's wealthiest countries.[2] By 1830, British GNP exceeded that of all European countries except Russia, and its per capita GNP was approached only by that of the Netherlands.[3] Britain also had the world's largest merchant shipping fleet, and a thriving and profitable merchant and trade services sector.[4] The nascent industrial revolution, beginning in the middle of the eighteenth century, had given the British a distinct qualitative advantage over other countries in many areas of manufacturing, to such an extent that they were beginning to think of themselves as the "workshop of the world."[5]

At this time, though, Britain had had strongly mercantilist policies for over a century. Combined with a global empire, these policies had created an economy based substantially on trade with, investment in, and exploitation of its colonies, over which Britain had direct political control.[6] The English East India Company operated on the same general principles as its Dutch equivalent.[7] Political devices such as the Navigation Acts, which restricted most trade involving Britain to British ships, were designed specifically to take advantage of this position of direct control over the Empire to promote the growth of both its shipping and its trade and financial services sectors.[8] Britain dominated its empire both politically and economically, and economic policy focused on mechanisms of authoritative control designed to promote monopoly profits, rather than the provision of structural public goods to encourage the expansion of the international economy.

This foreign economic structure based on mercantilism and formal empire was already showing strains by the beginning of the French Revolutionary Wars at the end of the eighteenth century. The British economy had simply grown too large for the Empire. In particular, the British shipping and trade services industries, which had flourished under the protectionism of the Navigation Acts, began to reach the limits of growth possible through intra-empire trade. They needed a larger international economic arena in order to maintain and further their traditional rates of growth. This phenomenon can be seen as a controlled experiment in what happens to internationalist economies when government policy is designed to prey upon or exploit their economic partners. Britain's mercantilist, protectionist policies did allow for faster economic growth than would otherwise have been the case for a period of time. They did so to a certain extent, though, at the expense of the rest of the Empire. This eventually resulted in a situation in which the continuing expansion of the British economy required further economic growth within the empire, while at the same time British policy prevented that growth. This contradiction was apparent to British merchants at the time, a major factor in the subsequent changes in British policy that will be discussed later.[9]

A final factor contributing to British financial predominance in the nineteenth century was the creation of the Bank of England in 1694. The bank was designed primarily as a mechanism to fund the national debt. It acted as an intermediary between the government as a borrower and individual lenders, serving to both decrease the cost of borrowing for the government and increasing the confidence of lenders that their investment was secure.[10] As a result, by the middle of the eighteenth century England had developed the world's most advanced and efficient public finance sector.[11] This sector provided a secure outlet for the large pools of investment capital generated by such profitable sectors of the economy as colonial trade and the colonial agricultural industry.[12]

This capital was absorbed primarily by the state. Throughout the eighteenth century, the British government ran substantial budget deficits. It had to do this to pay for an adventurous foreign policy and a domestic patronage system on the one hand, and to mollify aristocratic interests by keeping the land tax low on the other.[13] It paid for this consistent pattern of deficit spending by increasing the national debt to levels that would not have been possible without the creation of the Bank of England. This debt grew so much over the course of the century that it absorbed much of the investment capital available on the London financial market. By the end of the century the national debt had become the investment of choice for substantial financiers.[14] The debt mushroomed during the Napoleonic era, as the government borrowed even more heavily to pay for an enormous war effort: the cumulative national debt increased from £244 million in 1790 to £840 million in 1820.[15] The residual effect of this increase was to absorb surplus capital throughout the war and for a short time afterwards.

Normal patterns of international commerce were interrupted for almost two decades by the Napoleonic wars, and the British government suspended both the convertibility of its currency and economic interaction with much of Europe for the duration.[16] At the end of the wars, governments had to resume peacetime economic policies. Britain had the options of resuming the prewar economic structure of mercantilism and empire trade, of adopting a structure based on industrial policy and the protection of British industrial advantage, or of working toward a liberalized economic structure that would promote the British commercial position internationally. For reasons that will become clear later on in this chapter, it chose to liberalize.

British economic policy, implemented gradually in the three decades following the Napoleonic wars, focused on liberalization with respect to foreign relations, and what came to be known as "orthodoxy" domestically.[17] The liberalization of its foreign economic policies followed the standard pattern of reducing barriers to the free flow of trade and factors of production. This involved rescinding legislation restricting imports, exports, and trade services. The process began with the gradual weakening of the chartered trading companies, export controls, and Navigation Laws, and culminated with the repeal of most agricultural tariffs in 1846. Liberalization in foreign economic policy coincided with a new approach to managing the domestic political economy—financial orthodoxy. This new approach entailed a set of policies including bureaucratic reform and the maintenance of a balanced budget. This aspect of orthodoxy, the balanced budget, was to have a direct impact on the growth of British international financial dominance.

The British government put financial orthodoxy into effect much more quickly than liberalization policies. The eighteenth-century pattern of government deficits stopped quickly following end of the French wars in 1815. By 1820, the budget was in surplus, where it remained throughout the century.[18] Thus the pattern of investment favored by the London financial markets in the previous century had to change; the national debt was no longer growing, and thus could no longer absorb increases in available investment capital. Nor could this investment readily be transferred to domestic industry. British industrial concerns tended to be fairly small, and thus they were inefficient outlets for large-scale investment. These concerns could usually finance their investment through equity and regional borrowing, thus obviating any need for investment capital from London.[19] Therefore, balancing the budget had the direct effect of encouraging British investment abroad, first within the empire and then, as the funds available began to exceed the ability of the empire to absorb them, internationally.

INTERNATIONAL FINANCE

Much of the capital that was no longer being absorbed by the national debt made its way into international finance. At first, this investment was largely in trade services, such as insurance; Lloyd's, the London insurance market that established itself as the primary insurer of international commerce at the time, remains important in that role to this day. But one of the effects of the industrial revolution was to create a whole range of opportunities for foreign investment outside areas of national political and military control, a process that was greatly expanded by the popularization of the railroad in mid-century.

Infrastructural investments such as railroads absorbed pools of capital comparable in scale only with those absorbed by the chartered merchant companies in the previous century. With the global expansion of the industrial economy came a parallel expansion of investment opportunities abroad.

As a result of these factors, Britain's financial stake in the international economy grew rapidly in the period from 1815 to 1850. By the end of this period, it constituted a critical element of the British economy. From the mid-1850s to 1914, income earned abroad, derived from financial and trade services abroad and dividends from foreign investments, combined to constitute well over 10% of the British GNP, reaching a peak of 16% in the 1890s.[20] This figure constituted more than a third of the total profit generated by the national economy. Throughout this period foreign investment grew at a phenomenal rate, while the international services sector, composed primarily of shipping and financial services, expanded at a more moderate pace. Given, though, that the international services sector was expanding from a well-established base, while international investment was growing from almost nothing, services remained the primary British commitment to the international economy. In fact, it was not until the early 1890s that total income from investment began to exceed total income from international financial services,[21] although, as will be discussed, the domestic political process did not necessarily reflect this.

Britain between 1850 and 1914 displayed all the characteristics of a financially predominant country, both in the financing and servicing of international commerce, and in foreign investment. It was the world's largest trader, accounting for between one-fifth and one-quarter of total world trade for most of the nineteenth century. A high fraction of this trade was re-exports, suggesting that there was an active entrepôt trade, and thus that high levels of trade did not simply reflect manufacturing power. Britain throughout this period was also the world's predominant servicer of international trade. Roughly half of the world's shipping tonnage was British throughout the century. In 1850, Britain was the only large-scale foreign investor outside of a formal empire. By 1914, British foreign investments totaled nearly £4 billion. The next largest foreign investor was France, with £1.7 billion, followed by Germany with £1 billion and the United States with £400 million. Thus even by the end of this period, Britain was by far the world's largest foreign investor, holding more such investments than all other countries combined.[22]

The degree of British international financial predominance remained relatively stable from the 1860s to 1914. It was almost entirely unaffected by the long depression of 1873–1896. Trade services fluctuated somewhat, but showed a pattern of slow growth in absolute terms, slow decline as a proportion of the national income, and a rather more marked decline as a proportion of global trade services. Foreign investment followed a pattern of rapid growth in absolute terms, and substantial growth as a proportion of the national income. It declined as a proportion of world totals, but only because other countries started with almost no such investment at all. In sum, the two taken together followed a pattern of slow but steady increase as a proportion of the national income, and remained predominant as a proportion of world totals.[23]

INSTITUTIONAL SOURCES OF POLICY

The growth of Britain's international financial role was mirrored by a growth of the role of the British internationalist financial sector in government foreign economic policy-making institutions. From the late eighteenth century to the early twentieth, the growth of financial predominance and the ability of British internationally oriented financiers to affect foreign economic policy-making had mutually reinforcing effects. Prior to the Napoleonic wars, those merchants involved in empire trade were able to begin a slow, gradual process of dismantling the eighteenth-century system of British mercantilist protectionism. This in turn allowed for the more rapid growth of British involvement in the international economy. This growth resulted in an increase in access by the internationalist financial sector to government policy, leading to further growth, leading to greater access, and so forth.

Two institutions in nineteenth-century Britain were primarily responsible for generating foreign economic policy: Parliament and the Bank of England. Parliament was responsible for commercial policy, creating mechanisms such as tariffs and export controls, and for maintaining fiscal policies. Through these mechanisms it had been the orchestrator of the mercantilist system in the seventeenth and eighteenth centuries. The Bank of England was responsible for much of England's monetary policy, and was the body responsible for underwriting the British currency, sterling,[24] as the primary currency for international exchange. Much of the differential rate at which Britain adopted leadership policies, starting with financial policies and moving only gradually to tariff reform, can be explained by the differing structures and memberships of these two institutions.

The Bank of England was unusual for an institution with autonomous national policy-making powers in that it was, throughout the period in question, privately owned. It was established and chartered in 1694, and was granted monopoly powers over the management of the national debt. This provided the British government with a stable, reliable, and efficient source of funds at relatively low rates. By the nineteenth century the Bank had adopted most of the functions of modern central banks.[25] The government had considerable leverage over the Bank; the monopoly on which the Bank's profitability was based came from government legislation that occasionally needed renewal, and the government was not above threatening to withhold this renewal as a means of coercing concessions from the Bank. Nevertheless, it was owned and operated privately. The Bank's management was overseen by its Board of Governors, whose membership was drawn from among those who owned stock in the Bank. In practice, these governors came almost exclusively from the City of London's merchant and merchant banker community.[26] In other words, internationalist financial interests had a direct and definitive voice in the creation of those areas of monetary policy that the Bank controlled. This direct control helps to explain Britain's enthusiasm for the gold standard and for acting as a lender of last resort internationally, as will be discussed.

Parliament was subject to more variegated interest group pressures. It consisted of two Houses, the Lords and the Commons. The former was populated by titled aristocrats, either hereditary or appointed, who kept their parliamentary seats for life. The latter was a body of elected representatives. For the purposes of this story, it is important to remember that not all Englishmen could vote in elections for the commons;[27] there was a minimum property requirement in order to be eligible to vote. This requirement was gradually reduced over the years, so that whereas in the eighteenth century only the upper middle class was eligible, by the early twentieth century most of the middle class and much of the working class could vote. Over time, as well, the balance of power between the two Houses shifted, in favor of the Commons. As such, by 1914, Parliament was a very different institution from what it had been at the end of the eighteenth century. The House of Lords had become much less powerful than the Commons, suffrage had increased dramatically, and the party system had developed, solidified, and come to dominate political life.[28] These developments had various and mixed effects on parliamentary responses to internationalist financial motivations.

One particular aspect of parliamentary tradition that remained fairly constant over time was the normative separation of high and low politics. The "low politics" of economic policy tended to be thought of quite apart from the "high politics" of alliances and wars. Britain carried out its international economic role unilaterally; economic policy tended not to be used to support the high politics of treaties and diplomatic maneuverings. The development of this norm may have reflected the historical division of powers within the British government, with Parliament responsible for economic policy and the monarchy responsible for diplomacy and war. It may simply have been a historical quirk. Other governments tended not to separate these two realms in the same way. France, for example, was prone to channeling foreign investment for political ends, such as loans to the Russian government to encourage an alliance.[29] The British government was far less prone to use economic policy to effect diplomatic or security goals.

DOMESTIC POLITICS

British mercantilism in the eighteenth century was based on control of a politically formal empire. This system evolved as a compromise between the landed interests of the old, conservative aristocracy, and the merchant and commercial interests that had become an important and growing element of the English economy. The merchant and commercial interests were given a captive market in which to grow and prosper. The landed interests were given protection for agriculture, and were provided considerable opportunity for patronage in the management of a large imperial structure. The costs of this system were paid primarily by consumers, both through taxation in the form of tariffs and through the higher prices that resulted from protection and government-sponsored monopolies. This compromise reflected the balance of power in Parliament. The landed aristocracy dominated the House of Lords with its hereditary membership, at first almost exclusively but gradually less so as financiers became ennobled. The wealthier of the merchant and commercial classes made up the bulk of those eligible, given the high capital requirements in force at the time, to vote for representation in the House of Commons. Similarly, public office in London at the time was disproportionately filled with the wealthier among the merchant class.[30] The mass of consumers had no representation in government at all. This is not to say that their interests were ignored. Inasmuch as unemployment leads to social instability, British governments throughout this period were committed to high employment policies.[31] But it was much easier to make consumers subsidize the system than either merchants or the nobility.

The one area of economic policy not dictated by this mercantilist compromise was monetary policy. Beginning in 1717 and continuing, except during the Napoleonic wars, for two centuries, the value of sterling was fixed against and convertible to gold.[32] Convertibility and the gold standard were not requirements of a mercantilist policy. In fact, they detracted from the ability of the state to manipulate its currency to pursue its fiscal needs and mercantilist goals.[33] They were, however, in the interests of the private owners of the Bank of England, who required a stable and reliable currency for their own purposes. One of the primary advantages to governments of devaluating their currencies is to devalue their debt. Since the Bank held the national debt in sterling, it had a strong interest in not letting the government devalue. Its primary goal was to generate profit for its owners, and the net effect of a devaluation would be that the Bank's owners would end up subsidizing the national budget. Thus one important prerequisite of international economic leadership—the maintenance of a strong and stable currency—was undertaken by Britain throughout the eighteenth century. It was not done for internationalist reasons, but it was done nonetheless.

By the time of the Napoleonic wars, it was becoming clear that the merchant and industrial sectors of the British economy were growing too fast for the constraints of formal empire. Both needed a broader international economy within which to operate. Merchant interests clearly favored international leadership policies, weakly right after war ended in 1815 but more strongly by the early to mid-1820s.[34] Industrial interests were mixed, but many were not opposed to these policies, especially industries that did not face direct competition from abroad. There is some evidence that these interests were split fairly evenly on the subject of protection. "In 1817, the president of the Board of Trade, Frederick Robinson, lamented that many of the burdens on imports operated to hurt British exports by depriving foreigners of the means of paying for British goods. But he felt he could do nothing. Whenever he proposed to reduce restrictions he had half the manufacturers in the country in arms against him. Each claimed it would ruin him."[35] The old landed interests favored a continuation of the status quo.[36] Of these three groups, merchant interests were in the strongest position to effect their policy choices, for three primary reasons; their interests were the most coherent, they conformed to an accepted notion of the national interest, and the financiers who held these interests were very well suited to the culture of British politics at the time.

Internationalist merchant and financial interests tended to agree to a great degree on international economic leadership as their preferred foreign economic policy.[37] There was also a substantial agreement on the part of landed interests, but this was tempered by two factors. The first is that many of the more successful of the old landed nobility had branched out into finance, and thus were beginning to share financial interests.[38] The second is that, with respect to many aspects of foreign economic policy other than agricultural tariffs, such as exchange rate policy, landed interests did not have reason to care much one way or the other. Industrial interests, on the other hand, were much more mixed. Leading-edge industries, such as cotton early on and railroads by the middle of the nineteenth century, were more interested in creating purchasing power abroad than in combating competition that did not exist. They therefore tended not to be opposed to international leadership policies.[39] Industries that were not qualitatively different from what existed abroad tended more to favor mercantilism (by the end of the nineteenth century traditional mercantilism had been replaced by a protectionism called "imperial preference," which involved tariffs only on producers not within the British Empire).[40] Internationalist interests, which encompassed some industrial as well as merchant and commercial interests, were thus more coherent than mercantilist interests. It is interesting to note in this context that leadership policies that did not conflict directly with agricultural interests were adopted much faster than those that did.

British government was not, though, simply an open battleground of competing interests. Policy-makers did act on their conception of a broader national interest, which in turn reflected the social construction of nineteenth-century British political discourse. The maintenance of social stability often featured as a prominent element of this discourse. Stability in turn required minimizing unemployment, as the political classes perceived that large numbers of idle unemployed posed a great social threat. Agriculture was not a growth industry;[41] it could not contribute much to expanding employment. Industry was a rapidly growing employer; between 1841 and 1911, roughly the era of British leadership, manufacturing employment grew by 258%.[42] There was, however, no general agreement on how to maximize this employment. Moreover, most industrial employment was in northern England, far away from the London populace that was the most visible problem as far as the government, also in London, was concerned. Internationalist interests, primarily merchants and trade servicers, were also large and rapidly growing employers; employment in commerce and finance grew by 786% between 1841 and 1911, and in transport and communications by 802%.[43] Employment in these industries was also disproportionately large in London, and there was general agreement as to how to maximize it.[44] Governments in London concerned with social stability therefore tended to pay disproportionate heed to the concerns of the international financial sector.

British political culture more broadly at the time was also conducive to the influence of the financial sector on government policy. This culture was characterized by a phenomenon that P. J. Cain and and A. G. Hopkins have referred to as "gentlemanly capitalism,"[45] in which financiers were particularly suited to participation in government. The British parliamentary system of the time allowed for considerable overt access by the economic elite to the legislature, both directly in the case of the House of Lords and representationally in the Commons. Participation in this system required three things: substantial wealth, considerable free time, and access to London. Landed interests generally had all three, and were thus a potent political force well into the nineteenth century. Beginning in mid-century, though, the ability to sustain aristocratic lifestyles on agricultural incomes began to fail. Even the most substantial of industrialists, however, were less suited to participate in this system. They were generally located in the north, far away from London, and were engaged in running businesses that were full-time occupations. Furthermore, factory work was seen as something dirty, vulgar, and thus an unsuitable pursuit for a "gentleman."

Financiers did not share these stigmas. The City of London is within walking distance of Parliament, and merchant banking allows for considerable free time.[46] It is also a more Platonic pursuit than industrialism; like imperial administration, it was seen as suitable work for an aristocrat. British political leaders, generally aristocrats themselves, were often in fact directly hostile to industrialism. Lord Liverpool, prime minister after the Napoleonic wars, saw the industrial revolution as a "malignant aberration," and tariff reform as a way to reduce, rather than expand, exports.[47] This attitude was reflected in the fact that many financiers were elevated to the peerage, while industrialists, for the most part, were not.[48] The greater affinity of financiers than industrialists with British political culture gave them better and more direct access to the mechanisms of policy-making.

Over time the policy demands of the internationalist financial sector came to be adopted as a new economic common sense through the more generalized economic ideology of laissez-faire liberalism. Policy reflecting these motivations could therefore be expressed through attention to the ideology, without the government appearing to favor the City of London over other vested interests. It is interesting in this context to note that laissez-faire liberalism was much more deeply internalized as an international than as a domestic common sense. As international leadership policies were solidifying around mid-century, the government was enacting several pieces of legislation intended to interfere with the domestic market for reasons of social welfare, aimed primarily at improving minimum working conditions.[49] Liberal ideology served as much as an expression of economically internationalist motivations as it did as an independent input into policy. Adam Smith had originally argued the laissez-faire case with respect to policy abroad, and the patterns of British domestic politics tended to reinforce this international focus.[50]

A final related note on the politics of Great Britain's foreign economy policies is that they tended to be unilateral; the British persevered in them irrespective of the actions of others. There was a brief period in the 1860s when there was an attempt to achieve reciprocity in free trade, which met with some success. This success, though, had more to do with the domestic needs of the other parties than with British power per se. France and Prussia, each for its own reasons, autonomously preferred lower tariffs at the time.[51] This success was also short-lived; with the depression of 1873, most of Europe reverted to a higher level of protectionism as their interests changed due to an international glut of manufactures. Britain did not raise tariffs, partly for normative reasons, but also because its interests had not changed.[52] The British did not attempt to achieve reciprocity in tariffs again. This unilateralism, which is the exception to the pattern seen in other cases in this book, reflects both the compromises reached in the domestic political process, and the strength with which the laissez-faire ideology in which leadership policies were embedded came to dominate thinking on international economic policy in Britain at the time. It also serves to highlight the degree to which the industrial sector, which would have the greatest interest in tariff reciprocity, was effectively excluded from the foreign economic policy-making process.

THE EVOLUTION OF POLICY

British mercantilist policy in the eighteenth century was consciously exploitative, seeing the gain from international economics as coming from a zero-sum victory over others rather than from increased efficiency through comparative advantages. Being a zero-sum interaction, mercantilism worked best within the sphere of British political and military control, in other words within the empire. As suggested earlier, this system is self-limiting; because it hinders growth in one's international economic partners, mercantilism inevitably limits the amount that can be extracted from them. As this became clear to British policy-makers, and as the point of diminishing returns was reached near the end of the eighteenth century, the philosophy underlying British foreign economic policy began to change.

The first of the policies that were to characterize British leadership in the later nineteenth century to be enacted was the maintenance of a stable, highly valued currency. The Bank of England maintained the convertibility of sterling to gold at a fixed par. This was done throughout the eighteenth and nineteenth centuries, with the exception of the period of the Napoleonic wars. The next major step was the weakening of the East India Company's monopoly in 1793. The company had been criticized for decades for its inefficiency; as early as 1776, Adam Smith could indict it "for all the extraordinary waste which the fraud and abuse, inseparable from the management of the affairs of so great a company, must necessarily have occasioned."[53] The concern that motivated the dismantling of the mercantilist system was for British competitiveness rather than for the needs of the international economy. It was, though, the first step toward a liberalized economic policy structure that could lay the basis for international macroeconomic policy coordination.

The magnitude of the threat of revolutionary France, both in terms of physical security and in terms of ideology, was such that all elite interests in Britain could agree on the suspension of business as usual until Napoleon was dealt with. There is some evidence to indicate that mass interests viewed the situation similarly.[54] The return to a civilian economy shortly after the war was conducted as a compromise between the interests of the internationalist and agricultural sectors. The interests of the industrial sector were largely excluded. "Commercial reform and the return to gold were designed to make Britain the warehouse of the world rather than its workshop."[55] Currency convertibility was reestablished as quickly as was practical, in 1819. Since the reasons for a strong currency were not originally internationalist, it was only gradually, over the course of half a century, that the Bank of England adopted sole responsibility for underwriting the international monetary system as a whole. Commercial reform and the termination of most export controls also began fairly quickly. This included the revocation of the Navigation Acts and the dismantling of the monopoly trading companies. These new policies were enough to spark a rapid growth of the internationalist elements of the British economy.

The spate of commercial and fiscal reforms that followed the Napoleonic wars created a monetary and commercial structure that provided a model for international coordination. That the British thought of this model as "orthodoxy" implies that they saw it as something inherently proper, as something that both could and should be made universal. In other words, as a common sense. This aura of propriety was moral and ethical as well as purely economic; convertibility and balanced budgets, it has been suggested, conformed well with Protestant ideas of honesty and individual moral responsibility.[56] Whether or not this is the case, orthodoxy clearly became, in the realm of government policy, ideologically hegemonic. Remember, though, that orthodoxy referred primarily to monetary and fiscal policies, rather than tariffs. A country that maintained a balanced budget and the convertibility of its currency into gold at a fixed par would be considered financially sound even if it maintained protectionist tariffs. The United States, for example, maintained currency convertibility and a balanced budget for most of the era of British financial predominance, and this generated sufficient confidence to allow it to become the largest single recipient of of British foreign investment, despite consistently high tariffs and protectionist policies.[57]

Britain itself maintained substantial tariffs a full thirty years after the end of the Napoleonic wars. Merchant, investment, and most industrial interests, and in fact many agricultural interests as well, agreed early in the century that these tariffs should go. The landed gentry's need for protection and the government's need for revenue, however, were sufficient to block tariff reform. As the coalition in favour of free trade became broader and more vocal, it gradually succeeded in lowering Britain's tariff barriers, beginning with barriers to manufactured goods. The last set of major tariffs to be lifted, the agricultural tariffs known as the Corn Laws, were in many ways the most important, as many of Britain's major trading partners and investment recipients were primarily agricultural exporters. The infrastructural projects that tended to be the investments of choice for London's financiers served often to expand the scope of cultivation by opening up previously inaccessible hinterlands, and thus required a secure market for primary agricultural goods.[58]

There are two primary reasons that import controls such as tariffs were the last vestiges of eighteenth-century mercantilism to go. The first is that they were the primary source of governmental revenue. In the 1830s, customs and excise taxes accounted for an average of just over 70% of central government revenue, a figure fairly typical of peacetime budgets for over a century. Even with the reestablishment of the income tax (it had been created originally during the Napoleonic wars) customs and excise taxes remained the largest single element of government revenue until World War One.[59] Given that the government was committed to balanced budgets as part of its commercial reform, tariff reductions would have to be offset by increases in other sources of revenue. By 1841, Parliament had decided to impose an income tax, and this allowed for the elimination of most tariffs.[60] Until that time, most tariffs had been paid by the lower classes, but both the income tax and most remaining tariffs targeted wealthier classes, the classes that the parliamentarians themselves came from. This change, from a more regressive to a more progressive taxation, suggests a strong focus by decision-makers on the needs of international commerce and finance.

The second reason that tariffs, particularly the Corn Laws, were among the last vestiges of mercantilism to go is that they served the interests of the traditional landed aristocracy, who were still a potent political force. By the 1840s, though, the strength of the coalition opposed to the Corn Laws became overwhelming. As might be expected, it included the merchant and financial sectors and most of the intelligentsia. It also included most of the industrial sector. Agricultural tariffs, after all, do nothing to help local industries and, by making food more expensive, serve only to increase the cost of labor. Since it had by this point become clear that industry would not be protected by tariffs, no industrial interests had anything to gain by supporting tariffs that only protected other sectors. The coalition even included many smaller-scale farmers, who supported free trade in agriculture because it they felt that it would favor them relative to larger-scale agriculture. The repeal of the Corn Laws, in turn, did much to break the political power of the traditional nobility, and of the House of Lords.[61]

The effect of these policy changes was to remove barriers to a British international leadership role. Other aspects of leadership, such as promoting liquidity internationally by ensuring a stable flow of capital abroad and acting as a lender of last resort to foreign countries, required a more interventionist role on the part of the British government and of the Bank of England. These roles developed more slowly. They were both, however, well established by the 1860s. By the early 1870s, if not much earlier, London was recognized as the sole financial center of the world.[62]

INTERNATIONAL ECONOMIC LEADERSHIP

By the middle of the nineteenth century, then, all of the foreign economic policies that characterized the *Pax Britannica*, the laissez-faire international economic system that had London at its center, were in place. Great Britain acted as economic leader for the first, and arguably the only, historical global economic system; global in the sense that all countries that participated in an international economy took part in it. Leadership policies were maintained until 1914, and remained fairly steady throughout this period. In the more interventionist roles, required particularly of the Bank of England, few mistakes were made, if any, and these were errors of judgment rather than lapses of policy.[63] Other more protectionist foreign economic policy paths, more suited to defense against industrial decline, were occasionally debated but never came to be reflected in actual policy. British policy in this period fulfilled all three of the functions of international economic and monetary leadership much more comprehensively than had Dutch policy two centuries earlier.

The first of these functions is a currency for international exchange, which must be both stable and highly valued so that others will have confidence in it both as a medium of exchange and as a store of value. It must also be widely available, in sufficient quantities that shortages of it do not hinder international commerce. Sterling succeeded on both counts. It remained convertible to gold at a fixed rate that did not change at all between 1819 and 1914.[64] It thus served as a model of stability. Whether it was overvalued is difficult to say, but

Britain did run a balance-of-trade deficit each year in this period without exception, indicating that it might well have been.[65] An undervalued currency promotes exports of goods and services, and thus the import of foreign currencies. An overvalued currency does the opposite. By promoting imports of goods, it causes a greater export of the currency, thus putting more of it into circulation internationally. This creates confidence in the stability of the currency's supply as well as of its value. The convertibility of sterling at the fixed par was not maintained because of a lack of recognition of the alternatives; policymakers recognized what they might accomplish by adopting other monetary policies. The suspension of convertibility during the Napoleonic wars and World War One indicates that governments knew the revenue potentials of manipulable currencies, and industrialists who lobbied for a two-metal system knew the benefits to exporters of devaluation. Convertibility was maintained because it served the interests of the people who ran the Bank of England and they knew it, and, with time, because it was simply the way things were done.

The second function of international economic leadership is the provision of liquidity to the system. In the long term, this can be done by providing a core market for international trade. Britain kept its markets completely open to international trade, without tariff barriers, from 1846 to 1914.[66] The only exceptions to this rule were tariffs on a few luxury items for which there was little elasticity of demand, maintained for revenue purposes.[67] Britain was, through most of this period, the world's largest trader: its share of total international trade ranged from 25% in 1860, near the beginning of the period of financial predominance, to 16% in 1913, at its end.[68] It ran large and continuing trade deficits during this period, with imports always at least 25% higher than exports, at times more than 50% higher.[69] This means that its share of world imports was significantly higher than its share of total trade. It was therefore able to act effectively as an international consumer to fuel considerable growth abroad. Since much of this consumption was in primary agricultural goods, the British trade deficit served to provide the foreign exchange to finance considerable economic expansion in the periphery and on the frontiers of the international economy, and thus to provide considerable opportunity for infrastructural investment.

In the medium term, liquidity can be provided through countercyclical lending. Neither the British government nor the Bank of England did much to promote the provision of liquidity countercyclically in a direct, active sense. For example, neither tried to promote or control lending at particular times in order to maintain a certain level of capital flow into the system. They did not, however, need to do so. The British financial system was structured in a fashion that kept the international and domestic capital markets quite separate. As a result, cycles in the domestic economy did not affect the flow of capital internationally.[70] City of London financiers, who dealt primarily in government bonds and railway investments, were insulated from the business cycles of British industry. Therefore, neither the requirements nor the failures of industry affected the availability of capital on the London market. Since most British foreign investment was in fixed-rate instruments such as bonds, business cycles abroad did not affect it much either. Defaults occurred only rarely because of the quality of British international macroeconomic management, aided by effective collective action on the part of the internationalist financial community in the City of London, in the form of the (private) Corporation of Foreign Bondholders.[71] Thus, neither domestic nor international business cycles had much effect on the flow of British foreign investment. Consequently it tended to display quite stable patterns. Even during the long depression of 1873–1896, the flow of this investment was not curtailed,[72] which helped significantly to ameliorate the effects of this downturn in much of the less industrialized world.

The provision of liquidity in the short term entails underwriting foreign institutions in trouble during financial crises. Active participation by the Bank of England in underwriting financial crises abroad developed more slowly than other functions of leadership. The Bank began tentative efforts at intervening in crises internationally in the 1830s, often in partnership with others, such as the Bank of France. By the 1850s, this intervention had become standard practice, rarely requiring any help from abroad. By the 1870s, it was internationally recognized as being part of the role of the Bank of England to do so. By the 1890s, intervention had become such standard practice that in most smaller crises, private banks and financiers in the City were doing the actual underwriting, with the Bank of England providing only tacit backing. This pattern of international intervention continued up to 1914.[73] It was to fail in the 1920s, due to a lack of sufficient resources on the part of the Bank, but that is a subject for the next chapter.

The final function of leadership is the definition and enforcement of a common set of property rights internationally. Although the British government occasionally imposed fiscal and monetary reform abroad, through both diplomatic and military means, for the most part it led by example. By maintaining "orthodox" policies, such as convertibility and a balanced budget, Britain set a straightforward example of policy structure for others to imitate—which other governments often did, for two main reasons. The first is simply the structure's success; it clearly worked for Britain, and therefore should work elsewhere as well. The second is that it was in important ways a requirement for full participation in the international economy. The basic currency in which international exchanges were denominated was sterling. Therefore, participation in these exchanges was made easier by convertibility into sterling—that is, convertibility into gold. Policy convergence with Britain also tended to generate international confidence, aiding in the expansion of trade and the availability of foreign investment. In time, orthodoxy came to be accepted in many other places for the same reason that it was so firmly entrenched in Great Britain; it simply became the way things were done, the accepted common sense.

A related issue is the overlap between economic and security policy, the extent to which the latter was used to enforce property rights abroad. Britain did not expend enormous resources on its military relative to other countries at the time.[74] As tends to be the case in financially predominant countries, however, these expenditures tended to be capital intensive, and thus focus on projectable technologies.[75] In other words, Britain throughout this period maintained the world's largest navy, by a substantial margin.[76] Naval policy during this period was oriented to, among other things, keeping sea lines of communication and transit open, thus enforcing the right of all countries to access to these common resources.[77] The British government did occasionally use military means to effect economic policy changes abroad, but rarely. When it did, force was only used in countries within Britain's internationally recognized sphere of influence, its "informal empire," and then usually only in cases that involved traditional national security issues as well.[78] These were seen as administrative police actions as much as international military ventures.

The discussion to this point has been of policy with respect to the global market economy. Yet Britain throughout this period remained an imperial power, and at times actively expanded its empire. Economic policy toward the Empire was mercantilist in the eighteenth century, but what happened with the dismantling of the mercantilist system in the decades around the start of the nineteenth century? The economic policies that Great Britain imposed on its imperial possessions throughout most of the nineteenth century were modeled on the policies that it attempted to internationalize more broadly, such as financial orthodoxy, and those that it adopted itself, such as free trade. Given these similarities, the motives for this imperial expansion are unclear. Some analysts argue that the impetus to this expansion was economic, that British imperial policy, or for want of a better term grand strategy, was driven by the demands of high finance.[79] Others argue that the impetus was not economic, that was driven by a form of nationalism and that it was actually a drain on the British economy.[80] In either case, in practice British policy was in most cases to impose the social construct of a money/market system of exchange on its imperial possessions wherever possible.

POSTSCRIPT

With the demise of the Corn Laws in 1846, the era of fully fledged British international economic leadership began in earnest. All government policy that needed to be changed had been changed. Continued leadership therefore required only the maintenance of current policies, rather than the implementation of any new ones. The influence of the financial sector over policy continued to increase throughout the latter half of the nineteenth century along with the importance of international finance to the British economy. At the same time, the norms of orthodoxy became more and more automatically accepted. The degree of direct participation by international financiers in the institutions of leadership continued to grow apace. The Bank of England, for example, became dominated almost exclusively by merchant banking families; in the period from 1890 to 1914, 92% of the directors of the Bank were not only bankers themselves, but also the children of bankers and merchant bankers.[81] More financiers became ennobled, thereby gaining influence in the House of Lords as well as the Commons. The influence of agriculture waned, and industrial interests became more fragmented as a result of industrial decline. The depression of 1873–1896 had no major impact on this situation. Alternate policy possibilities intended to benefit industry, such as imperial preference rules or a bimetallic currency standard, were recognized and occasionally debated publicly, but never came to affect government policy.[82]

British international financial predominance did not gradually fade, as did Britain's industrial predominance. It disappeared suddenly in the cataclysm of World War One. The pattern of foreign investment and foreign economic policy-making continued unabated up to the eve of the Great War. As was the case with the Napoleonic wars, the immediate security crisis displaced commercial concerns, both in the eyes of government and the financial community itself, as the crisis developed into war in 1914. The civilian economy was suspended for the duration of the war, as was the convertibility of sterling, and by the time it was over Britain had lost its position of international financial predominance. It had not lost its motivation to lead, and British foreign economic policy attempted after the war to recreate the international system that had been in place at its beginning, but that story will be told in the next chapter.

During the war, Britain was called on not only to finance its own war effort, but also to subsidize the war efforts of its major allies, France and Russia, and to cover almost entirely the financing of the war efforts of some of its smaller allies, such as Serbia and Rumania.[83] Although the British may have been able to meet the costs of their own war effort domestically, they could not afford to act as primary underwriters of the entire war effort. Since most of London's foreign investments were outside of Europe and the Near East (these accounted for only 6.8% of total investment in 1913),[84] little of it was physically destroyed by the war, and most remained accessible. Yet the British government was forced to liquidate much of this investment to pay for the allied war effort. For example, foreign portfolio investment in the United States, most of which was British, declined from $5.4 billion in 1914 to $1.6 billion in 1919.[85] It is estimated that Britain liquidated roughly 25% of its total foreign investment during the war.[86]

After the war, the British government forgave the Allies their war debts. The American government refused to do the same.[87] Since the bulk of the British foreign war debt was held in the United States, Britain ended up paying for a disproportionate share of the entire Allied war debt. Assets liquidated to pay for this debt were therefore never recovered. In the meantime, the war had stimulated many economies into rapid industrial and financial growth, not the least of which was the American. Thus the British in 1919 had substantially fewer financial resources, and faced a substantially larger international economy. The motivation to lead the international economy remained following the war, but the capability to do so had faded.

CONCLUSIONS

In the latter half of the nineteenth century Great Britain was globally predominant both in the servicing of international commerce and in foreign investment. The British gradually overtook the Dutch in the financing and servicing of international trade in the eighteenth century, and began large-scale investment abroad in the decades following the defeat of Napoleon. Throughout this period British policy came increasingly to reflect the demands of international economic leadership. The degree of dependence of the British economy on international commerce and finance went through a period of explosive growth from 1850 to 1860; in that decade alone the percentage of British national income derived from trade services and foreign investment increased from 7.7% to 11.5%.[88] This was partly a result of the adoption of free trade policies in the mid-1840s, an example of the mutual positive feedback between financial predominance that results in leadership policies, and leadership policies that create favorable conditions for increasing international investment. The dependency of the British economy on income from international commerce and finance continued to grow after 1860; that income constituted over a tenth of total GNP from that time until World War One.[89]

Britain played a number of roles in the international politics of the latter nineteenth and early twentieth century. These include imperialist, leading industrialist, and balancer of power as well as provider of international economic infrastructure. There has been a tendency in the literature on leadership and hegemony in international relations theory to conflate these roles, to relate Great Britain's high stock of a variety of power resources to its generally central role in the international politics of the time. But in this conflation we risk losing useful analytical nuance. The first three roles listed preceded economic leadership by a century or more, and the industrial role had already begun to decline as the financial leadership role developed. If international economic leadership is part and parcel of a broader hegemonic role, why this temporal gap?

The answer suggested here is that different stages in the evolution of British foreign policy reflect different policy milieus. Although the milieus that led to balancing policies in Europe and imperial policies elsewhere had begun to develop in the seventeenth century, one of the key background conditions that led to policies of international economic leadership did not mature until the mid-nineteenth century. This condition was the development of a strong financial interest in the international market economy, and the evolution of the political system to allow those sharing this interest at first access to, and then predominance over, foreign economic policy-making. This new interest did not supercede or replace the earlier motivations, but rather joined them as a key input into accepted definitions and understandings of the national interest. British foreign policy from the mid-nineteenth century until World War One thus became an exercise in making the demands of leadership, balancing, and imperialism compatible. From the perspective of international relations theory, the interesting upshot is that leadership and hegemony as general categories can usefully be disaggregated, that while general bigness may lead to general centrality in international relations, identifying specific forms of bigness can tell us much about what sort of centrality the country in question will choose.

In speaking of leadership and hegemony, it is worth reiterating that leadership is defined here in terms of functions fulfilled and infrastructure provided, not in terms of the activism of government policy. British government policy was in fact not particularly active in managing the gold standard system, certainly much less so than was U.S. government policy in managing the Bretton Woods system, as will be discussed in Chapter 6. Giulio Gallarotti characterized the system as a "diffuse regime,"[90] reflecting the fact that some of the actors participating in maintaining the regime, including a key actor, the Bank of England, were private actors, not subject to active central government coordination. Much of the British leadership role was effected through the absence of policy that interfered with international commerce, rather than the presence of policy designed specifically in the interests of leadership. This lack of strong central coordination did not make British leadership weaker. If anything it made it stronger, by insulating it from too much interference from day-to-day politics.

The construction of the British system of leadership nonetheless reflected the structure of British politics at the time, and the nature of the compromises among various interests that had access to the policy-making apparatus. Whereas Dutch politics was notable for the extent of its confederalism, British politics were notable for their centralization—all relevant policy was made by the central authorities in London. The internationalist financial community had, for a variety of reasons, significant access to these central institutions of government, although the degree of access varied among institutions. Access to the Bank of England was most direct, and as a result monetary leadership was among the first of the leadership policies to be adopted. Access to Parliament and to the civil service had to be shared, more with traditional Tory landed interests than with manufacturers, and policy outputs reflected the greater need to compromise with the traditional nobility than with the new industrialists. This helps to explain the survival of imperialism despite the demise of mercantilist policy.

A key feature of British leadership was the ideology that it came to be embedded in. Through ideas of financial orthodoxy and laissez-faire the norms of the international financial infrastructure that was created came to represent, certainly in the minds of policy-makers in London but to a significant extent throughout the country, policy that was not only in the national interest, but also ethically appropriate. An economic morality developed around this normative structure, such that its proponents came to think of it as being not only in their own good, but in the general good. A variant of this school of thought, sometimes referred to as Manchester liberalism, developed this argument further, proposing that liberal orthodoxy led not only to economic growth, but also to international peace.[91] The social construction of British policy in the context of a broader economic ideology goes a long way in explaining the more comprehensive nature of British leadership than its earlier Dutch equivalent. This helps to explain not only policy within money/market systems of exchange, but also the creation of new money-based systems. The British, alone among European imperialists, imposed such systems, and with them the social constructions of orthodox economic liberalism, on their colonial possessions. The next chapter will argue that this normative structure of British leadership became so deeply embedded in the worldviews of policy-makers that they dictated policy choices long after these choices served the British national interest.

5

The Interwar Period and the Great Depression

The dynamics of international economic and monetary leadership can be illustrated by examples both of the presence of successful leadership and by its absence. The Great Depression of 1929–1939 represents perhaps the greatest failure of the global economy in the modern era. Its first few years are a classic story of international noncooperation and its potential effects. The period between the two world wars more generally was one of uncertainty in international relations, when leadership is needed most. This example is salient to the contemporary international political economy, with its financial implosions and its trade disputes. Now, as then, the international political economy appears to be in transition, and its leadership appears uncertain.[1]

The previous two chapters told the stories of countries that acted to varying degrees as international economic leaders. This chapter tells the stories of countries that might have, but did not. Charles Kindleberger speaks of the inability of Great Britain to resume its prewar role of international economic leader, and the unwillingness of the United States to do so.[2] David Lake categorizes France as a "spoiler" throughout the interwar period, suggesting that even though it did not have hegemonic capabilities in this period, it played at least a sufficiently important economic role to have a significant impact on issues of leadership of the international economic system.[3] These three countries were also the main players in the German reparations drama, the dominant international financial issue of the 1920s, and the central countries in the three currency blocs that resulted from the collapse of the international gold standard in the early 1930s. This chapter focuses on the role of Great Britain, France, and the United States in both the reconstruction of the international economy and monetary system in the wake of World War One, and the its collapse in the course of the Great Depression.

The three countries being studied in this case shared what at first glance seem to be similar political systems. They were all liberal democracies, with universal suffrage and free political debate, in which all men were equal under the law. Yet each had very different responses both to the demands of postwar reconstruction and to the onset of depression. These differences have been explained both structurally, as resulting from the different places of the countries in the global economy, and particularistically, as resulting from the peculiarities of the individual domestic political cultures and processes. The story told here suggests that these two approaches succeed only in combination in explaining the failure of the international economic infrastructure in the first years of the Great Depression. Structure is important. Great Britain simply did not have sufficient financial capabilities to maintain the infrastructure, and international commerce was not important enough to the American economy to expect it to motivate the American government to lead. France had neither the capabilities nor the motivation. But the specific policy responses, including some that contributed to the precipitousness of the collapse of the international economy, cannot be explained without historical context, including domestic political structures, different social responses to World War One, and loyalty to different historical roles within the global political economy.

RECONSTRUCTION AND DEPRESSION

The study of international economic leadership in the interwar period can be divided into two distinct parts. The first, the 1920s, was a time when real, and to a certain extent successful, efforts were made to reconstitute a global economic order along the lines of the system centered on London that had worked so well until 1914. The second, the Great Depression era of the 1930s, saw the collapse of the international economy. It was a time of self-help, beggar-thy-neighbor policies, and of the emergence of exclusive economic blocs, groups of countries that interacted with each other but only marginally with countries outside the group. To understand the progression from the

1920s to the 1930s, one must first look at the antecedent to the 1920s, the situation coming out of World War One.

Following World War One, three countries had the financial wherewithal to have a major impact on the reestablishment of an international political-economic system: Great Britain, the United States, and France. Great Britain, as we saw in the last chapter, had been the international economic and monetary leader through 1914. London retained both a reputation as the center of international finance, and significant capital abroad. The United States had been a net debtor at the beginning of the century, and continued to be one until the outbreak of World War One. During the course of the war, though, many American foreign debts were liquidated, and after the war new loans were made, leaving the United States as a substantial net creditor shortly after the war. The United States was also the predominant net supplier of allied governmental war loans. France had been the world's second largest foreign investor at the beginning of the century, and remained the second largest net creditor well into the 1920s.

The pattern of international financial commitment in the aftermath of World War One, however, was more complicated than it had been during the earlier period of British financial predominance. In that earlier era, the bulk of international capital transfers were private. All of Britain's foreign investment was made by private investors, and most of it was in nongovernmental enterprises. During the war, however, private international financial flows were swamped by intergovernmental loans made to finance the war effort. Total foreign borrowing by governments to finance military spending amounted to some $26 billion, a figure equal to roughly two-thirds of total outstanding foreign investment in 1914.[4] This situation was further complicated by the question of German reparations, a question that remained unresolved for more than a decade. The Treaty of Versailles that marked the end of the war held Germany responsible for paying reparations to cover the costs of war damage and reconstruction, and created a committee to set a specific amount. The original figure arrived at by the Reparations Committee in 1921 was 132 billion gold marks, which translates roughly into $31 billion, or just over £6.5 billion, all at prewar par exchange rates.[5] There was never any real chance that this total sum would be paid, but it was still the official baseline for German reparations debts. Great Britain, the United States, and France retained among themselves the political control of both the reparations and war debts issues.

No other countries had major financial commitments to the international economy. The remaining large-scale foreign investor before the war was Germany, but the policy motivations generated by this commitment to the international economy were replaced by those derived from the obligation of reparations. German foreign investments have been estimated at $5 billion, as of 1913. Because there were few foreign investments in Germany, this figure is net as well as gross.[6] Accurate figures for the stock of German foreign investment between the wars, however, are difficult to find. A substantial amount of the prewar investment seems to have survived the war, although it is unclear how much. Even figures for income from foreign investments are difficult to come by. While all other countries at the time reported both gross income from foreign investments and gross payments abroad on foreign capital, Germany reported only the net figure of these two. In the mid-1920s this net figure averaged almost nothing.[7] In any case, any returns on foreign investment would have been dwarfed by Germany's reparations bill. If all German foreign investment survived the war, the ratio of reparations owed to foreign investments held would have been six to one. The real ratio might be as high as twice that. As a result, it was the issue of reparations, rather than concerns for its foreign investment, that came to dominate German foreign economic policy-making.[8]

The total foreign investments of countries other than Great Britain, the United States, France, and Germany similarly totaled roughly $5 billion in the mid-1920s.[9] The countries from which this investment came were small European ones with large financial sectors, such as the Netherlands and Switzerland, and large economies with a few minor foreign holdings, such as Italy and Japan.[10] The recipients of this investment as well as the sources were widely dispersed geographically. This dispersion meant that while the income from these investments might have been an important part of national income for countries like the Netherlands and Switzerland, it was not concentrated enough to have a significant systemic impact. All told, Great Britain, the United States, and France were the source of close to three-quarters of global foreign investment in the 1920s.

The 1920s saw some efforts to reconstruct a global economic system. The Great Depression era of the 1930s was a time of pointed economic regionalism. The disintegration of the international economy in the early 1930s resulted in five major economic blocs. Two of these were centered on Germany and Japan, and were predominantly nonmonetary in orientation. Both countries decided to construct regional economic systems that were not based on patterns of market exchange. Both, but particularly the German bloc, were motivated by political as much as, or more than, economic motivations, and were based on authoritative as much as (or more than) monetary exchange.[11] In other words, both were essentially authoritative rather than market-based systems. As a result neither bloc fits into the analytic framework being used here.

The other three blocs were centered on the three countries discussed in this chapter. The sterling bloc consisted of the countries that followed Britain's defection from the gold standard in 1931 (to be discussed). There were twenty-five of them, consisting of the empire (except for South Africa and, partially, Canada), the Scandinavian countries, much of Eastern Europe, and some of Britain's traditional raw materials suppliers, such as Argentina, Portugal, and Egypt.[12] These countries were mostly in the formal and informal empires, where over two-thirds of British foreign investment was concentrated. Most of these countries were to be included in the imperial trading structure created over the course of the next two years. The dollar bloc consisted of the United States and those countries, predominantly in the Americas, that chose to follow the dollar's lead. The gold bloc consisted of France and its possessions, the Netherlands, Switzerland, and Belgium. Italy was a member, but only nominally. The Netherlands, Switzerland, and Belgium were all substantial foreign investors in proportion to their size, and thus had their own independent reasons for maintaining overvalued currencies. The gold bloc thus was a group by default rather than by intention, as was reflected by the absence of cooperation in the regionalization of trade, cooperation that was in evidence in the other two blocs.

This devolution from a global system to a set of mostly exclusive economic blocs was in direct response to the effects of global depression. There is no general consensus on the specific origins and causes of the Great Depression. Although the historiographic debate on the subject is both interesting and thought-provoking,[13] it is tangential to our discussion of international economic and monetary leadership. By, contrast, most explanations of why the depression was so severe and persistent hinge on the absence of leadership. Charles Kindleberger's classic history of the Great Depression makes this argument explicitly.[14] Explanations that focus on beggar-thy-neighbor policies generally, or specifically on the infamous American Smoot-Hawley Tariff of

1930, are also making leadership arguments; they are suggesting that if a country of sufficient capabilities such as the United States had not adopted these policies, but rather had behaved responsibly, the Great Depression in all likelihood would not have been so severe and persistent.

Even those explanations that seem to take different approaches usually boil down to a lack of international economic leadership. Barry Eichengreen's argument that it was the nature of the gold standard itself, rather than an absence of leadership, that exacerbated the depression appears to challenge this view.[15] He argues that the gold standard was technologically and socially obsolete, and therefore no longer credible. This obsolescence itself, though, was created by a lack of leadership. In the Dutch and British cases discussed in the last two chapters, the nascent leaders created new monetary technologies that reflected the practices around which the policies of other countries converged in the new international economic system. In the language of international regimes, the leaders created the institutions (sets of principles, norms, rules, and decision-making procedures) around which expectations converged in the issue area of international monetary coordination.[16] Eichengreen's approach does not replace explanations centering on leadership; rather, it focuses on the absence of one specific function of leadership.

The absence of international economic leadership is thus the most common explanation for the magnitude of the Great Depression. This leaves unanswered the question of why no leadership was forthcoming. The absence of leadership has been explained by factors as diverse as plain irresponsibility,[17] the prevalence of misguided economic theory,[18] and a time lag required for states to adapt to new structural positions in international politics.[19] The argument here is that no country acted successfully as an international economic and monetary leader because none had the necessary combination of financial capabilities and internationalist motivations. In other words, no country was financially predominant. The ways, and the extent, in which countries failed to lead reflected both their domestic identities with respect to international relations, and their responses to World War One. To make this argument, the stories of the three countries from which leadership might have been possible must be told individually.

GREAT BRITAIN

We left Great Britain in the last chapter with its international financial capabilities undermined by World War One, both from foreign borrowing and from the physical damage caused. In the aftermath of the war Britain regained its motivation to lead, and British policy-makers retained the mindset of international leadership that they had internalized over the better part of the last century. But the capabilities were lost, never to be recovered.

Britain entered the Great War with some $20 billion in foreign investments, which amounted to just over half the global total, nearly half of the world's shipping capacity, and a healthy lead in the provision of services to the international economy. During the course of the war roughly a quarter of British private foreign investment was liquidated to pay for the war effort, leaving a total of some $15 billion, both gross and net as there was little foreign private investment in Britain.[20] The global total also declined during the war, but the British share by the early 1920s had nonetheless fallen below half.[21] Similarly, almost half of the total British tonnage of shipping was lost during the war. Although much was replaced, the net loss was 2.6 million tons, or roughly one-seventh of the prewar total. As a proportion of the world total, the British merchant fleet declined from two-fifths to one-third.[22] Great Britain nonetheless emerged from the war both the world's predominant foreign investor and the world's leading servicer of international trade and commerce.

This situation was not greatly affected by the war debts issue. The British government had lent large sums to its European allies to pay for their war efforts, and had had to borrow from the American government for the same reason. This debt came to $4.7 billion, equal to roughly a third of British foreign investment. Britain was in turn owed about $9.4 billion, but of this $3.1 billion was owed by a Russian government that no longer existed and was therefore unrecoverable. A further half-billion dollars was owed by Eastern European governments of dubious solvency. The net British position in war debts, net of debt that was functionally unrecoverable, was thus less than $1 billion, a small fraction of foreign investment outstanding.[23] The British government showed an interest in the early 1920s in canceling all war debts, but could not do so as the American government would not go along.

After the war City of London financiers resumed lending abroad at a rate that averaged just over $500 million a year until the beginning of the Great Depression, at which time foreign lending generally slowed considerably. This rate was only half that of the immediate prewar rate, but was similar to the average rate in the first decade of the twentieth century.[24] British foreign investment was fairly concentrated within the sphere of British political predominance. Some two-thirds of the investment was within the empire and the "informal empire," while less than one-tenth was in Europe.[25] By 1930, the total stock of British foreign investment had regained and slightly surpassed its prewar peak.

This investment was, however, proportionally less important than it had been, both internationally and domestically. The global total of foreign investment had increased by almost half during the 1920s, primarily as a result of the rapid growth of American international financial investment. As such, the British proportion of the total had by 1930 fallen to little over 40%.[26] Domestically, Britain's GNP had continued to increase throughout this period so that the ratio of foreign investment to national income had declined from 2:1 in 1910 to 1:1 by 1938.[27] Similarly, while income from investments abroad considerably exceeded their prewar peak in absolute terms throughout the late 1920s, they never again attained a similar level of importance to the British economy. Returns on investment in the international economy as a percentage of the British economy fell by almost half from their peak, from 16% at the turn of the century to little over 8% in the early 1920s, the earliest time after the war at which meaningful measurements could be made. They had recovered substantially by the late 1920s, to almost 12%, though they never again did reach prewar levels. This percentage crashed, from almost 12% in 1929 to just over 6% by 1932,[28] for two reasons. A decline in lending with the onset of the Great Depression combined with a marked decrease in the profitability of investments already made. And income from services to a rapidly contracting international economy declined precipitously.

As such, Britain continued to have the motivation for leadership throughout much of the 1920s, but this motivation was somewhat weaker than it had been in the latter nineteenth century. Although income from international investments and services remained a large part of the economy, the internationalist financial sector was no longer able to preempt the national foreign economic policy debate the way it had half a century earlier. This relative weakness was expressed by a greater government willingness to think in terms of the needs of other sectors of the economy, primarily industry, and by a stronger tendency to think in terms of economic security rather than just economic leadership. This willingness was weaker in some areas of policy than in others. In monetary policy, for example, the commitment of the government to the traditional sterling par in the 1920s was complete; there was never any discussion whatsoever of resuming convertibility at a different rate. Interestingly, there was some debate as to when, and to a certain extent whether, to reestablish convertibility, but no consideration of reestablishing it at a devalued rate.[29] This commitment seems to have gone beyond a conscious policy choice; an overvalued pound was an article of faith, in the government as well as with the Bank of England.[30] In trade policy, on the other hand, the government was much more willing to entertain departures from policies of leadership. Even in trade policy, however, change was restrained by the extent to which leadership was part of the social construction that was the British identity and self-image at the time.

Meanwhile, Great Britain's domestic political structure and processes of foreign economic policy-making remained relatively unchanged from the period prior to World War One. Shortly after the war, suffrage was granted to all adults, and the House of Lords continued to decline in importance. But the essential features of the British system remained the same. A number of factors did change, though, that affected the British foreign economic policy-making process. The importance of leadership to the British identity was weakened by the war, and by the expansion in political participation that followed.[31] With the decline in importance of income from investment in the international economy, opposition to free trade from other sectors of the economy strengthened. A form of protectionism crept in under the guise of national security planning. And finally, a realization of the critical decline of British capabilities altered basic assumptions about Britain's role in the international economy.

The protectionism that crept into British trade policy weakened but did not completely undermine Britain's role as a market of last resort. Market-driven trade patterns had of course been suspended for the duration of the war, not least because a naval blockade of Germany was a central element of allied strategy. Free trade was for the most part reestablished after the war, but tariffs on certain manufactures deemed essential for national security were imposed in 1919 and gradually increased during the 1920s. It remains unclear whether the primary motivations behind these tariffs were security-oriented or economic; if the latter, they would constitute traditional protectionism. Either way, however, they were very specific, and efficient at protecting only threatened industries while doing a minimum of damage abroad.[32] They also tended to bypass primary products, for which a market of last resort is needed most.[33]

Britain rejoined the gold standard in 1925. The lag of several years in resuming the convertibility of sterling was made necessary by the need to deflate after wartime inflation, to replenish gold stocks, and to regain control of the money supply. Despite this lag, the British government was eager to resume its role as international economic leader, in order to ensure London's continued role as the financial center of the world. This role had clearly been internalized as part of the British national identity. If anything, the British were much more overt and self-conscious in their role as leader then they had been before the war.[34] This was the case, perhaps, because they saw leadership as part of London's role as financial center, and felt that that role was threatened by America's newfound financial wherewithal. The return of sterling to convertibility, however, did not succeed in recreating the prewar gold standard, for two reasons; there was a shortage of gold available to be held in reserve by central banks, and there was too much sterling in circulation internationally. A major factor contributing to the shortage of gold was the accumulation of gold stocks beyond what was necessary for adequate reserves by the United States and then France, the reasons for which will be discussed later. The excess of sterling in circulation was a direct result of the war, during which Britain had run balance-of-payments deficits beyond those paid for by the liquidations of investments.

Both of these problems were dealt with by the creation of a new twist on the gold standard, called the gold exchange standard. The Bank of England continued to hold gold as its primary reserve, but other central banks were encouraged to hold a combination of gold and sterling. This both increased the availability of reserves to central banks and soaked up some of the excess sterling, inasmuch as holding a currency as a central bank reserve has the effect of taking it out of general circulation. It also fit well with the British view of London as the financial center of the world, because it made of sterling the official, rather than just the de facto, linchpin of the international monetary system.

Great Britain thus self-consciously attempted to fulfill all of the functions of leadership in the 1920s. It maintained a currency for international exchange, keeping sterling both stable and overvalued as soon as it was able, and actively encouraging the use of sterling abroad to an even greater degree than was the case before the war. With a few exceptions, Britain kept its markets open, although the number of exceptions grew over the course of the decade. The exceptions, mostly advanced manufactures, were generally those types of goods least likely to need a market for distressed goods. It resumed lending abroad almost immediately upon the end of the war, and continued doing so at a steady rate throughout the decade, although at a slightly slower rate than the prewar peak. The British government also took steps to encourage international liquidity by encouraging moderation on both the reparations and war debts issues,[35] and by leading and coordinating the underwriting of central banks abroad in crises. Finally, the British encouraged macroeconomic policy coordination by espousing fiscal orthodoxy as religiously as they had before the war.

Great Britain's attempt to resume its leadership role, however, was not entirely successful. The British market, greatly shrunk in relative size by spreading industrialization and the expanding frontiers of the international economy, could no longer absorb enough imports to make it a viable market for distressed goods. British financiers could no longer sustain the volume of capital exports that they had been able to at the beginning of the century. And finally, the Bank of England no longer had the resources necessary either to maintain sterling as the primary international reserve currency or to lead underwriting activities in major international crises. In fact, the gold exchange standard had made sterling far more vulnerable, because crises in central banks that held Sterling as a reserve currency magnified the pressure on the Bank of England's reserves of gold. An expedient solution thought necessary to allow the recreation of an international gold standard thus had the unintended consequence of creating a more brittle monetary system.[36] In other words, British commitment to the norm of leadership that had become part of its international identity had, in the absence of sufficient capabilities, the effect of making the system more vulnerable to crises.[37]

These weaknesses became painfully obvious with the onset of depression throughout the industrialized world in 1930. As a result, over the course of little over a year in 1930 and 1931 the British abandoned their commitment to the two pillars of their foreign economic policy, the gold standard and unilateral free trade, remarkably quickly and remarkably thoroughly. The British attempted to lead underwriting activities in the Central European monetary crises, and failed.[38] This failure in turn contributed to a crisis of confidence that led to the run on sterling that forced Britain off the gold standard in 1931. The forced floating of sterling made clear to the British that they no longer had the capabilities necessary to underwrite a currency for international exchange. This being the case, they abandoned entirely any pretext of doing so. The floating of sterling, surprisingly enough, had the full support of the Bank of England. Without either the capability or, by 1932, the national motivation for leadership, the governors of the Bank realized that retrenchment within the structure of the international economy could succeed only in doing further damage to British finance.[39]

At the same time, the domestic effects of free trade became so onerous by 1932 that the first comprehensive new tariff in over a century was introduced, although many primary products were exempted, as was most trade within the Empire.[40] The decline in income from international financial activity in 1930 and 1931 was in part directly responsible for forcing the tariff issue. Britain had traditionally run balance-of-trade deficits, which remained relatively stable through the first years of the depression. These deficits had, however, always been more than made up for by income from international financial activity. When this income suddenly plummeted, it left Britain in a balance-of-payments crisis. The new tariff was meant in part to alleviate this crisis.[41]

Once Britain had been forced off gold, there was no great pressure, even from the City of London, to go back on.[42] The sterling bloc and the imperial trading system served the interests of the internationalist financial sector adequately, and nothing would be gained by an attempt to reestablish a globalism that was no longer viable. Although the new system instituted in 1931 and 1932 was an abdication of global leadership, however, it was not a complete abdication of international economic and monetary leadership. It can more precisely be thought of as a regionalization of leadership.[43] The British continued to provide leadership within the empire and the sterling bloc. Sterling continued its role as the currency for international exchanges within the sterling bloc, retaining its relative value because bloc countries were tied to it. Imperial preference rules, and a continued relative openness to primary imports, kept the British market available to exports from regional countries, and in fact made it more viable as a market for distressed goods from within the region by restricting goods from elsewhere. Although long-term investment activity was drastically curtailed, the British did encourage short-term liquidity within the bloc, and maintained a policy of supporting currencies associated with sterling.[44] And finally, the British government fulfilled the function of macroeconomic policy coordination by consciously adopting and promoting the idea of a sterling bloc and imperial trading area.

The norm of leadership that had made its way into the British national identity had essentially been transferred from a focus on global commerce to a focus on imperial commerce.

Interestingly (from the perspective of historical continuity), the British acted unilaterally in declaring the imperial trading area, in much the same way as they had unilaterally become free traders in the 1840s. It was not a negotiated or a multilateral agreement; it was a British creation. In promoting this regionalization it did help to undermine global economic cooperation; this much is true. However, at the same time it allowed access by sterling bloc countries to a system of regional cooperation that they otherwise would not have had in a disintegrating international economy.

FRANCE

French foreign economic policy between the wars was constrained by two overriding factors that limited the range of French governmental behavior in this period. These factors were the legacy of the Great War and the chronic weakness of governments within the political structure of the Third Republic. The Great War left French society inwardly focused and burdened by the costs of reconstruction, and left the government with the expectation of large reparations payments that never materialized. The government, in the meantime, could do little in the way of major policy planning, unless the policy in question was uncontested by any major domestic interest group. If it did, it would fall, as happened dozens of times in this period.

France had long been an important but not predominant foreign investor. Before World War One it was the world's second largest foreign investor. By 1913, total French private holdings of foreign investment totaled some $8.25 billion.[45] The French government had followed mixed policies with respect to international economic and monetary leadership, reflecting the interests of a country that was a major but not leading foreign investor. Both monetary and fiscal policies were similar to the British model. The franc was convertible and fairly highly valued, French budgets were balanced, and the Bank of France often acted in support of the Bank of England in financial crises. French tariff policy, however, was clearly protectionist. It was similar to that of the United States, both in general magnitude of protection given and in the use of differential rates to secure tariff concessions abroad.[46]

Not much over half of this investment survived World War One. Of French foreign investments immediately before the war, approximately 27% was invested in Russia, 35% in Central and Southern Europe, 24% in the Middle East and North Africa, and the remaining 14% in the United States. Roughly $1 billion of this total was liquidated during the Great War to help pay for the war effort. After allowing for the expropriation of all the investments in Russia following the Communist revolution, this left French private investors with some $5 billion in foreign investments after the war. Almost all of this total was in Central Europe, Southern Europe, the Middle East, and North Africa. There was little inward foreign investment, so the net figure is little less than $5 billion.[47]

The French government, on the other hand, had substantial debts from the war. It was owed $3.5 billion by its allies, but almost half of this was from Russia and therefore unrecoverable. It owed $7 billion, of which $4 billion was to the United States and $3 billion was to Britain. France was, however, supposed to receive the bulk of German reparations payments. Of the total reparations bill of 132 billion gold marks, 52%, or 69 billion gold marks, was apportioned to France.[48] This works out to just over $16 billion. Which means that had full reparations been forthcoming, income from French foreign holdings would have been dwarfed by foreign income generated by reparations payments.

The French foreign investment position did not change greatly during the course of the 1920s. There was no pressing reason for French investors to repatriate their capital, and thus the stock of investment abroad was maintained. On the other hand, the French economy during this period did not generate sufficient liquid capital to markedly increase this stock. The paucity in new foreign investing was exacerbated by the decline of the French franc, which resulted in substantial losses for creditors and investors.

The government of France did recognize an interest in international economic stability. This interest, however, was never strong enough to displace other goals of economic policy, such as the maintenance of high employment levels, particularly during times of economic distress. Furthermore, the chronic weakness of French governments limited their ability to effect long-term coherent economic plans. Except when emergency measures were passed, the government was limited to piecemeal policies and expedients. Thus France was unable to act even as a supporter of leadership, as it had before the Great War.

In fact, French behavior in the interwar period is often pointed to as a model of irresponsibility and obstructionism. One observer has described the stereotype of French behavior in the period as follows. "The French are dogmatic, obstinate, selfish, and jealous. Their passion for impractical logic combines with their envy of the British, short-sighted greed, and general bloody-mindedness. They gloated over Britain's discomfort until the system collapsed. In any international system, the French, it is suspected, can be counted on to play the dog in the manger."[49] Its international financial position predicts that it would not be a leader. Its governmental problems and security fears explain why its behavior seemed so erratic and shortsighted at times.

Unlike Great Britain and the United States, France had suffered substantial physical damage in the war, and repairing this damage was, along with preventing new damage by ensuring the continued military security of France from Germany, the national obsession after the war. Reconstruction was an uncontested policy, and therefore the natural policy course for structurally weak governments.[50] Furthermore, it was seen as essentially costless; expenditures on reconstruction would be met by the more than one billion marks France expected from Germany annually in reparations.[51] The reparations payments, however, never arrived in the expected quantities. This left the French government both fiscally and financially weak, and was a major factor contributing to a series of currency crises between 1924 and 1926.[52] In the last of these crises there was a real fear that the franc would collapse completely in a hyperinflationary spiral in the manner of the German mark three years earlier.[53] The franc was finally stabilized, but at a fairly low value and only through extraordinary political measures (as is discussed below). Thus the postwar reconstruction left France financially weakened, and with its monetary policy process politically paralyzed.

The war also left French society in general with an inward focus, a greater concern with domestic stability and security at the expense of concern with international stability and security.[54] As the world's second largest foreign investor before the war, the French government had often been willing to actively participate in British leadership. The prewar support of English leadership policies had never been based on the sort of ideological commitment to internationalism found in Britain, and therefore was more easily displaced by domestic concerns. After the war, despite remaining a major investor, France was no longer willing to do so. An internationalism that appealed to the French public at large until the war, no longer did so in the narcissistic environment of interwar France. This change of popular mood brought about by the war created a constraining effect on French foreign economic policy.

French economic policy in general, furthermore, suffered from a strong tendency to incoherence. This resulted in large part from the political structure of the Third Republic, which was a parliamentary system elected by proportional representation. The parliamentary form meant that there was no strong executive power separate from the legislative process, and proportional representation meant that the parliament usually contained a wide variety of parties, none of which had voting majorities. As a result, governments were made up of coalitions of several parties, each with their own agendas and dominant personalities. This in turn led to a succession of weak governments, in the sense that no government could enact new policies that were at all contentious without losing the support of either its own left or right, and as a result usually falling. During the height of the currency crisis of 1924–1926, for example, France had eight finance ministers in little over two years.[55] With such a rate of turnover, consistent policy was difficult to achieve. Most of the time the government seemed to muddle through on a business-as-usual basis, but it tended to become paralyzed during crises. For example, during the fiscal and currency crisis of 1926, the government in the end could only respond by taking the extraordinary measure of voting decree powers to the premier for the duration of the crisis.[56] Aside from this exception, government economic policy was usually restricted to temporary expedient.

The Bank of France was similar to the Bank of England in that it was relatively autonomous, highly respected, and influential in the making of monetary policy. It might even be suggested that it was more respected than the French government. Raymond Poincaré, the premier granted decree powers to solve the currency crisis, justified his insistence on convertibility by pointing out that the directors of the Bank of France demanded it. "If these directors were to resign, the entire world would say the government was wrong, because the prestige of the Bank abroad is enormous, greater than that of the state."[57] It was also similar to the Bank of England in that it was run by internationalist financiers (the governor of the Bank in the late 1920s was one of the Rothschild barons),[58] and tended to adopt internationalist policy stances. It was, however, constrained both by the chronic weakness of the government and by the legacy of the Great War, as discussed earlier.

The Bank was as a result more often in the position of trying to avoid worst-case outcomes than in the position of effecting first-choice policies. In other words, it was too constrained by the need for crisis management to be able to adopt an active role in support of leadership. For example, when the franc was to be restored to convertibility in 1928, the first preference of the Bank of France was to revalue it first, to compensate for wartime and postwar inflation and achieve a value closer to its prewar parity. It became clear, however, that such a revaluation might sabotage the attempt to reestablish convertibility. The Bank was faced with a choice between an uncertain probability of achieving a highly valued convertible franc, with continued monetary chaos should the attempt fail, or a high probability of achieving convertibility at an undervalued rate. The Bank chose in the end to support the latter option, to avoid any risk of continued chaos.

The franc had fallen in value fairly consistently from the end of the war through to 1926, and was quite unstable.[59] Had Germany continued to pay reparations according to the original schedule, the French currency may well have remained strong. But the reparations were never paid consistently, leaving a choice between reining in the reconstruction program or allowing downward pressure on the franc to build. Until the governmental crises of 1924–1926 the French government chose to subordinate currency stabilization to the needs of reconstruction—in other words it subordinated internationalist to domestic concerns. When the franc was finally once again made convertible, it was at a small fraction of its prewar par. The desire for a strong currency was subordinated to the need for a stable currency. Once the crisis was finally resolved, in part by reestablishing the convertibility of the franc to gold, the fear of future currency crises, and of repeated governmental paralysis, was so great that popular opinion would allow no depreciation of the franc, for whatever reason. Convertibility was maintained at an unchanged rate until 1936, but for domestic political, rather than internationalist financial, reasons.

The financial weakness resulting from the war and reconstruction also left France unable to participate in maintaining the liquidity of the international economy to the extent to which it had before the war.[60] The French government, moreover, also displayed a lack of interest in such participation. In terms of short- and medium-term liquidity, little was done either by the government or by the Bank of France to attempt to stabilize capital outflows, and the response of the bank to the currency instabilities of the 1920s was to hoard gold, so that by the end of the decade it had the world's largest reserves.[61] This withdrawal of monetary gold from international circulation had the effect of forcing other central banks to hold a larger proportion of their reserves in sterling, increasing the pressure on sterling and thus making the system as a whole less stable and resilient. In other words, the response of the bank to international instability was to attempt to create a buffer against it, rather than to try to help alleviate it.

In terms of long-term liquidity, France had never (with a minor exception in the 1860s) kept a particularly open market for international trade goods. During the war, French trade policy drifted from an emphasis on price, through tariffs, to an emphasis on quantity, through quotas and outright import prohibitions. These latter policies were relaxed after the war, but not eliminated. Quotas are significantly worse than tariffs as obstacles to a market for distressed goods. Tariffs distort the market so that a lower quantity is demanded at any given price. However, as a good becomes increasingly distressed, its price will probably fall, which, even with the tariff, will lead to an increase in the quantity demanded. Thus at least some of the excess supply that caused the good to be distressed will be soaked up despite the tariff. Quotas, and to an even greater extent prohibitions, do not allow this flexibility. Prices fall, but quantities imported cannot rise. Furthermore, these more stringent forms of protection were often used by France on primary products, particularly agricultural goods.[62] Thus the French market became even more closed in the 1920s, and in a way that made it of particularly little use as a market for distressed goods. The preference of many French governments in this period for quotas over tariffs may reflect the tendency of the system toward political paralysis. Tariffs are usually enacted through some sort of general legislation, whereas quotas are more conducive to being imposed on purely case-by-case bases, administratively rather than legislatively—that is, by the bureaucracy rather than the government.

Finally, the French did little to coordinate macroeconomic policies internationally. They participated in all the major international conferences, but their aims were more to secure defense against and reparations from Germany than to coordinate policies more broadly. They were not for the most part pointedly obstructionist, as were the Americans, but they were not in any notable way constructive either. The biggest exception to this rule was the French role in the currency crisis that led to the demise of the Gold Exchange Standard in 1931. The crisis started in Austria, leading to efforts by the Bank of International Settlements to coordinate a loan to the Austrian central bank in support of the schilling. At the same time, the Austrian government was considering a customs union with Germany, which France saw as a potential security threat. The French government thus vetoed any coordinated international action in support of the Austrian currency. In the end, the Bank of England tried to fulfill the role of lender of last resort alone, but failed. In other words, when the demands of the international economic infrastructure came up against French fears of Germany, the French focused narrowly on their security concerns.[63]

Aside from the currency crisis of 1931, the French government's response to the Great Depression was muted, largely because its foreign economic policies had not been particularly internationally oriented in the first place, obviated any defensive policy response. The franc clung to convertibility without devaluing, even when, by 1932, it became extremely overvalued, because this was demanded by the electorate. However, the franc never became a major currency for international exchange, partly because it was not in wide enough circulation, and partly because of French trade policies.[64] Trade policy became a little more bilateralist and tended toward quotas and exclusions, as opposed to tariffs, somewhat more than in the 1920s.[65] But this represented a change in degree, not a change in kind as was the case with British and American trade policies. And finally, the French attitude to international policy coordination remained the same. If anything, in fact, it became somewhat more oriented to such cooperation as the various German issues became less immediate. The French approached the first successful depression-era international monetary agreement, the Tripartite Agreement of 1936, reasonably well disposed toward cooperation. It can be argued that they needed such an agreement to devalue the franc, which was in turn a necessity for France to begin recovering from the depression. Given the French public's attachment to the *franc fort*, the government felt that it could only devalue under the cover of an internationally sanctioned agreement. Thus, the French were cooperative, but for reasons of helping the domestic economy, rather than for reasons of leadership.[66]

A result of the attachment to convertibility until 1936 was the French role in the gold bloc, a grouping of those countries that resisted devaluation until well into the 1930s. This bloc was, however, not a coherent regional economic system, as was the sterling bloc, or even one coalescing around a dominant economy, as was the dollar bloc. It was simply a group of countries that followed a similar monetary policy, each for its own reasons. The other major participants in the gold bloc, Switzerland, the Netherlands, and Belgium, were all particularly large foreign investors in relation to the sizes of their own economies. They were relatively small countries, and therefore even their cumulative foreign investments were not a major proportion of the international total, but their investments nonetheless gave them the motivation to maintain overvalued currencies. In this sense, France was not at all a leader of the gold bloc, but rather simply the largest country in it. Since the gold bloc consisted primarily of countries with strong currencies, there was little opportunity for France to act as lender of last resort, a role they were unlikely to have played anyway.

THE UNITED STATES

The United States came out of World War One with the only major currency that had not been devalued by the pressures of financing the war,[67] a majority of the world's gold reserves,[68] and its lowest tariff structure since the beginning of American industrialization.[69] Wilsonian idealism provided the focus for the major postwar international institutions.[70] The United States was not, however, financially predominant. Much of the world looked to the United States for international leadership, both political and economic. Yet that leadership was not forthcoming. Despite Wilson's internationalism, the United States withdrew from international leadership and focused its economic policies on the needs of domestic industry and agriculture.

While in the 1920s the United States surpassed Great Britain as an exporter of capital, and by the 1930s came close to rivaling Britain in the total stock of foreign investment held, these investments never assumed the same importance to the American economy as they did for the British. At the outset of World War One the American investment position abroad totaled $2.5 billion, one-eighth of the British total. Over three-quarters of this investment was in the Americas, primarily Mexico and Canada. At the same time, foreign investment in the United States totaled some $7 billion, over half of which was British. Thus in 1913 the United States was a net debtor of $4.5 billion.[71] By the early 1920s, over $6.5 billion in new private foreign investments had been made. After deducting $1.5 billion in defaulted Russian and Mexican loans, this left just over $7.5 billion in American private foreign investment. By this time as well, foreign investment in the United States had decreased to $4 billion, leaving the United

States a net private creditor of $3.5 billion. The geographic distribution of American investment had by this time shifted somewhat, with less than two-thirds being in the Americas and 30% in Europe.[72]

The American government also became a substantial creditor during the war, because of its loans to allied governments to finance their war and reconstruction efforts. These loans totaled $11.9 billion, of which $4.7 billion was to Great Britain, $4 billion to France, and $2 billion to Italy. As only $240 million of these loans were to Russia, almost all of the aggregate sum was considered recoverable. The American government claimed no reparations. Throughout the 1920s, American private investment abroad increased at an average rate of roughly $1 billion a year, or about twice the rate of the British equivalent.[73] Thus by the onset of the Great Depression Americans held approximately $14 billion in foreign investment. The flow of this investment was somewhat different than previously, with 44% going to the Americas, 46% to Europe, and the remaining tenth to Asia.[74] As a result, by the eve of the Great Depression 55% of American private foreign investment was in the Americas (about two-thirds of which was in Canada), 37% was in Europe, mostly Germany, and the remaining 8% was in Asia, particularly the Philippines, Japan, and Australia.

By 1930, then, American private holdings abroad equaled two-thirds of the stock of British foreign investments. The American economy, though, was three times the size of the British.[75] Assuming that the returns on these investments were similar, these returns as a proportion of the American GNP would be less than a quarter of the returns to investment as a proportion of British GNP. Income from services to international trade and commerce were of an even smaller proportion; throughout this period, in fact, the United States was a substantial net importer of services, on the order of roughly half a billion dollars worth a year.[76] In short, by the early 1930s, American leadership capabilities approached the level of British capabilities, but American levels of internationalist financial motivation remained a small fraction of British levels.

These motivations were filtered through a political structure that differed from the British and French in two particular ways that had significant impacts on foreign economic policy. The first is the structural division of powers that is the hallmark of the American system of government. The executive and legislative branches each have their own areas of jurisdiction with respect to foreign economic policymaking. Each at the time also had substantially different political concerns. This tended to distract from the coherence of policy outputs. The second is the decentralized design of the American central bank, the Federal Reserve Board.

A key feature of government in the United States is the separation of governmental powers between the executive and the legislature. Both branches have substantial powers over foreign economic policy. As a result, the policy-making process often reflects the inputs of both, sometimes at the expense of its overall coherence. Congressional policy tends to be an amalgam of specific regional interests, whereas presidential policy tends more to reflect the 'national interest' as a whole.[77]

Two particular aspects of the structure of Congress had a major impact on American foreign economic policy in this period: the ability to logroll and a strong agricultural bias. Logrolling refers to vote-trading, which was much easier in the American than in the British or French systems because of both the absence of strict party discipline, and the ability of individual members of Congress to attach amendments to legislation. This meant in effect that they could hold an entire bill hostage to their own particularistic and parochial concerns.[78] This phenomenon can be particularly important in the passage of tariff legislation. If, for example, a tariff bill is introduced that reflects a coherent national tariff strategy, it can be amended by members of Congress representing regions with strong special interests that feel that they need special protection. Although the executive can have substantial influence on the design of the original tariff bill, by the time the final bill reaches the president, it may be a hodgepodge of special interest tariffs that bears little resemblance to the original design. The president at this point has the option either of signing it as is, or vetoing it, leaving the country with no tariff policy at all.[79]

Congress, and particularly the Senate, also had a traditional pro-agriculture bias, because thinly populated agricultural states have the same two senators as heavily populated urbanized states. Thus New York, where most international financial activity was centered, had two senators, while the group of primarily agricultural states, with a combined population of less than New York, might have over twenty. This agricultural overrepresentation, combined with the ability to logroll and a decline in American agricultural competitiveness, caused Congress to have a consistent bias toward agricultural protection that continues to this day.

The American presidency is structurally less permeable to regional and special interests than Congress, and thus one might expect it to act more in keeping with some idea of a national interest. Throughout the interwar period presidents did favor more open international trade regimes than Congress, primarily because of their greater distance from the politics of regional protection and logrolling. Presidential tariff policy, and foreign economic policy more generally, actually remained fairly consistent throughout this period in its focus on reciprocity as a primary goal. What varied was the willingness of different presidents to challenge Congress on this issue. This varying degree of willingness can be traced to changing perceptions of the effect of American policy on the policies of other countries. When presidents thought that limited, rational tariff structures would encourage others to reciprocate with nondiscriminatory tariff structures, then they actively promoted restraint in Congress. When they thought that foreign tariffs would be discriminatory anyway, they tended not to get involved.[80]

The American monetary policy-making process was, like the legislative process, structurally more fragmented than the British and French models. The Federal Reserve system was set up in 1914 to fulfill the functions of a central bank, in order to distance monetary policy management from the political process.[81] Unlike many other central banks, the Federal Reserve system consisted of several semiautonomous regional banks overseen by the central Federal Reserve Board in Washington, rather than a single national office. These different banks reflected different sets of interests. Because each regional bank was responsible for the regulation and health of the commercial banks within its region, each had an institutional interest in maintaining the economic health of whatever those commercial banks invested in. Thus, if a Reserve Bank was responsible for banks that were heavily involved internationally, it would have an institutional interest in the health of the international economy. If few of the banks that it was responsible for were involved internationally, it would have no reason to care about the international economy.

The Federal Reserve Bank of New York contained within its area of jurisdiction most of the American financial institutions with major international commitments. It often did attempt to fulfill some leadership functions, such as underwriting abroad in financial crises and stabilizing international capital flows.[82] The other reserve banks, however, dealt to a far lesser degree with banks lending, and other institutions investing, abroad. As such, they took very little interest in leading the international economy, a lack of concern mirrored by the Federal Reserve Board.[83] The existence of a system of several reserve banks thus had a mixed effect on American international economic leadership. It allowed the New York Fed to be more internationalist than a single central bank would have been, but it denied the individual Feds both the resources and the political clout that a single central bank would have had.

It is interesting to note in this context that the American bank most committed to the international economy did on occasion attempt to act on its own as an international leader. J. P. Morgan & Co. made a number of attempts at international policy coordination with respect to the reparations issue, and even bailed out foreign central banks on occasion.[84] The bank clearly recognized its interest in international economic leadership, and was in turn recognized by the international financial community in a semiofficial capacity. Morgan & Co. often acted as a bellwether for private lending activity, much in the same way the International Monetary Fund does today; a Morgan loan was considered an approval of creditworthiness. Morgan was so central to international financial activity in this period that it, alone among private bankers, participated at meetings of central bankers.[85] However, despite this ability to act in a quasi-official capacity, as a private bank it simply did not have the resources to act as a stabilizer without government support during major international crises.

In short, although the Wall Street banking community and its Federal Reserve Bank had both the interest and the autonomy to act in support of the international financial infrastructure, its access to the ear of the government in Washington was limited. So that even though the dollar was the only major currency that remained officially convertible throughout the war (although some nonstatutory impediments to gold exports were created), it did not become a reserve currency in the way that sterling was.[86] In the first place it was undercirculated abroad, particularly given the value of allied war debts owed in dollars. And though the dollar remained stable in relation to gold throughout the 1920s, at $20 an ounce, it was probably undervalued.[87] Some observers have suggested that it may have been significantly undervalued, and that this undervaluation was a significant contributory factor to the monetary instability that led to the crisis of the Great Depression. In the early to mid-1920s, there was a significant inflow of gold to the United States. According to the etiquette of the gold standard as practiced by the Bank of England, the Federal Reserve should have lowered its reserve rate, inflating the domestic economy and stabilizing gold reserves. To shield the domestic economy from the effects of inflation, however, the rate was kept high. This had the effect of "sterilizing" the gold (taking it out of international circulation), which in turn exacerbated liquidity problems elsewhere, particularly in Europe. Finally, the Federal Reserve Board managed monetary policy in response to domestic concerns. It is interesting, for example, that in a quasi-official history of the Federal Reserve System, the chapter dealing with the 1920s does not mention international financial or monetary issues at all.[88]

American private banks did provide a substantial and fairly constant flow of liquidity to the international economy throughout most of the 1920s. This flow was driven primarily by market forces, and the government did little to promote a stable flow of funds abroad, let alone countercyclical lending. In fact, American governmental representatives stressed on a number of occasions that it would not do so on principle.[89] As a result, lending declined precipitously at the first sign of crisis in 1929. In net terms, U.S. long-term capital exports in 1929 were little over a tenth of their peak in the 1920s, and by 1931, again in net terms, Americans had begun repatriating long-term capital.[90] The Federal Reserve Bank of New York did undertake to act as an international lender of last resort to a certain extent through most of the 1920s, but even this role was curtailed as the government in Washington took more interest in monetary politics as the crisis of the late 1920s loomed. The American response to the international liquidity squeeze associated with the Great Depression was to cease almost entirely sending funds abroad. This was true not only of private banks, but of the American government as well. With capital needed both at home and abroad, the American government chose to encourage its retention at home.[91]

But the primary focus of the American government's foreign economic policy was on the export of goods rather than of capital. American policy-makers never embraced free trade in the way that the British did. Tariffs were always seen as a valid tool of industrial development rather than as ideologically odious, and tariff reduction was seen as useful only insofar as it was reciprocated abroad, allowing for a growth in exports. The fad throughout much of the first half of this century in executive tariff policy was for "scientific" tariffs, which were tariffs that compensated for unequal production costs. These were popular with the executive (and elsewhere) because they ostensibly depoliticized tariffs—that is, removed them from the jurisdiction of Congress. But "scientific" tariffs still end up highest with respect to those goods that need a market of last resort most. Even when the United States sought multilateral tariff reduction it was not really acting as a leader, because these reductions would likely be reversed when they no longer served the interests of exporters.

American trade policy immediately after the war, still governed by the Underwood Tariff of 1913, was the most liberal it had been in half a century. It nonetheless did not make the American market a bona fide market for distressed goods, for two reasons. First, although lower, tariff rates were still substantial. Second, the tariff was based upon reciprocity and nondiscrimination, meaning that it was contingent on the policies of America's trading partners. This tariff structure was modified by the Fordney-McCumber Act of 1922, which was similar in kind and in intent to the Underwood Tariff, but revised the rates upward in response to the uncertainties of increased international economic instability.[92] But the onset of depression in 1929 changed the interests of industry. Export growth was no longer possible, so industry demanded import protection instead. They got it, with the infamous Smoot-Hawley Tariff of 1930.[93]

When, as a result of the onset of depression internationally, the executive branch could no longer elicit trade reciprocity, it allowed control over the setting of tariff levels to gravitate to Congress. Once subject to congressional logrolling, American policy became actively internationally destabilizing. The Smoot-Hawley Tariff raised tariff rates precipitously, particularly on those primary commodities most in need of a market for distressed goods. Its worst features resulted from congressional logrolling rather than conscious planning, but they became national policy nonetheless. The executive branch regained control of trade policy with the Reciprocal Trade Agreements Act in 1934, which did open American markets somewhat, but on a purely bilateral basis.[94] The convertibility of the dollar was suspended in 1932, at a time when it was not under heavy pressure in international markets; the executive branch managed a gradual depreciation to $35 for an ounce of gold.[95] This devaluation was, like American tariff policy, driven by concerns over exports.

Finally, the United States showed little interest in leading international macroeconomic policy coordination. There was American involvement in the reparations issue, but this can be traced to an interest in securing American investments in Germany rather than an interest in the international economy as a whole. Furthermore, American loans to Germany tended to be to local governments rather than to industry, usually for public works projects. American lenders thus had a greater commitment to the political stability of the Weimar Republic than the economic health of Germany.[96] This interpretation is supported by American inflexibility on the war debts issue, seen by most other governments as being related.[97] Moreover, while Great Britain consistently showed an interest in creating international forums for macroeconomic policy coordination, the Americans as often as not seemed to go out of their way to undermine these forums.[98] And, while American multilateralist trade policy can be seen as a basis for policy coordination, as it was after World War Two, in the 1920s it was a much less appealing model than British trade unilateralism. The United States was no more active at coordinating macroeconomic policies internationally in the 1930s than it had been in the 1920s. In fact, American responses at international coordinating forums in the 1930s were remarkably similar to what they had been in the 1920s. The focus of American participation at these forums was negative rather than positive, avoiding commitments rather than fostering cooperation.

A currency bloc did coalesce around the American dollar, consisting primarily of those countries in the Americas that depended on the United States for trade and capital. However, the dollar bloc was not a smaller international system with a purposive leader in the way the sterling bloc was. The sterling bloc was generated by a recognition on the part of Great Britain that it no longer had the capabilities to lead internationally, and was an attempt to lead regionally instead. The dollar bloc consisted of countries that perceived themselves to be so economically dependent on the United States that they chose to follow even though the United States did not attempt to lead. American capabilities were great enough that these few countries could free ride on American policy without creating significant costs for the American economy, but American policy remained focused on the needs of domestic producers.

CONCLUSION

By the time of World War One the classic gold standard system had been a fact of life for generations, and it set the baseline of expectations for most of the participants in the international economy. Neither the technology and organization of international commerce nor financial capabilities had changed radically over the course of the war. As such, at the end of the war, it was the late nineteenth-century system that was the social norm around which views of a postwar system converged. Before the war Great Britain had been clearly financially predominant, with France and Germany as the next two most important investors in the international economy. Britain had acted as leader, France had actively cooperated in facilitating that leadership, and Germany had played a relatively passive role. After the war Britain remained the financial center of the world, but with its degree of financial predominance significantly weakened, and the United States supplanted Germany in the top three international financial powers.

But the gold standard proved to be a Humpty Dumpty; it had had a great fall, and it just could not be put back together again. Analysts have argued that Britain could no longer act as a leader even though it wanted to, the United States would not act as a leader even though it might have been able to, and France went from being an active supporter of British leadership to an active spoiler. Why the change? Why could a system that had worked so well not be effectively reconstructed a decade later? The answer to these questions involves changes in the international financial structure, domestic political priorities, and changes in the relationship between economic ideologies and potential policy practice.

Three key changes in the international financial structure undermined postwar international economic leadership. The first was the weaker position of Great Britain. The war had left sterling more vulnerable, both structurally and psychologically. The circumstances that led to the expedient of the gold exchange standard also made sterling more vulnerable in crises,[99] and the process of suspending convertibility for the war and the time required to resume it undermined sterling's aura of invincibility. The second was the replacement of Germany by the United States, with its unique domestic system and its isolationism, as a major international creditor country. The third change in the international financial structure that undermined postwar leadership was the status of intergovernmental finance, particularly the issues of war debts and reparations. Even though these issues had lost much (though not all) of their salience by the onset of the Great Depression, they had already made their impact in the form of a structurally weak international economic system.

As a final observation on the effects of the structure of international finance at the time, it is interesting to note that the geographic distribution of investment had a major impact on the formation of the various currency blocs in the 1930s. It is for the most part those countries that looked to Great Britain for finance that followed it into the sterling bloc, and those that looked to the United States for finance that followed the dollar (Canada, which looked to both countries for finance, ended up trying to straddle both blocs). And it was those countries on the periphery of French finance, as well as smaller European creditor countries, that maintained convertibility longest. This suggests that the structure of international finance affects not only who will be able to act as leader in an international economy, but also who will choose to follow them. But it is also interesting to note that countries could choose not to participate in market-based international economic systems at all. Germany and Japan chose to construct, and succeeded in constructing, regional economic systems based more on authoritative than on market exchange. This suggests that we not simply assume the presence in the international economy of the social construct of money/market systems of exchange in which the logic of financial predominance operates.

The key features of domestic political structures affecting the brittleness of leadership in the interwar period were the weakness of French governments and the division in American government. Both of these features undermined the ability of the respective governments to create consistently internationalist foreign economic policy. The American executive usually could do so when it was a priority, but there was always a consistent anti-internationalist pressure from Congress that proved easy to yield to in times of crisis. The chronic weakness of French governments throughout the interwar period did not allow for much in the way of policy leadership, be it international or domestic, when there was any significant domestic opposition. And the relative unimportance of revenue from international commerce and finance to the economies of both France and, to an even greater extent, the United States, compared with Great Britain, meant that domestic support for internationalist policies would be relatively weaker than in the traditional leader in the first place.

But the story cannot be fully told without looking at the ideological setting, at the social constructions that defined reality as seen in these three countries at the time. British and American policy responses in the interwar era were conditioned by domestic foreign policy norms, of international engagement and unilateralism in Britain, and of isolationism and reciprocity in the United States. These norms account for leadership behavior that was stronger than can be explained by the logic of financial predominance in Britain, and weaker in the United States. At the same time, in both Britain and the United States financial orthodoxy and a commitment to convertibility at par remained accepted economic dogma. This is true particularly in Great Britain, where even the Labour Party remained committed to balanced budgets at the height of the Great Depression, and where devaluing sterling with respect to gold was never considered as an option, either in the process of resuming convertibility after the war or in the process of ending it in 1931. In both instances it was convertibility at par, or not at all. This commitment has no particular logical explanation, but it was a social fact underlying monetary policy. Whether or not one accepts the argument that the commitment to a gold standard in general was obsolete by the 1920s and was a major contributing factor to the Great Depression, the inflexibility created by Britain's commitment to par and the almost moralistic stance in the United States that financial orthodoxy was a national responsibility[100] cannot but have contributed to the brittleness of the system.

Accepted conventional wisdoms, "common senses" in Gramscian terms, strongly reflected recent historical experience in all three countries. Great Britain's experience had been as a successful leader, and policy tended to follow this experience whenever possible. This explains both the conscious attempt to recreate an international gold standard in the 1920s, and the creation of a smaller international system within the sterling bloc with Britain at the helm once it had become clear that leadership on a global scale was no longer in the cards. The United States' experience had been as a follower, as an importer rather than an exporter of international finance and commercial services, and as a country on the periphery of the Eurocentric international political system. This experience proved a great hindrance to the process of adjustment of American policy to match its newly acquired international financial wherewithal. American responses to the international system in general were traditionally isolationist, a preference for withdrawal over engagement, and these traditions for the most part overwhelmed impulses to leadership. Finally, French recent experience was dominated by World War One to a far greater extent than was true of either Great Britain or the United States. This experience was reflected by a French focus on reconstruction and later on security, and goes a long way to explain France's willingness to undermine international leadership and cooperation when these threatened either policy goal.

6

The Postwar Period
American Leadership?

The attempt to create international institutions in the aftermath of World War One failed. The attempt in the aftermath of World War Two succeeded. International relations in the period following the end of World War Two showed a number of seemingly contradictory trends. Economically, this period ushered in an era of clear American hegemony. In the aftermath of the war, the United States had over half of the world's industrial capacity and a majority of the world's monetary reserves.[1] Militarily, it witnessed the beginnings of the Cold War, the bipolar confrontation that was to set the tone for international security relations for almost half a century, and also created the basis for two separate and largely exclusive international economic systems. Yet at the same time it saw the creation of a set of multilateral economic institutions and norms that continue to have a major impact on the international political economy today. The International Monetary Fund (IMF), International Bank for Reconstruction and Development (IBRD), and the General Agreement on Tariffs and Trade (GATT), all of which were negotiated and institutionalized in this period, continue to be the official organs of the international community in the fields of international monetary, financial, and trade affairs.[2] They do not necessarily work as originally envisioned, but they remain to some extent reflections of the intentions of their designers.

It is conventional wisdom that the United States was the key international leader in the construction of the postwar settlement. The United States emerged from the war as the world's predominant economy, largest exporter, overwhelming monetary power, and sole source for much of the capital and technology, and many of the resources, needed for postwar reconstruction.[3] Most of the countries of the world looked to the United States for leadership in creating the new order, and in sustaining them until the equilibrium of the new order could be reached. Furthermore, American resources gave the United States a de facto veto over at least the major features of the new order.

The previous three chapters discussed clear connections between international economic leadership (or absence thereof) and international financial capabilities (or absence thereof). But that story does not work as straighforwardly in this case. In the late 1940s, the United States was the classic hegemon, in the standard international relations theory sense of the word.[4] This does not necessarily mean, however, that it was financially predominant in the same way as Great Britain a century earlier and Holland two centuries before that. American capabilities gave the United States the predominant role in the creation of new international economic institutions and norms. But these institutions did not provide as solid an international economic infrastructure as had British and Dutch leadership.

Why did the Unites States use its hegemonic position to create a set of formal international institutions rather than the more informal system the British had favored a century earlier? And why design these institutions in a way that failed to provide as solid an infrastructure as might have been done? The answer lies in the weakness of American financial motivations. The United States was never driven by the logic of international finance in the same way that the British and the Dutch were. As a result, other foreign policy motivations came to predominate in its leadership. Its capabilities allowed it to play the leading role in coordinating the postwar international economy, but the absence of internationalist financial motivations meant that it chose to focus that role on issues other than the creation of a stable international commercial and monetary infrastructure. The story of the American role in the postwar reconstruction and its aftermath is the story of the interaction of its various motivations with the constraints of the international system.

THE DEMAND FOR LEADERSHIP

Three events provide the background context for the reconstruction of an international economic order in the 1940s: the Great Depression,

World War Two, and the emergence of the Soviet Union as a major international player, both militarily and ideologically. The Great Depression was important as an object lesson of what can happen to the global economy in the absence of effective international cooperation; it was generally accepted that the "beggar-thy-neighbor" policies of the 1930s had gone a long way toward making a bad situation worse. It was also important for the developments in economic theory that it spawned, particularly in getting Keynesian ideas of demand management accepted by both the academic and policy-making mainstream. This provided, for the first time in a century, a theory of liberal/market economics that was an acceptable alternative to financial orthodoxy.

The war had a number of effects that served to enable the multilateral economic system constructed in the 1940s. It clarified the answer to the question of where the center of the system should be; there was no longer any question that to be functional, a system had to be built around American economic capabilities. It helped to counteract traditional American isolationist tendencies; popular opinion could no longer hesitate to get involved in Europe because the United States was clearly already heavily involved. And finally, the outbreak of the war served as a historical example from which policy-makers drew lessons. One of these lessons was that the League of Nations had failed not because the concept was inherently flawed, but because the institution itself was too weak. Future multilateral cooperation would therefore have to be based on more robust institutions. Another lesson, drawn more strongly by American policy-makers than those elsewhere, was that economic conflict, if poorly managed, can lead to military conflict, and therefore that an effective way of promoting military security in the international system as a whole is to promote economic security as broadly as possible.

The emergence of the Soviet Union as a superpower also had a profound effect on the creation of the new international economic order. In both the Dutch- and British-led international economies discussed earlier, there was no direct overlap between systems of security alliances and systems of economic infrastructure. But in the bipolar confrontation of the Cold War there was a direct overlap. The United States and the Soviet Union saw each other at the same time as military, economic, and ideological threats. Both poles created distinct international systems around themselves that combined both security and economic elements. The Soviet system was not fundamentally money-based. In the Soviet style of economic planning, the value of investments is defined by the central plan rather than by market mechanisms,[5] which is the reason for the focus on the U.S.-centered system in this chapter.

The onset of the Cold War had both a constraining and an enabling effect on the creation of this system. It was constraining in that it was to an extent inherently exclusionary. The limitations of an ideological confrontation meant that economic logic was subordinate to the political goals of containment. The enabling effect was to draw the United States into international politics, and into international economic politics, much more than would have been likely without the ideological motivation.

In short, the demand for commercial infrastructure that one would normally expect in a money-based economic system was both amplified and channeled, in the United States and among its allies, by a new respect for multilateralism based on the effects of its absence in the spread both of the Great Depression and World War Two. It was also inextricably intertwined with a fear, both physical and ideological, of the Soviet Union and of Soviet communism. These experiences lent a greater immediacy to the demand for leadership, particularly among the governments of Western Europe. They also led to a far greater openness to multilateral approaches and formal, institutionalized models of cooperation than had been common earlier. The context for the development of leadership during the war and the reconstruction meant that issues of the international economic infrastructure were addressed explicitly, through formal intergovernmental negotiation.

INTERNATIONAL FINANCE

The United States at the beginning of World War Two was not heavily invested in the global economy compared with Britain or Holland in their heydays; it mattered less to international commerce, and international commerce mattered less to it. Furthermore, the United States was significantly less invested than it had been a decade earlier. In the interwar period the stock of American long-term private foreign investment peaked in 1930, at roughly $14 billion. It slowly declined through the depression, and by 1939 was down to $11.5 billion.[6] Income from this investment was just over half a billion dollars annually, still substantially less nominally than Britain earned from its foreign investments.[7] Total gross annual income to the United States from foreign investments and services to the international economy by this time was roughly a billion dollars, little over 1% of the national economy. The net figure, income from foreign investments and services less payments to foreign investors in the United States and for services provided abroad, was negligibly small, a credit of $183 million.[8]

The war did not have a great impact on the United States' private financial position abroad. Many of the war years actually saw American long-term disinvestment.[9] This is the opposite of the pattern seen in World War One, probably because most allied purchases of war materiel in World War One had had to be paid for by the purchaser, while the American government paid much of the bill for Allied purchases in World War Two through the Lend-Lease program. While there was little new investment, however, the appreciation of existing investments was sufficient to increase the total foreign investment position of the United States at the war's end to over $13 billion.[10] But by the immediate postwar years income on that investment plus income on international services remained at around the 1% level it had been at prior to the war.[11] Thus the war did not have a great impact on the importance of international finance to the American economy.

What did change significantly during the war was the relative importance of the United States in global foreign investment totals. That it increased was almost entirely a reflection of declining financial capabilities on the part of other countries, rather than any major increase in private international financing on the part of the United States. The war caused a marked reduction in global levels of foreign investment. Investments by nationals of the Axis countries, especially those of Germany, were eliminated, and investments by many other creditor countries were repatriated to pay for the war effort and reconstruction. Thus while in 1938 American foreign investments generated less aggregate income than British investments alone, by 1947 they generated more than those of all other countries combined.[12] This contraction of global foreign investment and the absence of major international financial claims on the United States left the United States with an overwhelming predominance in international financial capabilities. Furthermore, the only other country with investments of a similar order of magnitude, Great Britain, was hampered by outstanding liquid war debts of some $14 billion, which put enormous strain on sterling's international position.[13]

Flows of new American private foreign investment took a couple of years to gather momentum after the war, but by 1947 they had surpassed $1 billion annually, and they continued at a rate of between

$1 billion and $1.5 billion for the rest of the decade.[14] These outflows of investment capital, however, remained consistently lower than income from existing investment. This meant that overall more money was coming into the country from existing investments than was going out in the form of new investments or, in other words, that in net terms foreign investment and the income it generated exacerbated rather than ameliorated the United States' persistent balance-of-payments surplus.[15] Meanwhile, income from international services declined somewhat as European financial institutions and trade servicers began to recover from the war. As a result of this decline, income from foreign investment and international services as a fraction of the national economy fell from its peak in this period of 1.7% in 1947 to 1.5% in 1949,[16] a figure less than a tenth of the equivalent British figure at its peak in the late nineteenth century.

An interesting note on the relationship between financial commitment to the international economy and foreign policy is suggested by the geographic distribution of American foreign investments. Investment patterns were concentrated in the Americas; over 40% of income earned on American foreign direct investment came from Latin America, another 20% from Canada, and almost 30% from Asia and Africa. As late as the early 1950s, only 3% of these earnings came from Continental Europe.[17] Thus to the extent that the United States was financially motivated to lead the international economy, its leadership should have focused strongly on the Americas, with much less concern for Europe.

The broader context of this discussion of the American international financial position is the American international economic position more generally, in particular its trade position. The Unites States was a large net exporter. Its export surplus peaked in 1947 at over $9 billion, an order of magnitude larger than income from foreign investment.[18] Since the overall balance on services was also positive, and Americans did not seem inclined to invest abroad at a very high rate, this left the United States, as already suggested, with a substantial balance-of-payments surplus. This in turn left the rest of the world with no way to finance imports from the United States without some form of American aid.[19] In the short run, importers could finance their trade with the United States with liquid assets such as gold, but these would eventually run out, more likely sooner rather then later. In fact, figures show dramatic decreases in gold holdings by a number of European countries until the arrival of American aid in the late 1940s.[20]

The United States in turn could not afford a drastic curtailment of exports for fear of a recession. The issue of financing American exports thus loomed larger in American foreign economic policy-making motivations than strictly financial concerns; the export dilemma posed an immediate threat to the American economy, a threat that the American private international financial position did not.[21]

DOMESTIC POLITICAL INSTITUTIONS

The basic institutions within which American foreign economic policy was made were similar to those in the interwar period, as discussed in the previous chapter. Some differences from the interwar period did develop, however, that had notable impacts on the course of American decision-making. In particular, the relative political strengths of various branches of government changed, their bureaucratic-political relationships evolved, and the personal characteristics and ideas of the various decision-makers involved differed.

The most important institutional continuity in this context is the separation of powers and the resulting absence from Congress of party discipline of the sort found in parliamentary systems. This structure leaves individual senators and representatives free to represent their particular constituency interests at the expense of the national interest. When combined with the ability of individual members of Congress to propose that amendments be added to bills regardless of any relevance to or harmony with the intent of the bill, this often results in legislation that reflects an assortment of disparate parochial interests logrolled together, rather than a single coherent perceived national interest.

The four particular parochial interest groups that had the greatest effect on American foreign economic policy-making in the second half of the 1940s were those dominated by export-driven industries, by import-competing industries, by agriculture, and by regions that had very little interaction with the international economy. The interests of the first two groups are, as would be expected, open markets and liquidity abroad on the one hand and protected markets at home on the other. The interaction of these two sets of interests can explain much about the particular content of the multilateralist approach favored by American policy-makers, as we will see. During the depression and the war, American agriculture had achieved a broad set of price supports and quantitative regulations that helped to ensure stable levels of income and employment throughout the industry.[22] Legislators from agricultural regions, which remained disproportionately represented in Congress, were consistent in wanting to keep as many of these support mechanisms as possible in the postwar era. Finally, significant parts of the American economy had fairly little interaction with the international economy. Legislators from regions in which these insular interests predominated tended to favor a focus of policy on purely domestic issues, and a withdrawal from involvement of whatever kind with international economic institutions.[23]

Perhaps the single most important institutional difference from the interwar period was that the Administration successfully froze the Federal Reserve System out of the process of negotiating the new international monetary and financial institutions. This stemmed from a desire on the part of the Administration to gain direct control of international monetary policy, and to remove said control from international bankers, at a time when seminal international institutions were being created. The Administration feared that the bankers would use control of monetary policy for parochial rather than national interests. One of the more vehement statements of this desire was expressed by Henry Morgenthau, Roosevelt's Secretary of the Treasury, who wanted "to drive . . . the usurious moneylenders from the temple of international finance."[24] This was more easily done in the American system than might have been the case elsewhere, because American monetary reserves were held by the Treasury Department, rather than by the central bank, as was the case in most other industrialized countries.[25] One of the results of the consequent move of the locus in decision-making in international monetary issues from New York to Washington was the politicization of the new international financial institutions (the Federal Reserve Board itself is in Washington, but it was the Federal Reserve Bank of New York that was always the most active in managing international monetary relations). The effect of this move is debatable, but no less an authority than John Maynard Keynes thought it to be of great importance. He considered the decision to locate the IMF and World Bank headquarters in Washington rather than New York, which he felt would serve to politicize them further, to be a personal defeat.[26]

Other differences between the interwar and the postwar policymaking structure stemmed from the interactions of the various bureaucracies involved in foreign economic policy-making, particularly during the war. The Treasury Department and the State Department, for example, had very different ideas for the postwar settlement. State favored a more traditional, laissez-faire approach to international trade that emphasized nondiscrimination, derived, as we shall see, from security concerns as well as financial motivations. Treasury was much more willing to experiment with mechanisms for maintaining international employment and liquidity.[27] These differences stemmed in part from differing bureaucratic interests, and in part more particularistic differences. Treasury was populated with people sympathetic to New Deal approaches whereas the people at State tended to be more conservative,[28] and the respective secretaries of the two departments, Cordell Hull at the Department of State and Henry Morgenthau at Treasury, had very different personalities and belief sets.[29] They resultant bureaucratic infighting caused a lack of clarity in the conceptualization of the goals that the United States was attempting to achieve in its foreign economic policy.

Finally, individual personality made perhaps more of a difference in the process of the development of American foreign economic policy in this period than in many of the other cases looked at in this book. A good example of this, and the most notable instance of a change of personality affecting bureaucratic policy in this chapter, is the change from Henry Morgenthau to Fred Vinson as Secretary of the Treasury in 1945. Morgenthau was an East Coast businessman, a childhood friend and lifelong confidant of Roosevelt. He had little feel for popular politics, and considerable sympathy with New Deal economics. His Treasury Department was open to ideas of international institutional innovation, and focused its attention on what was most likely to work to stabilize international financial relations. Vinson was a career politician from the South, a political populist who tended to economic conservatism. His criteria for policy rejected economic theory in favor of what the voters back home would want.[30] Much of the change in American policy from the idealist institutionalism of wartime planning to the more isolationist stance of mid-1945 to mid-1947 can be traced to these personal differences, and their impact on Treasury Department policy.

DOMESTIC POLITICS AND INTERNATIONAL INSTITUTIONS

Three issue areas in which these various structural and individual factors affected American foreign economic policy-making are particularly relevant to this story; the creation of international financial institutions, the creation of international trade institutions, and the creation of international liquidity in the period of transition from war economies to a new peacetime equilibrium.

In the creation of the new international financial institutions, five particular issues were of expressed importance to American policymakers. These included the question of whether the new institutions would tend more toward being inflationary or deflationary, and the related questions of whether they would be financially orthodox or liquidity-producing, and whether they would require adjustment in cases of balance-of-payments disequilibria primarily from the debtor or creditor country. In the gold standard, or "orthodox," system, a country that ran persistent balance-of-payments deficits and that wanted to maintain the parity and convertibility of its currency would be forced to deflate its economy, often by raising interest rates. This would decrease imports, and thus help to balance national payments. In a more liquidity-producing system, a country in deficit would be able to defer any deflation by using the source of international liquidity to cover the deficit. This might, however, have inflationary effects on nondeficit countries, transferring the burden of adjustment from the debtor to the creditor. Thus all three of these issues are directly interrelated. The other two issues of concern were ensuring an acceptable level of American political control over the resources of the new institutions, and ensuring that the United States did not end up paying too much for them.[31]

The two main institutions of international monetary and financial management set up during the latter part of the war, the IMF and the World Bank, were designed during the course of predominantly bilateral negotiations between the United States and Britain, at the resort town of Bretton Woods, New Hampshire, in 1944. With respect to the three related issues previously listed, the British at these negotiations favored institutions that were liquidity-producing, required adjustment primarily of creditors, and that were biased toward inflation rather than deflation. The Americans, on the other hand, favored the opposite: more orthodox institutions that required adjustment of debtors and were biased more toward deflation. Significant variations existed within both national positions, but the most liquidity-oriented of the American positions was less so than the most orthodox of the British positions.[32] Both sets of positions reflected the existing economic conditions in the respective countries. The United States was a large net exporter with no need of liquidity assistance from international sources, in which inflation was a greater perceived threat than deflation. Great Britain was a net importer facing major international liquidity problems where there was a much greater fear of the economy cooling down too much than of it overheating.

American policy-makers were willing to bear some costs to create institutions to stabilize international financial and monetary relations. They also, however, wanted to ensure that other countries bore the brunt of adjustment to the new order. The executive branch was willing to make some concessions to the needs of international economic leadership, but was cognizant that the legislative branch was more interested in limiting American financial commitments abroad. One of the more colorful expressions of Congressional opposition on this issue was provided by Senator Robert Taft, who suggested that participation in the IMF would be tantamount to "pouring money down a rathole."[33] This Congressional check on resources available for international economic leadership became a conscious constraint on executive policy. Economic leadership was also hampered by a desire to politicize the new institutions. Both branches of government felt that the financial commitments being asked of the United States were too large to be managed for purely economic ends, reflecting the weakness of internationalist financial motivation. They felt that funds of such magnitude should give the United States certain additional political clout as well.[34]

An interesting postscript to the issue of American monetary policy at Bretton Woods is an alternative plan suggested by the New York banking community, with the support of the Federal Reserve Bank of New York. This group was clearly interested in international economic leadership, as the community would be among the primary beneficiaries of an international financial system centered on the United States. Their proposal was essentially to recreate the traditional gold standard, with the dollar replacing sterling as the primary reserve currency.[35] Such a plan would have constrained American domestic economic policy in much the same way as the role of sterling in the gold standard system had constrained British domestic economic policy in the nineteenth century. It would have also, its proponents felt, created a more reliable currency for international exchange. This plan was almost completely ignored by American policy-makers, reflecting the relatively small role of the New York internationalist banking community within the American economy.[36]

The creation of new international trade institutions was, from the perspective of creating American foreign economic policy, more problematic than new monetary and financial institutions. Any new agreement on tariffs invariably hurt particular national industries directly. A number of major issues faced negotiators in creating a new international trading order, in most of which the United States adopted positions that supported either its industrial interests or its political autonomy. Three of these issues were the relationship of tariff rate reduction with tariff nondiscrimination, the relationship between trade and employment, and the position of agriculture in the new trade order.

Multilateralism in the new international trade order, as envisioned by most of the participants in the creation of the new order, had two components; decreasing absolute levels of tariff protection, and decreasing levels of trade discrimination.[37] There was, however, no similar consensus on what the relationship between these two components should be; opinions ranged from strong support for tariff reduction combined with the retention of trade blocs, to a hesitancy about tariff reductions mixed with a strong antipathy to trade blocs. The American negotiators were solidly in this latter camp, giving definite priority to nondiscrimination over tariff reduction. There were two reasons for this, one derived from traditional economic concerns and the other stemming from security concerns.

The economic concern seems to have been quite simply the protection of the American export surplus. No one had a commitment to the idea of a surplus per se, but export industries wanted to be able to maintain wartime levels of exports, while import-competing industries wanted to avoid any precipitous drop in their levels of protection. The government as well saw the maintenance of export levels as necessary to avoid recession during the process of transition from a wartime to a peacetime economy. Trade discrimination had not been much of a problem during the war, as most American exports had been given to allied countries to support the war effort, rather than sold. However, many Americans felt that a return to interwar-style economic blocs would cripple American exports, as many of the blocs, particularly the sterling bloc, would operate to conserve dollars by limiting dollar imports. At the same time, import-competing industries, working through Congressional lobbies, strictly limited the scope of possible tariff reductions.[38] Since American trade law was already substantially nondiscriminatory, an emphasis on nondiscrimination rather than tariff reduction served the interests of American exporting industries while at the same time hurting import-competing industries fairly little.

In contrast, positions on the issue in Britain ranged from ambivalence between tariff reductions and nondiscrimination, to strong support for Imperial trade preferences. The British government in its bargaining position tended to the view that both were important, but were more inclined to push for decreased tariffs rather than nondiscrimination, as this would help most exporters but hurt few importers. They saw, though, no reason to give one component philosophical or ideological priority over the other.[39] There were many in Britain, however, on both the political left and right, who favored retaining Imperial preference as a means to insulate Britain from the global economy. Others in Britain strongly supported Imperial preference for ideological reasons. They felt that the Commonwealth had really come through for Britain during the war, and thus deserved British preferences during the peace. Interestingly, shortly after the war, the United States signed preferential trade agreements with the Philippines and Cuba. It justified these agreements by pointing out that both were recent American possessions, and thus the United States bore a special responsibility for their economic health. The difference between this and the British relationship with the empire was never made entirely clear.

The security motivation underlying the strong American support for nondiscrimination was the belief that nondiscrimination in international trade would contribute to global peace. There were many people in the U.S. government, particularly in the State Department, led by the wartime Secretary of State Cordell Hull, who strongly believed in this idea. They saw the discriminatory, sometimes exclusive, trade blocs of the 1930s as a significant contributory factor to the onset of World War Two. By excluding Axis countries from trade blocs, they argued, the Allies had hindered the ability of Germany and Japan to ensure the supply of necessary commodities through trade, leaving them little choice but to fulfill these needs through military expansion. A new international trade order based on the idea of nondiscrimination would eliminate any economic motivations to expansion, and therefore eliminate a major cause of war. William Clayton, Assistant Secretary of State for Economic Affairs, argued that "the international economic policies of nations have more to do with creating conditions which lead to war than any other single factor."[40] Thus the American commitment to trade nondiscrimination was an exercise in security leadership as much as an exercise in economic leadership.

The relationship between trade and employment issues was another one that created contention between the United States and many of its partners in international trade negotiations. These negotiations were officially convened as discussions of trade and employment as interrelated issues. They did not begin until well after the war had ended, and, unlike the Bretton Woods negotiations, they included a majority of the world's countries. The Americans were much more hesitant than representatives of other countries, though, to accept an international agreement that constrained countries' freedom of action with respect to their domestic economies. American negotiators were also more inclined than those of other countries to believe that the more important causal arrow was from trade to employment rather than vice versa, meaning that if trade discrimination were overcome, this would solve employment problems as well.[41] As a result, American delegations to international trade negotiations tended to oppose references to full employment policies, and organizational charters referring to such policies faced difficulty in Congressional ratification.

The final item on the list of issues in the creation of new international trade organizations was the least contentious. None of the major participants in international trade negotiations in the late 1940s favored a drastic liberalization of trade in agriculture. This was not because no one was interested in it; rather it was because those interests were not well represented at the negotiations. All the major voices at these talks were from industrialized countries, where agricultural protection was favored for primarily parochial or political reasons—that is, either because the maintenance of a large agricultural sector was popularly seen as a good in itself or because the political structure in some way favored agricultural protectionist interests. Most of those regions of the world that would benefit most from free trade in agriculture were either not represented, or were represented by new governments that did not carry much political weight. As a result there was little expressed support for a liberalization of trade in agricultural products. The American government was one of those most strongly encouraging the exclusion of agriculture from the new international trade order, because any agreement that included it would face insurmountable opposition in a traditionally and structurally agriculturally biased Congress. In fact, provisions were inserted into both the International Trade Organization charter and the GATT to make them compatible with the existing price support mechanisms authorized by section 22 of the American Agricultural Adjustment Act.

The third major issue area of the postwar economic reconstruction was the question of international liquidity, and the extent to which the

United States should underwrite it during the transitional period. The war had left a situation in which international commerce was hindered by a shortage of currency for international exchange. The primary problem was a shortage of dollars outside of the United States, and thus the United States was in the best position to rectify the problem. There were three primary vehicles of American financial aid abroad during the 1940s. The first was the Lend-Lease program, in which the United States gave military supplies as aid-in-grant. The American government valued this aid at a total of $38 billion.[42] The second was the loan to Britain of $3.75 billion at below-market rates in 1946, supplemented by a loan of $1.25 billion from Canada on the same terms. The third was the granting to Western Europe, beginning in 1947, some $12 billion in matching funds under the Marshall Plan.

The national interest underlying the Lend-Lease program was straightforward; winning the war. The stated Anglo-American philosophy for financing the war was based on the concept of equality of sacrifice, dating back to the pledge of "each government . . . to employ its full resources, military or economic, against those . . . with which such government is at war," contained in the original Declaration of the United Nations in early 1942.[43] The British felt that this meant equality throughout the course of the war effort, meaning that American aid should help to compensate both for British efforts before Lend-Lease began, and for the proportionately greater dislocation to the British economy from the war. The American government disagreed, reflecting popular opinion that the United States had been generous enough during the war, and should concentrate on domestic problems afterward. As a result, Lend-Lease was terminated abruptly with the surrender of Japan, leaving foreign governments unable to pay for goods already ordered without depleting irreplaceable hard-currency reserves. The narrowness and security orientation of the interests underlying Lend-Lease thus led to a premature end to the program that exacerbated problems of postwar international liquidity.[44]

The sterling bloc had survived the war intact. As a group, the members of the bloc pooled all available dollars to be able to use them most efficiently. Thus any dollar shortage in Britain affected the other sterling bloc countries as well. By late 1945, it had already become clear that Britain was facing a balance-of-payments crisis that could prove crippling to the international monetary and trade position of the sterling bloc as a whole. The British government developed the expectation that the United States would bail it out, and requested a $6 billion grant-in-aid, or at least an interest-free loan.[45] Should no aid have been forthcoming, the sterling bloc may well have had to resort to a set of currency controls designed primarily to limit economic interaction with the United States. This threatened the American export position directly. There were two primary American responses. Many voices, in Congress and elsewhere, favored simply saying no, and focusing American resources domestically.[46] Others, including the relevant part of the Administration, favored using a loan (the idea of a grant was never seriously considered in the United States) as bargaining leverage to gain a British commitment to trade multilateralism as defined by the United States, and to making sterling convertible as soon as possible.[47] These commitments, it was felt, would both ensure that American exports did not get frozen out of a new trade regionalism, as had happened in the Great Depression, and help improve international security by alleviated economic motives for expansionism. Thus the two main sets of responses triggered by the British request for balance-of-payments assistance in 1945 were a traditional American isolationism on the one hand and a concern with ensuring export levels on the other. The latter response prevailed, resulting in the Anglo-American Financial Agreement of 1946, more commonly referred to as the British Loan.

The third major American contribution to international liquidity in the transition from war to the new international order was the Marshall Plan. This resembled Lend-Lease inasmuch as it reflected serious underlying security concerns. In justifying the Marshall Plan, the Administration made it clear that while the economic goal was supporting European reindustrialization, this was the corollary of a definite political goal, stemming Soviet expansionism.[48] It resembled the British Loan in that the immediate crisis that forced American action was a general European balance-of-payments shortfall stemming largely from the American export surplus. Thus both security concerns and export concerns seem to have contributed to the decision to grant Europe large-scale aid in 1947. It was different from the two earlier programs, however, in its demands on the recipients of the aid. Marshall Plan grants required matching funds from recipient governments, and could by and large only be used in ways that expedited and reinforced the development of market-based systems of exchange within the national economies of those countries. In this sense, the Marshall Plan was not only an attempt to shore up the liquidity of postwar Europe, it was an attempt at creating property rights by reinforcing the norm of market exchange in Europe.

INTERNATIONAL ECONOMIC LEADERSHIP

What were the effects of these domestic political debates and consensuses on the provision of a financial infrastructure to the international economy? The United States clearly provided leadership in some areas, most notably security cooperation, to a greater degree that the leaders that we saw in earlier chapters. But the demands of security leadership do not necessarily correlate with the demands of international economic and monetary leadership. The United States did nonetheless provide some infrastructure to the international economy. The question remains, however, of how effective this leadership was at fulfilling the three functions of leadership discussed in Chapter 2: the provision of a currency for international exchange, the provision of liquidity, and the coordination of property rights.

The first of these functions of leadership is the maintenance of a currency for international exchange. To act as such, a currency must be both highly valued and available internationally in sufficient quantity that it can be readily used by third parties in exchanges. The United States did fulfill this function to a certain extent; the dollar, throughout the postwar period, was at all times either highly valued or widely available. It was, however, rarely both.

Even though it was technically based on a gold standard, the monetary system created at Bretton Woods was for all practical purposes dollar-centered. It made the dollar the currency of international exchange in the sense that it was the benchmark for other currencies.[49] This had the advantage of transparency; it was clear to everyone that the system was based on the dollar, in contrast to the interwar period, when there was no clear single currency of international exchange. It had the disadvantage of structurally favoring the dollar as the central currency. This meant that the United States could externalize adjustment to changes in its economy and balance-of-payments; in other words, it could make other countries pay for them. For example, in the nineteenth century, if Britain's current accounts balance deteriorated to the point where it threatened the value of sterling, the Bank of England would be forced to raise interest rates and deflate the economy. The United States, in a similar circumstance, could force other countries to lower their interest rates and inflate their economies.[50] The United States availed itself of this ability increasingly as its balance-of-payments situation worsened.[51] This became a particularly acute problem in the 1960s, with the growth of American spending in Vietnam.

Two of the primary concerns of American negotiators at the Bretton Woods conference, as indicated above, were ensuring domestic political autonomy and ensuring political control of the international financial institutions. Both concerns reflected the positions of those within the United States who had little interest in international finance. The resulting institutions reflected these concerns. The political control of the institutions was more important to the question of international liquidity, which will be discussed below, than to the currency issue. The domestic autonomy they allowed the United States permitted the American government to create policies driven by a variety of interests without taking into account in the short term their effect on the position of the dollar.[52]

It was to a large extent security concerns that ended up weakening the position of the dollar as the central currency of the Bretton Woods system. Most of the damage done to the dollar by American security commitments abroad was done after the postwar reconstruction was substantially complete; these commitments began to be a significant burden with the onset of the Korean War in 1950. Direct military expenditures abroad rose from just over half a billion dollars in 1950 to almost $3 billion a year by 1955, stayed at roughly that level for a decade, then increased to almost $5 billion by 1969.[53] A monetary system designed to limit the short-term policy constraints that the international monetary system could put on American policy autonomy resulted in a situation in which the United States could use the position of the dollar in the system to defer the costs of international security leadership. This behavior reflects a combination of security concerns and isolationism—security concerns in that the American government was committed to its security expenditures abroad, isolationism in that it wasn't willing to deflate its own economy to pay for them.

The second function of leadership is the provision of liquidity to the international economy. In the long run this is best done through the provision of a market for international trade goods. This is the element of international economic infrastructure that the United States provided least well. As suggested earlier, three basic sets of interests drove American trade policy: security concerns, based on the idea that nondiscrimination in trade would eliminate a major cause of war; export concerns, seeking to protect markets abroad for American goods; and protectionist interests, seeking to prevent international competition for import-substituting industries and agriculture. There were several phases to the development of American trade policy in the

1940s, beginning with attempts to gain British commitments in principle to multilateralism in trade during the war, continuing with the negotiations for the charter of the International Trade Organization and the General Agreement on Tariffs and Trade after the war, and culminating in the withdrawal by the American administration of the ITO charter from consideration in 1950. Since then, and until the creation of the World Trade Organization in 1994, the GATT, originally intended as only one aspect of the ITO, was the primary institutional mechanism for cooperation in international trade.

The first phase encompassed the trade aspects of the Atlantic Charter of 1941, the Lend-Lease settlement, and the British Loan. All three made reference to multilateralism in trade as a basis for the postwar economic order. To a certain extent, British acceptance of a commitment to multilateralism in these documents was a quid-pro-quo for the various kinds of aid they contained.[54] Or, in other words, the United States used the bargaining leverage afforded to it by its wartime and reconstruction aid programs to extract concessions to multilateralism from the British. As previously noted, there remained a consistent misunderstanding between the British, who saw their imperial preference system and American tariffs as equal obstacles to multilateralism, and the Americans, who saw discriminatory preferences as the primary evil. This difference of opinion was to place a stumbling block in the way of more substantive negotiations on a trade charter, begun in 1946.[55]

American negotiators felt that Congress would be unwilling to pass fundamental tariff cuts even in exchange for an end to imperial preference. The U.S. Reciprocal Trade Agreements Act, as amended in 1947, gave the executive branch the authority to negotiate reductions of up to 50% in most American tariffs, from 1945 levels, except where such a reduction would cause injury to domestic industry. Given the high starting levels of American tariffs, along with the escape clause, this reduction still left the United States with substantial barriers. In exchange for this, American negotiators expected to eliminate, or at least gut, imperial preference.[56] The compromise eventually reached on this issue at the tariff negotiations associated with the ITO charter talks was to move very slowly on both issues. Discrimination, as a general rule, would not be increased, and had to contract as tariffs contracted.[57] But an elimination of most preferences on manufactured goods, coupled with large, across-the-board tariff cuts, would not occur until 1967.

The charter of the ITO as a whole, as agreed to at Havana in 1948, was never formally presented to Congress for ratification, as the administration recognized that it was a lost cause. Three particular groups combined to oppose it. Economic conservatives opposed the employment provisions of the charter, in that they delimited the freedom of action of the American government with respect to its domestic economic policy. Some export interests opposed it because it provided too many loopholes for trade discrimination. Legislators representing agricultural interests opposed it because it threatened the agricultural support system of the New Deal, which had since become institutionalized.[58] The negotiations on tariffs on manufactured goods specifically, though, were more acceptable to all of these groups, and were institutionalized as the GATT. This provided a forum for multilateral negotiations on tariffs and trade, but no immediate breakthroughs.

Thus until 1967 American tariff levels on manufactured goods remained relatively high, in some cases prohibitively so. As late as 1960, for example, the average American tariff rate on manufactured goods was 20.2%, as compared with an European Economic Community (EEC) common tariff of 14.3%. The American figure was higher than any of the EEC or European Free Trade Area countries except for Portugal. There were some manufactures on which American tariffs were as high as 81%, and a number on which American rates were more than double the EEC equivalents.[59] In agricultural goods, the only potential export for much of the less industrialized world, the American market was protected not only by tariffs, but by quotas as well. It could not as a result act as a market for distressed international trade goods.

The provision of liquidity to the international economy in the medium term can be achieved through ensuring the provision of liquidity countercyclically abroad and to the international economy. This is the function of leadership that the United States fulfilled perhaps best of all. There are a number of possible reasons for this, one of which is a compatibility of policy suggested by security, export, and financial concerns with respect to this function.[60] As was the case with the previous function of leadership, though, when the demands of providing countercyclical liquidity came into conflict with security concerns in the 1960s, the security concerns won out.

There were two distinct ways in which American policy promoted international liquidity: directly, through government aid programs, and indirectly, through incentives for private investment. The aid programs were most important in the immediate aftermath of the war, and included transitional aid, primarily the British Loan and the Marshall Plan. They also include, in a way, American military spending abroad, which increased dramatically in the early 1950s. Indirect promotion of international liquidity occurred primarily through tax incentives for corporate direct investment abroad.[61]

The British Loan and, to an even greater degree, the Marshall Plan were clearly effective at stabilizing the economies of the recipient countries through the provision of countercyclical liquidity.[62] They were targeted, however, only at Europe. It is true that the European countries bore the brunt of the damage from the war and suffered the greatest economic dislocation.[63] Many economies elsewhere, however, suffered significant dislocation as well. These two programs, being driven primarily by security and export-insuring concerns, focused on Europe because that is where American export levels were threatened, and where the greatest security threat was perceived to be.[64] Thus because of the motivations driving their creation, the British Loan and the Marshall Plan stabilized the European economy at a time of particular need, but did little for the rest of the international economy. Development aid programs were more widely dispersed, but were often driven by security concerns, rather than economic rationales, and have always been of a magnitude too small to make a difference on a global scale.

Tax incentives for foreign direct investment reflected both security and balance-of-payments concerns. Increased investment abroad helped ensure American control over resources internationally,[65] and also helped to alleviate the balance-of-payments surplus. These incentives did help to create a relatively stable flow of liquidity to the international economy. This flow, however, was to an extent based on the compatibility of the demands of leadership of the international economy on the one hand and of Western security on the other. When security demands had, by the mid-1960s, contributed to a fundamental deterioration of the American balance of payments, the government maintained its security expenditures, but acted to control the outward flow of foreign investment.

The final function of international economic leadership is the creation and enforcement of a set of basic property rights around which the expectations of participants in the international economy can converge. This involves the creation and enforcement of a set of norms for international economic interaction. The United States fulfilled this function partially. The American government used a number of forums to articulate the tenets of an international economic regime around which it wanted international economic behavior to converge. It was more willing than leaders in the past had been to use international institutional structures and aid programs as leverage to enforce this convergence abroad. It frequently did not, however, play by its own rules.

The regime around which the United States attempted to coordinate international economic behavior was based on nondiscrimination in international economic interactions, an emphasis on market forces over government involvement in the economy, and formal international organizations as the mechanism for maintaining equilibrium in the international economy. Nondiscrimination, as previously discussed, was promoted in most international economic agreements that the United States signed, from the Atlantic Charter and the Lend-Lease agreement through to the British Loan and the GATT. Support for market forces over government intervention was promoted through both the design and the implementation of the IMF and World Bank, and through various provisions of the Marshall Plan that determined how the aid could be used.[66] Supranational institutionalization was supported through the very creation of the various postwar economic institutions, the distancing of American domestic monetary and financial institutions from international leadership roles, and a persistent tendency on the part of the American government to create new and formal agreements and institutions to deal with new situations and crises as they arose.

The United States did succeed in getting a substantial degree of convergence of international economic behavior around these three tenets in much of the world, particularly in Western Europe. Success was more modest elsewhere, and declined almost to nothing in the communist bloc. In much of the developing world these tenets were less appealing. For developing countries, an emphasis on market focus over government involvement meant that it was difficult to get a start creating an industrial base, nondiscrimination meant that a relatively weak industrial base had to compete globally, and international institutions in which votes were based on subscriptions meant that the poor had no say in how they would be run.[67] The United States was not willing to commit sufficient resources or make sufficient concessions to make the tenets more appealing in areas where American security interests were not perceived to be involved.

The United States was fairly consistent in its macroeconomic policy coordination as long as its tenets remained compatible with both security and export concerns, and did not require a level of resource commitment that would trigger an isolationist backlash. When they conflicted with these concerns, the American government showed a willingness to stray from these tenets itself, or allow its allies to do so, while still requiring adherence from other countries. During the period being discussed here, for example, the United States began to encourage European regionalism, which helped both American security and export interests, at the expense both of the norm of nondiscrimination and of many extra-European economies whose trade would be displaced as a result. It also exempted agriculture and, in ways, military industries from the requirements of market-orientedness. The United States did not violate its own norm of working through the international institutional structure during the immediate postwar period, but was certainly willing to do so beginning in the 1960s, when the institutional structures began to interfere with the demands on the American economy of ensuring security without compromising domestic economic growth.

DENOUEMENT

By 1953, the basic institutions of the postwar reconstruction were in place. The Bretton Woods institutions were up and running, and the GATT was in force. The history of this international economic system after this point can be divided into four general episodes. The first, from 1952 to 1958, was a period of adjustment from the centrally controlled and managed economies of the war and the reconstruction to the multilateralism envisioned by the new economic order. The second period, from 1958 to 1964, was in many ways the heyday of the Bretton Woods system, when the IMF and World Bank worked pretty much as planned. The third, from 1964 until the early 1970s, was a period of increasing strain on the Bretton Woods monetary and financial order, beginning with the first voluntary restraints on American capital exports in 1964 and ending with the closing of the gold window in 1971 and the official end of the gold standard in 1973. Paradoxically, it was also the period when the GATT really came into its own as a forum for major, across-the-board international tariff reductions. The final period, beginning in the early 1970s can be thought of as the post-Bretton Woods era, which is addressed in the next chapter.

The period from 1952 to 1958 was a period of slow adjustment from the special institutions of postwar reconstruction to the institutions designed for a longer-term equilibrium. It was also in many ways the height of the Cold War, in terms both of ideological enmity and of perceived threat from the Soviet bloc.[68] From the point of view of a study of international economic and monetary leadership it is not as interesting either as the period before it or the period after. The basic thrust of the foreign economic policies of the major economies did not change much, and there were few major new institutional developments in the international political economy. The United States did begin to face a slowly worsening balance-of-payments situation, which resulted from both a deteriorating balance of trade and gradually increasing security commitments abroad. But this situation was not yet bad enough to pose a problem for an international monetary system based on the dollar.[69]

In 1958, the major Western European currencies became convertible. This allowed the Bretton Woods institutions to function essentially as planned.[70] The six years from 1958 to 1964 marked the high point of the dollar-based, fixed exchange rate, mobile capital regime envisioned in 1944. This period can be viewed as one of stable equilibrium broken by the war in Vietnam. More realistically, though, it can be seen as the period in which a strengthening European and Japanese balance-of-payments position and weakening American position allowed the system to function for a short while. Not a stable equilibrium, but a temporary conjuncture. As early as 1960, in fact, Robert Triffin suggested that the international monetary system was based on an internal contradiction, in that it simultaneously required an American international payments deficit and was undermined by the same deficit. He argued, in an analysis that came to be known as the Triffin dilemma, that as such the system could not last.[71]

The U.S. government was, by 1964, forced by its deteriorating payments situation and the ensuing pressure on American gold reserves to take action to deal with the Triffin dilemma. The American government responded in that year by suggesting voluntary restraints on foreign investment by U.S.-based companies. By 1968 the deficit and the pressure had increased sufficiently that mandatory capital controls were instituted, and the United States stopped supporting gold at $35 an ounce on the free market.[72] By this point, the combination of the chronic balance-of-payments problem and evaporating confidence in the dollar made any long-term continuation of the Bretton

Woods system infeasible. In 1971, the United States abdicated its structural position in the Bretton Woods international monetary system by "closing the gold window" even to foreign central banks and ending entirely the convertibility of the dollar to gold.[73] The postwar monetary system had come to an end.

CONCLUSION

There is a substantial historiographic debate as to the primary set of concerns that motivated American policy-making in the aftermath of World War Two. The traditional view is that security concerns predominated, that American foreign economic policy was subordinate to the demands of the Cold War. The revisionist view is that the confrontation with the Soviet Union was to a certain extent a cover for American economic imperialism, a way of ensuring American export markets.[74] Although the traditional view is the more compelling, it is likely the case that both sets of concerns played some role in the social construction of the Cold War. To these issues must be added a lingering isolationism, reflecting both the United States' historical role in international relations and the isolation of much of the country at the time from the international economy. It is not in any case of fundamental importance for the purposes of this chapter which of the historiographic positions on the sources of American postwar foreign policy is the more accurate. The key point here is that the United States was not financially predominant. While it had the requisite capabilities, it did not have the associated level of financial motivation. As a result, the demands for an international commercial infrastructure were only tangentially supplied.

The centrality of security concerns in the making of American foreign economic policy is suggested by geography as well as by content. In both the Dutch- and British-led systems, the focus of foreign economic policy-making tended to be on those areas in which investment in international commerce was concentrated. In the balkanization of the global economy in the 1930s, the new economic blocs tended to match existing patterns of investment as well. Of American foreign investment following the war, some three-fifths was in the Americas and only 3% in continental Europe. One might as a result expect a financially motivated United States to focus its attention everywhere but Western Europe. This was, however, not the case. In fact, in as major a policy initiative as the Marshall Plan, all of the American aid went to Europe. Foreign economic policy in general tended strongly to focus on those areas of the world, both in Europe and in Asia, where the security threat was deemed to be the highest.[75]

The focus of U.S. policy on the creation of multilateral institutions can only be understood within the social context of American political thought at mid-century. The impetus to multilateralism originated to a certain extent in the lessons drawn both from the Great Depression and World War Two. It may also have stemmed in part from a particularly American form of idealism, a constitutionalism that generates the belief that creating the right political institutions is the key to establishing a well-functioning society. Finally, the content of the new international economic institutions owed a significant debt to Keynes, and the general acceptance of Keynesian theory at the time as a supplement to traditional orthodox economics.[76] The norm of multilateralism allowed for the incorporation of all of these ideological priorities, and had a major impact on the development of the postwar international political economy. The American constitutional idealism suggested above, though, has always sat uncomfortably with the isolationist strain discussed earlier. It may well be the case that the magnification of the Soviet threat by American elites in the 1940s and 1950s was as much a tool for supporting the internationalism of the idealist impetus against the traditional isolationist bent.

The United States began the postwar era fulfilling all of the functions of leadership to some degree or other, but some to a much lesser degree than others. The immediate postwar period, though, was one in which financial, export, and security needs all made compatible demands on American policy, tempered only by the isolationist leanings of a relatively self-contained economy. It was also a period in which leadership did not place enormous demands on American capabilities. Even so, there was a considerable hesitation to adopt some of the functions of leadership. As the demands of trade and security needs diverged from those of economic leadership, and as the demands on its capabilities became greater, American leadership weakened. In the series of international economic crises that followed and were precipitated by World War Two, the United States performed adequately as a leader. As security and trade needs pulled American policy away from economic and monetary leadership, it began to perform less and less as a provider of international economic infrastructure, until by the late 1960s and early 1970s it abandoned its own monetary regime when confronted by a crisis requiring a choice among these needs.

Thus despite appearances during postwar reconstruction, the United States in this period never really led a stable, reequilibrating international economic order. The postwar system began to unravel almost as soon as it was first put into place. The roots of its eventual failure stem from both its original design and American security policy. The design of the system from the outset gave the United States the ability to externalize macroeconomic adjustment in a variety of ways. Were the United States financially motivated as an economic leader, this ability to externalize adjustment might not matter much. But the predominance of other concerns meant that as soon as major adjustment was required, the United States did indeed begin externalizing the costs. In the end, the extent to which the United States did so became unacceptable to some of the other major players in the international economic system. This is not meant as a judgment of American foreign policy choices—the sacrificing of economic infrastructure for military and ideological security may have been an appropriate choice. It is, however, meant as an example of the relationship between motivation and policy, and more particularly between internationalist financial motivation and the provision of international economic and monetary infrastructure.

In sum, there were clearly some factors motivating the United States to act in support of the international economy. These factors were for the most part, not financial; they stemmed primarily from security and export concerns. Even these internationalist motivations, though, were tempered by both isolationism and a hostility to the international economy in parts of the country, and a domestic institutional structure that tended to bias legislative outputs toward the interests of import-competing industries and agriculture. The extent to which both these institutional quirks and the preferences of individual decision-makers were able to affect policy may well reflect the proliferation of American concerns and motivations in this period, and the inability of any one of them to predominate. This suggests that it is important to look behind the short-term content of foreign economic policy and examine the motivations that underlie it as well. And when these are not financial, it is important to determine the social constructions that underlie the motivations that do predominate. Policies that in the short term approximate the functions of leadership will not necessarily prove to be stabilizing in the long term, if they are driven by nonfinancial concerns.

7

Conclusions and Implications

The last four chapters have traced, on a case-by-case basis, the link between financial predominance and policies of international economic and monetary leadership in four historical eras, from 1600 through to the 1950s. The link remains relevant today. The voluminous literatures on such issues as hegemonic stability theory and American hegemonic decline, and more recently on globalization and governance, suggest that questions of international economic management remain a focus of the field of international political economy. To the extent that this study shows the way in which the logic of financial predominance affects questions of leadership, and how this logic can interact with the relevant contemporary social constructions, it should also be useful in addressing questions of the current state and direction of the management of the international economy and monetary system. In other words, an examination of current levels of international financial commitment, and of the relevant contemporary social constructions, should give us some indication of where, and where not, to look for international economic leadership in the near future. This chapter thus has two functions; to review the case studies and draw conclusions from them, and to suggest the implications of these conclusions for international economic leadership in the near future.

CONCLUSIONS

There are two core arguments in this book. The first concerns financial predominance, the idea that there is a logic to monetary/market systems of international exchange that creates a demand for economic and monetary leadership, and which makes it likely that financially predominant countries will be the ones to supply this leadership. Both capabilities and motivations are integral parts of the logic of financial predominance. The second argument is methodological, that we can best understand leadership behaviors by using a combination of rationalist and constructivist methodologies. With respect to the first of these arguments, all four of the case studies both illustrate and support the contention that the logic of money informs the decisions of agents with respect to both the demand for and the supply of international economic and monetary leadership. The degree of leadership provided by a country reflected its financial predominance in all the cases.

The first case, the comparison of the Netherlands and France in the seventeenth century, serves to isolate financial predominance from other more traditional measures of hegemony, both economic and military. France was the predominant power in Europe by most measures, including the size of its economy and its military capabilities. The Netherlands predominated in little other than the financing and servicing of Europe's commerce. It was thus not hegemonic by most definitions, but was financially predominant. During this period, France behaved as a quintessential economic nationalist, while the Netherlands fulfilled many of the functions of an international economic leader. By isolating financial commitment to the international economy from other suggested measures of hegemony, this comparison strengthens the argument that it is finance specifically that drives the logic of international economic and monetary leadership.

The case of Great Britain from the middle of the nineteenth century to the outbreak of World War One is in many ways the classic example of international economic leadership. The British fulfilled all of the functions of leadership well, and they continued to do so until confronted by a world war. The conventional historiography attributes British foreign economic policy to Britain's predominance in industrial production and export. Yet this predominance does not correlate with British leadership; at the height of industrial predominance British foreign economic policy remained substantially mercantilist, and leadership policies were not fully emplaced until industrial decline had begun. Leadership correlates not with industrial predominance, but with financial predominance. This distinction is relevant to the current implications of the argument; those countries that dominate international exports are not necessarily financially predominant as well.

The examination of the interwar period is interesting in this context in three ways. The first is that it is the setting for Kindleberger's seminal discussion of the absence of leadership in the Great Depression. He argues that the United States could have led but chose not to, whereas Great Britain wanted to but could not. The logic of financial predominance puts this conclusion into a broader theoretical setting, by pointing out the distinction between capabilities and motivations in investment in the international economy. The second is by providing a good illustration of the differential effects of capabilities and motivations. The third is that it gives an example of geographically exclusive international economies, geographically exclusive regions of financial predominance and leadership.

The final case is of methodological note because it allows for a greater degree of separation of the two components of financial predominance—capabilities and motivation—than do most of the other cases examined. The United States in the period of postwar reconstruction possessed the capabilities associated with financial predominance, but its financial motivations were weak. It was, however, motivated to lead in other ways, notably militarily and ideologically. As a result, even though it acted the role of a superpower, it was an unreliable international economic leader at best. It constructed an international monetary system to provide necessary infrastructure, but failed to implement over time the policies necessary to support that infrastructure. This suggests that both aspects of financial predominance are in fact integral parts of the logic of monetary leadership. Capabilities alone, even when associated with motivations other than those of financial predominance, are unlikely to result in consistent economic leadership.

All four cases, then, clearly associate the provision of leadership with financial predominance. At different times, two countries have had both the capabilities and the motivations associated with financial predominance: the Netherlands in the seventeenth century and Great Britain in the nineteenth. The ratio of investment in an international system required for a country to have financially predominant capabilities cannot be specified precisely. In any case, there is not a clear cutoff point. But a plurality of investment would certainly be necessary, and more than half of the systemic total should usually be sufficient.[1] We can be even less specific about levels of motivation in general; these depend on contextually specific factors, as will be discussed below. Great Britain became strongly motivated when the proportion of its national income generated by its international financial involvement passed the 8–10% range. The United States did not become strongly motivated when this ratio peaked at about 3%.

The distinction between capabilities and motivations is a key part of the argument of financial predominance. Some smaller countries not looked at in detail in the case studies have had the motivations associated with financial predominance without the capabilities. Switzerland throughout most of the twentieth century is a likely example.[2] Still other countries have had the capabilities without the motivations. As previously suggested, the United States in the postwar period is a good example. In other words, the two elements of financial predominance need not necessarily covary. Simplifying capabilities and motivations to the ideal types of yes or no yields four possible results in determining the status of a country's financial predominance. A country can have both the capabilities and the motivations, in which case it will likely act as an international economic leader. A country can have neither, in which case it will likely not act as a leader. The two other possibilities are more ambiguous. Both the logic of financial predominance and the evidence from the cases suggest that when a country has the capabilities but not the motivations it is more likely to fulfill the role of coordinator of an international system, but less likely to be a reliable leader in the sense of providing a stabilizing foreign economic policy that fulfills the functions of leadership in the long run. A country that has the motivations but not the capabilities, on the other hand, should (other things being equal) maintain a stable foreign economic policy intended to secure financial commitments to the international economy as much as possible, but without trying to behave as a leader in the sense of coordinating an international system. For example, it might attempt to maintain the value of its currency in the international market, and a stable or countercyclical flow of liquidity abroad, but not attempt to coordinate international macroeconomic policies. In matrix form, the relationship between capabilities and motivations would look as shown in:

		CAPABILITIES	
		Yes	No
MOTIVATIONS	Yes	INTERNATIONAL ECONOMIC LEADER e.g., Great Britain in the nineteenth century	STABILIZING POLICY, BUT FEW ATTEMPTS TO COORDINATE e.g., the United Kingdom between the wars
	No	COORDINATOR, BUT NOT NECESSARILY A STABILIZER e.g., the United States after World War Two	NO LEADERSHIP BEHAVIOR Most countries, most of the time

Figure 7.1: Capabilities and Motivations

A related question is the way in which nonfinancially predominant countries can be expected to behave in crises. A comparison of financial and other contextually specific sets of motivations can help to a certain extent to explain (and predict) the degree to which a nonfinancially predominant country will act in support of a leader in such situations. Countries that play a major role in the international economy can have an impact on the success of leadership even if they are not financially predominant themselves. To use David Lake's terminology, these countries can range from "opportunists," whose actions are ambiguous, to "spoilers," focused on other economic concerns even at the expense of undermining the leadership of the system.[3] Lake distinguishes between opportunists and spoilers based on labor productivity, whereas the distinction here would be better drawn in terms of motivations for leadership. Within the category that Lake labels opportunists, a country will likely behave as a supporter of leadership if internationalist financial motivations are the strongest set of motivations driving the country's interactions with the international economy, and its capabilities are significant, but not predominant. If other motivations outweigh financial motivations, the country is more likely to act as a spoiler.

This conclusion helps to explain Britain's role as the key supporter of the new economic institutions after World War Two despite its many economic difficulties. A good example illustrating a transition from supporter to spoiler is the case of France. Before World War One, France was the world's second largest foreign investor, and the strongest supporter of British leadership. After the war, national security considerations came to loom larger in the French psyche, while the potential income from reparations became far greater than the potential from investment, and France became a spoiler.[4] This hypothesis of course begs the question of relative motivations, which are affected by financial commitment to the international economy but are also contingent on domestic institutional structures and the social construction of the country's foreign economic policy at that point in time.

This contingency leads to the second major argument of this book, the idea that international economic leadership can best be studied through a combination of constructivist and rationalist research methodologies. The relationship between these two methodological approaches has tended to be one of opposition, rather than reconciliation. The constructivist critique of rationalism is that international political realities are based on social constructions rather than objective logics, and therefore analysis based on objective logics will not in the end succeed in explaining what happens. The debate between the two research communities tends to be one of epistemological priority; constructivists argue that the social constructions are what really matter, and that rational action is largely a residual category, while rationalists tend to use terms like culture as their residual category.

The methodological premise of this book is that social constructions and inherent logics of behavior may in fact be in a recursive or dialectic relationship with each other. In other words, some socially constructed institutions create their own logics, which inhere to these institutions as long as the social constructions underlying them hold. But these logics can themselves be actualized in a wide variety of ways, which ways are in turn social constructs. When an international institution, broadly defined, develops within a community that holds both similar knowledge structures and similar goals with respect to the institution, then the institution may well generate an inherent logic. This logic is objective in the sense that it can be derived from an understanding of the institution, but it will not apply once the intersubjective consensus on which it is based ceases to be. As a research methodology, the question then becomes a threefold one, of discovering these intersubjective consensuses, and then of discovering what their inherent logics might be. The final step is finding the way in which the form and content of specific instances of leadership are affected by their historical context, including among other things both the forms of domestic and international political structure, and the social construction of competing identities, interests, and knowledge structures. The extent to which this methodological approach applies beyond the logic of international monetary systems is a question that calls for further research. It should, however, apply in any case in which a common set of goals within a given social construction of international politics creates a recursive, or semihomeostatic, logic.

This methodological argument may at first seem like common sense—you need a deductive argument to get the big picture, but you need to know the details to know the details. There is more to it than that, however, for three reasons. The first is that it reminds us that the deductive argument presumes a normative and institutional setting that is itself socially constructed, and thus subject to change. The second is that the argument shows us more precisely which methodology explains what, where the explanatory line lies between rationalist and constructivist analysis. The third reason is that it does yield some important generalizable conclusions. In particular, it suggests some answers to questions often seen in the literatures on leadership and hegemonic stability theory, particularly questions such as the relationship between leadership and ideology, and between leadership and identity.

In terms of the first of these reasons, the logic of financial predominance operates only within those international economic systems based on monetary and market exchange. Market-based systems of international exchange are social constructs, rather than assumptions or teleologies. They are neither always there, nor the logical conclusion of economic advancement. As such, a necessary prior step to looking at questions of economic and monetary leadership is establishing whether or not such a system is in place. This is particularly true since leaders can, and in all four cases examined here have, manipulated this social construct for various purposes. The Dutch dispensed with market systems wherever they could get away with it, the British imposed them wherever they could manage it. In response to the Great Depression, the French grasped onto monetary orthodoxy more strongly, the Germans dispensed with it altogether. The United States during the Cold War tried at the same time to reinforce such a system among their allies and prevent their adversaries from participation as much as possible. The reasons for these behaviors with respect to money-based systems of international economic exchange are historically specific and contingent. But this variety of reasons reinforces the argument that we must look at the social construction of international systems before asking whether they have inherent logics, and what those inherent logics are.

In terms of the second of these reasons, the rationalist argument is that the logic of financial predominance is linked to international economic and monetary leadership, defined as a set of functions to be fulfilled by the financially predominant country's foreign economic policy. The logic does not identify the specific policy sets that will be used to fulfill these functions, only that the policy sets chosen will fulfill them. In other words, the logic of international economic leadership is one of functions fulfilled by policy, rather than one of specific policies. Other studies of leadership draw the line elsewhere. Kindleberger, for example, speaks of a logic of demand for leadership, but not a logic of supply, making it difficult to generalize from his study.[5] The end point of Krasner's logic is openness, a policy rather than a function, and his results are, partially in consequence, weak.[6] Conybeare discusses the provision of public goods, but not what functions those goods might fulfill.[7] The argument here is that the logic provides a framework on which only certain kinds of policy would fit, but does not determine what those policies will be.

An example of this distinction is Krasner's use of systemic trade openness as a dependent variable. The extent to which leaders have been concerned with systemic openness has, however, varied significantly. The United States has always been concerned with reciprocity, with the idea that others' market be open to a comparable degree as their own. Britain in the nineteenth century, with only a few exceptions, cared very little about reciprocity. It maintained unilateral free trade even when systemic average tariff levels were quite high. The Netherlands in the seventeenth century fell somewhere in the middle. And yet all three sets of policies fulfilled the function of promoting long-term international liquidity. It is by drawing the line between deduction and details at the point of distinction between functions fulfilled and policies chosen that we can maximize explanatory power.

Within the study of international economic and monetary leadership, this methodological approach yields significant results. In all of the cases examined, the particularities of national foreign economic policy-making beliefs and institutions affected specific aspects of policy. Different policies and policy choices were driven by the institutional structure of the foreign economic policy-making process, the paths of the process itself, the norms and ideologies of both specific institutions and national political cultures more generally, and even in many instances the personal ideas, beliefs, and ambitions of individual policy makers, and their interaction. In short, while the functions fulfilled by the foreign economic policies of financially predominant countries can be predicted structurally, the details cannot; they can only be fully addressed particularistically.

The sets of intersubjective understandings that affect foreign economic policy can be divided into two broad kinds: those that result in formal political institutions and those that result in "common senses," or more informal norm sets, beliefs, and identity structures. With respect to the former kind, the peculiarities of the domestic political structures, the formal political institutions, of all of the countries looked at affected policy outputs. For example, the loose confederal nature of Dutch politics in the seventeenth century meant that those functions of leadership that could be undertaken by the government of Amsterdam were undertaken more effectively than those that were within the remit of the national government. The interplay between the House of Lords and the Commons in nineteenth-century Britain goes a long way toward explaining why profitable trade monopolies were broken up more than a quarter century before the lifting of agricultural protection. The chronic weakness of French governments in the interwar period had much to do with the passivity of French foreign economic policy. And the fact that the American government is physically located in a different city than the center of international financial activity explains some of the relative lack of success of internationalist financial interests in penetrating state policy.

One can, to a certain extent, generalize from these observations. The more centralized a state is (in the sense of decisions being made in one place), the more coherent policy is likely to be. The more the internationalist financial community participates directly in government, the more committed a financially predominant state is likely to be to leadership. But beyond these broad generalities, the value added in looking at the construction of domestic political institutions is likely to be in the details of each specific case. Looking at the second sort of intersubjective understandings, those that operate on the level of beliefs, ideologies, and identities, however, can help to illuminate broader questions about international economic and monetary leadership. Two of these questions are the relationship between leadership and ideology, and the relationship between leadership and identity.

The question of the relationship between leadership and ideology is a recurring theme in studies of leadership. Studies often imply a link between the two, some suggesting that hegemony leads to a liberal ideology, other that it is a liberal ideology that causes a country to lead. This study suggests that neither is true. It suggests that ideology will not dictate whether or not a country will become a leader, but will provide the form through which leadership is carried out. In positivist terminology, it is an intervening variable between financial predominance and leadership policies. This relationship is evident in all four cases.

The Dutch case is perhaps the most straightforward in this context. It suggests that leaders need not necessarily either be driven by or adopt liberal economic ideologies. The Dutch were, on the whole, not particularly ideological in their economics, and were on the whole more sympathetic to mercantilist than to liberal economic ideas, but acted as leaders nonetheless. But a comparison of British and American liberal ideology also yields interesting observations. To simplify somewhat, British ideas of liberty tended more toward economic liberalism, of which Cobden provides a good example.[8] American liberal ideas tend to be more focused on the political. This distinction in liberal ideology affected the sort of leadership that each wished to project on the international stage, with the British more focused on economic openness and the Americans more focused on political freedoms. So even if the different levels of commitment to economic leadership can be traced to different levels of financial motivation, different contents of leadership, such as the British focus on unilateralism versus the American focus on rules, can in many cases be traced to different variants of liberal ideology.

Similarly, identity, the consensus view within a country of who the country is within the international community, also affects leadership policy choices.[9] The extent to which the British internalized the role of economic leadership helps to explain both the internal consistency of British foreign economic policy in the second half of the nineteenth century, and the need that British governments seemed to feel to be at the center of the restructuring of the international economic system after both of the twentieth century's world wars. The postwar American identity as anti-communist affected the basket of economic leadership policies that the United States was willing to undertake. Identity may also affect the question previously discussed of when a country is likely to support the leadership of another, and when it will choose to free-ride on that leadership. The enthusiasm of Britain for supporter roles in the twentieth century is one example. The hesitancy of Japan in the latter half of that century to become an active supporter has much to do with a tendency to disengagement born of the degree to which nonaggression is part of its postwar national identity. Stephen Krasner, in his seminal article on hegemonic stability theory, suggested a lag time between when a country should, logically, act as a leader, and when it has historically begun to do so.[10] The internalization of leadership, and a slow pace of the subjectification of new identities, may well account for this lag.

Beyond support for the two central arguments of this book, three other conclusions can be drawn from the case studies that are relevant to the discussion of the implications of this approach for international economic and monetary leadership in the future. The first concerns changes in patterns of financial predominance. Rapid changes in the status of financial predominance can be caused by major exogenous shocks, particularly security crises such as world wars, in unpredictable ways. Barring such shocks, changes in predominance tend to be slow and incremental. The second concerns the scope of leadership. Specifically, leadership need not be universal; it can be regional in its domain. Its geographic extent can be limited through conscious intent, technological limitation, or historical accident. The final conclusion concerns the relationship between international regimes and international economic leadership. International regimes have historically not been reliable mechanisms for crisis management. They have not adequately replaced a committed leader in this role.

With respect to the first of these conclusions, concerning change in financial predominance, the cases suggest two different patterns: slow change brought about by the gradual accumulation or dilution of international financial resources, and sudden major readjustment brought about by exogenous security shocks such as world wars. Dutch predominance, for example, petered out over the course of more than half a century, while British predominance ended abruptly with World War One. The corollaries of these observations are that in the absence of major international security crises, change in the status of financial predominance is likely to be slow and incremental, and that when such crises do occur, they are likely to result in a significant restructuring of the international economic order. This is because, quite simply, world wars are hugely expensive, and thus, unless the burden of this expense is shared equally, they will result in a significant reallocation of global wealth. World wars can also have the effect of adjusting national self-images more abruptly than would be expected during processes of incremental change, as can be seen in the increased acceptance by the United States of a central role in the international community after World War Two.

The second of these conclusions is that international economic leadership need not be universal or global. In three of the four cases, the nineteenth century being the exception, the international economic system in question was less than global. Subglobal regions can have financially predominant countries within them, even if those countries are not financially predominant globally. In turn, these countries should be willing to provide regional economic leadership when they would not have been willing and/or able to do so globally. Regionalization can result from limitations in technology or transportation, which limited the potential areas of penetration of Dutch policy; it can result from deliberate political design, as occurred after World War Two; or it can evolve around existing investment and trade patterns, which is to a certain extent what happened in the 1930s. All that is required is that those within the region identify with it and adopt the economic structure created by the leader. Since the various costs of leadership should decrease as the size of the region being led decreases, this also means that that a country not motivated to lead globally may possibly be motivated to do so regionally.

The interwar period is particularly interesting in this context. An examination of this case suggests that even when no country is financially predominant in a global economy, a country that is financially predominant within a specific region can act as an economic leader for that region. This suggestion is strengthened by a comparison of the three currency blocs that developed in the 1930s. Within the sterling bloc, Great Britain was relatively financially predominant, and chose to fulfill many of the functions of an economic leader. Equivalent levels of financial predominance did not exist within the other two blocs; the United States lacked the motivations and France the capabilities. Neither country was willing to act as a leader to a degree comparable to Britain. The degree of American capabilities within its region, however, meant that it could lead largely by default. It is also interesting to note here that, in general, recovery from the Great Depression began, by and large, shortly after the regional blocs formed.

The final of these conclusions is that international regimes have historically not been adequate replacements for committed international economic and monetary leaders. This inadequacy has shown through in the cases particularly in times of crisis. For example, the normal responses dictated by the international monetary regime failed to materialize during crises on a number of occasions, including the crises of 1890, 1931, and 1971. In 1890, the leader intervened in an active, forceful manner to support the regime, and it was successfully restored. In both 1931 and 1971, no motivated and committed leader existed, and the respective regimes collapsed. Although international regimes have become, particularly in this century, useful mechanisms for managing regularized patterns of interaction in the international political economy, they have not been as useful for managing crisis situations. They have in fact been most likely to fail during crises, when leadership is needed most. And when they have succeeded, it is when they have been underwritten by a country willing to take an active role to lead them through crises. When no leadership exists, regimes have been brittle;[11] a committed leader has increased the chances of the survival of regimes in the long run. This observation provides a bridge between the two parts of this chapter. The second part is concerned with the implications of the argument for the contemporary international political economy.

IMPLICATIONS

How does the logic of financial predominance interact with the social construction of international relations at the beginning of the twenty-first century? One of the great innovations in the discourse and practice of international relations in the second half of the twentieth century was the increasing acceptance of the norm of multilateralism.[12] This norm might seem strongest in the international political economy, given that this is the field of focus of three of the most venerable of multilateral institutions: the IMF, the World Bank, and the GATT/WTO. A response to the logic of financial predominance might reasonably be that it is being superceded by the social construction of the multilateral regime structure in the international political economy. As such, the relationship between leadership and international economic and monetary regimes is a good starting point for discussing the ramifications of multilateralist practices for this logic.

Unilateral Goods and the Logic of Groups

Can international institutions be effective economic and monetary leaders? The logic of leadership suggests that they cannot, for two reasons. The first is that some of the functions of leadership are unilateral in nature; they are not appropriate for collective provision. Either they must come from a single sovereign source, or they simply do not make sense as cooperative endeavors. The second is they are crisis-unstable. They are least likely to be effective when they are needed most.

The clearest example of a unilateral or single-source leadership function is the provision of a currency for international exchange. Currencies must come from a sovereign source.[13] Thus a cooperative provision of this good can be ruled out a priori. An agreement among sovereign states to cede authority over currency provision is possible, but this results in a single supranational currency rather than exchange rate cooperation. In such a case, because authority no longer rests with states, currency stabilization ceases to be an international issue. This is the case with the Euro; the European Central Bank has the ultimate authority over monetary policy decisions, short of decisions by member countries to withdraw.[14] A similar currency could in principle be created globally, but this as well would be subject to the logic of domestic rather than international monetary systems. There appears, in any case, little likelihood of the creation of a formally global currency in the foreseeable future.

Other functions of leadership, such as a market for distressed goods and the provision of countercyclical liquidity, simply do not make sense as cooperative endeavors. If everyone must participate in them, then they will not aid those who need them. Thus, in the case of these goods, collective provision is not simply unlikely, it is a contradiction in terms. Many states can contribute to the costs of providing them, but they become less efficient the more states participate in them, and one state must take ultimate and final responsibility for them.[15] Countercyclical lending or markets for distressed goods, for example, are useless if everyone participates in them equally. If all states were to participate in countercyclical lending equally, there would be no net transfer of funds, and thus nothing would have been accomplished. If only one state undertakes to lend countercyclically, then all but that one state will benefit from added liquidity when it is needed most. The more states participate, the fewer benefit. Thus the good, which promotes stability in such circumstances by limiting economic contractions due to lack of liquidity, is most efficient in its goal when the least possible number of actors participate in its provision. In relation to these functions of leadership, too much multilateralization can be counterproductive.

In relation to other functions of leadership, multilateralization is not counterproductive per se, but will likely yield less stability in crises, when leadership is needed most. This is the case because of the logic of collective action.[16] The norm of multilateralism implies that issues of global importance be dealt with through international regimes rather than through unilateral action by states. Regimes, as described by institutionalist theorists, foster cooperation by reducing its cost. But participation in regimes is, in the short run at least, nonetheless costly. It implies adherence to ways of doing things the elimination of which might lead to immediate savings, and the maintenance of institutions that use up resources. The long-term benefits presumably outweigh these short-term costs. For example, maintaining an open market for international trade goods is costly in terms of tariff revenues foregone and infant industries left unprotected. If everyone complies with an open market regime, however, aggregate wealth will presumably be maximized in the long run. Therefore, states acting rationally and planning for the long term should be willing to comply subject only to the assurance that others will comply as well.

Crises, however, tend to have both the effect of raising costs of compliance and of shortening the shadow of the future of participants. It is during economic crises that the most strain is put on the functions of leadership, particularly those related to liquidity that have high opportunity costs. For example, the long-term liquidity function of maintaining an open market for internationally traded goods and services becomes more costly as domestic industries become threatened, and the short-term liquidity function of last-resort lending becomes more expensive as financial crisis spreads. So crises drive the costs of leadership up. At the same time, whereas economic cooperation in normal times can resemble an infinitely iterated game, crises introduce an element of the one-shot play. This has the effect of shortening shadows of the future all round.[17] So that as the costs of cooperation go up, the perception of long-term benefits is likely to go down. Players should thus become increasingly tempted to defect. The difference between single leaders and multilateral leadership in this case has to do with the passing of bucks. Participants in multilateral leadership may be tempted to pass the buck to other participants, and this temptation will increase as the crisis worsens. But single committed leaders know that there is no one to pass the buck to. This makes the individual leader more reliable in economic crisis, when leadership is most important.

Multilateralism and Leadership

All this suggests that multilateral organizations are not adequate replacements for sovereign states as international economic and monetary leaders. But multilateralism in the contemporary international political economy is a social fact. The postwar construction of embedded liberalism and its gradual transformation to the competitive liberalism of the contemporary world have happened in the international social context of widespread intersubjective acceptance of multilateralist norms.[18] There is even evidence that the level of acceptance of these norms by policy elites is increasing; witness the acceptance by the United States of a binding dispute settlement mechanism in the World Trade Organization in the 1990s, when such a mechanism was unacceptable as part of the International Trade Organization in the 1940s. Meanwhile, the observation that multilateral institutions cannot fully replace committed leaders does not mean that these institutions are not useful or effective in helping to stabilize the international political economy. Leadership works best when supported by an active followership, and multilateral norms help to assure such a followership. Furthermore, multilateral institutions can make leadership more effective, by clarifying and strengthening cooperative norms and creating permanent institutional mechanisms.[19] But in crises, multilateral organizations supported by committed leaders are likely to be more effective.

This having been said, what role do the major multilateral organizations of the international political economy play in fulfilling the functions of leadership in the contemporary world? This differs with respect not only to the three major functions of leadership, but also to various aspects of these functions. On the whole, the organizations play roles that are supportive of, but not replacements for, attempts by the major international economic powers to lead.

The first of the functions of leadership is the provision of a medium for international exchange. The dollar remains the primary currency for international exchange, despite the loss of its structural position at the center of the international monetary system with the collapse of the Bretton Woods system. There are several indicators of the international position of the dollar, among them its continued strength as a reserve currency,[20] the continued use of the dollar as the reporting currency of the IMF and the World Bank, and the existence of large and active dollar markets abroad. The dollar easily fulfills the first requirement of a currency for international exchange, in that it is available internationally in sufficient quantities to be used by third parties in exchanges.[21] With respect to the second requirement, that it be highly valued within a policed system of relatively stable exchange rates, the performance of the dollar is mixed. It is valued in that it commands the respect and confidence required of a currency for international exchange. Its trading value, though, has gone through phases of both high and low valuation since it was floated in 1971. Thus the dollar successfully fulfills the liquidity function of a currency for international exchange, but since 1971 has been less consistently successful at the currency stabilization role.

Until 1971, the IMF played a central role in the provision of a medium of international exchange—it was designed specifically to police a system of stable exchange rates. But since then this institution has found new roles for itself, and deals at best marginally with stabilizing the core currencies of the international system. The G-7, the group of seven large industrialized countries that meet very publicly every year to discuss issues of multilateralism in international economic coordination, has attempted a more direct role in managing stabilization among these core currencies. But the G-7 has been effective only when its members have been in agreement ex-ante. In these situations it has served a useful role as a forum, but when prior agreement among the poles of the international political economy has not already existed, the G-7 as an institution has done little to promote cooperation.[22] The only international institution currently on the horizon that may displace the dollar in its role as the currency of international exchange, and thus the United States in its role as provider of such a currency, is the European Central Bank.[23] But this would mean competition from another currency, not the multilateralization of this leadership role.

The second function of leadership is the provision of liquidity to the system, in the long term by maintaining open markets for internationally traded goods, in the medium term by providing countercyclical liquidity, and in the short term by acting as an international lender of last resort. With respect to the maintenance of open markets, a relatively strong case can be made for the role of multilateral institutions, particularly the regime created under the GATT and continued under the WTO. Under the GATT, average tariff levels on manufactured goods have fallen both steadily and dramatically since World War Two, and may well be at historically low levels.[24] Although the work of the GATT has been continued under the WTO, its progress has been mixed. On the one hand, there has been some success expanding the trading system to cover new goods and services, and to deal with new issues, that had not previously been covered or dealt with. On the other hand, trade disputes among the core powers of the international economy threaten to undermine the credibility of the WTO.[25] Furthermore, the attempt in Seattle in 1999 to launch a new round of trade talks, the Millennium Round, not only failed, but also attracted a level of popular protest never before seen in developed countries on the issue of the multilateral trade regime.

In any case, however, the GATT/WTO regime cannot entirely fulfill the function of ensuring a market for distressed goods, because its rules are designed for nondistressed goods, and explicitly allow countries to protect themselves from distressed goods.[26] Even when the rules do not allow for protection, it remains unclear that countries will follow the rules when they perceive the results of protection to be important; recent examples include the Euro-American disputes over beef hormones, bananas and steel. Yet it seems to have been the case in recent international economic crises, most notably the East Asian crisis of 1997–1998, that the recovery of the economies most affected by the crisis was helped by, perhaps even dependent on, strong international demand for their exports. Their ability to export was certainly aided by the norms of the international trading system. But in the end the market that these recoveries depended on was not the international market in general, but the American market in particular. It is unlikely that the general recovery process from that particular crisis would have been nearly as successful had American demand for imports not been as insatiable as was the case. Again, we have leadership facilitated by a multilateral regime, but dependent on a single leader.

With respect to countercyclical liquidity over the medium term, the extent to which it has been provided to the international economy recently is open to interpretation. The IMF and the World Bank continue to have a stabilizing effect on international investment cycles.[27] This is the case particularly with respect to poorer countries, and takes the form of such things as assistance with debt rescheduling as well as lending per se. One can also speak of structural adjustment programs as a form of countercyclical lending guarantee. The arguments made in favor of creating a new multilateral regime for investment often include the idea that it would stabilize liquidity flows over the medium term. But these arguments are contested, and in any case the negotiation of a multilateral agreement on investments seems to be on hold.[28]

The level of financial flows has continued to grow, reflecting both the solidification of norms of capital openness internationally that is a key part of the evolving norm-set of competitive liberalism, and the development of new financial technologies. But this may partly reflect an increased velocity of money in short-term speculation, rather than increasing levels of long-term commitment to the international economy.[29]

And one of the key sources of recent countercyclical stabilization is governmental, rather than multilateral. Governments of the countries with the largest international financial capabilities have generally refrained from altering incentives for foreign investment during cyclical downturns. For example, the American government's tax incentives favoring foreign direct investment have generally remained in place through all phases of the American investment cycle, thus continuing the incentive to invest abroad even when investment lagged at home.[30] This is in marked contrast to the situation in the United States in the late 1920s and early 1930s, when foreign investment patterns tended to exaggerate rather than be buffered from domestic investment cycles. There are also indications, however, that investment patterns have become significantly more strongly linked with domestic savings patterns since the demise of the Bretton Woods monetary system in 1971.[31] This would mean that international long-term capital markets have become less tightly linked, and that foreign investment patterns are following domestic economic cycles more than had previously been the case. Thus while countercyclical liquidity is being provided to a much greater degree than in the interwar period, the multilateral economic organizations are not fully replacing a country willing to play a more active role in fulfilling the function of provider of countercyclical liquidity internationally.

The final aspect of the liquidity function is last-resort lending, and it is here that on the face of it one could make the best case for multilateral leadership, particularly in the form of the IMF. One of the Fund's primary roles is to ease exchange adjustments, which in practice often means the same thing as being a lender of last resort. The IMF clearly played a major role in crisis lending in the 1990s, particularly in the Mexican crisis of 1995 and the East Asian crisis of 1997. Even here, though, multilateral leadership is captive to leadership by individual states. The IMF could only act with the approval of, and in conjunction with, its most important members, particularly the United States. The discussion in the aftermath of the latter crisis of the need for a "new international economic architecture" also suggests that multilateral leadership in short-term liquidity was not as effective as it might have been.[32]

The third function of leadership is the definition and protection of a set of property rights, of the normative structure of commerce, internationally. Multilateralism certainly plays a role here. At the level of procedural norms, of principles of international political organization, multilateralism is itself a property right, in that it gives states a formal seat at the tables at which the rules of the international economy are formally negotiated. In this sense, multilateralism is a constitutive element of, rather than only a source of and enforcement mechanism for norms in, the contemporary international political economy. But international organizations, particularly the IMF, the World Bank, and the WTO, also play a strong regulative role. The IMF and the World Bank create standards of creditworthiness and actively approve particular macroeconomic policies for their members. The WTO exists primarily to facilitate and police property rights with respect to trade-related issues. Finally, collective security organizations, led by but not restricted to the United Nations, monitor, and occasionally sanction and organize the use of force in defense of, basic human rights, defined in the contemporary world as the set of individual rights needed to underpin market capitalism as practiced in the contemporary world.[33]

But again, as is often the case with multilateral leadership, one can question the extent to which international organizations have traditionally been independent purveyors of property rights norms, and the extent to which they have been agents of dissemination for American norms. This does not bring their centrality to the activity of managing the contemporary international political economy into question. It does, however, bring into question the extent to which these organizations could continue acting as leaders in the creation and policing of international property rights in the absence of active support and direction from the United States. The failure of the WTO to launch its Millennium Round of trade negotiations in Seattle in 1999 also suggests that multilateral leadership is vulnerable to disagreements among its key players. When there are multiple principals, rather than a leader and followers, modern multilateralism has been vulnerable to gridlock.

In sum, multilateralism as embodied in international organizations plays a key and central role in the provision of infrastructure, of leadership functions, to the contemporary international political economy. It has not, though, fully replaced the role of the international economic and monetary leader. It may well be the case that leadership in the absence of respect for multilateral norms would not be possible today, to the extent that multilateralism is constitutive of international politics in contemporary international relations. By the same token, though, this does not make the demand for sovereign leadership obsolete.

Financial Predominance and Potential Leaders

Who might we look to for such sovereign leadership? The answer that is suggested by the discussion of the role of multilateralism in leadership is the United States. The United States has been at the structural center of the international economy for over half a century, and most analysts are used to seeing it there. It provides the currency used most often as a medium of international exchange, it has the world's largest import market, it plays the most active role in orchestrating and funding international lending of last resort, and it more than any other country provides the model for contemporary international property rights. But can we expect the United States to be a reliable leader, particularly if its decade-long economic expansion begins to stagnate? And are there any other potential leaders out there?

A decade ago the natural answer to this question would have been Japan. Its international investment position and financial clout was growing rapidly, and it was threatening to replace the United States as the world's largest economy in currency terms.[34] Furthermore, the Japanese brand of capitalism seemed to be working better than the American. The decade-long Japanese economic crisis of the 1990s that coincided with the longest American economic expansion to date reversed most of these trends, although Japan's international investment position continues to grow. The other country that might have shown a plausible potential for leadership a decade ago was Germany. The German economic model has similarly not fared as well as the American in the past decade. But in any case its sovereign leadership potential is complicated by European Monetary Union; in the case of the Euro, it is no longer entirely clear whether sovereignty lies at the national level or at the European Union level. The same is true of many of the sorts of policies that factor into leadership, trade policy being a notable example. Yet the members of the EU do retain some sovereign policy-making capabilities, in areas such as fiscal and foreign policies. So when we look to Europe as a potential leader, it is not clear if we should be looking to European countries or to the European Union.

But the logic of money suggests that prior to discussing potentials for leadership, we should look at levels of financial predominance. The United States came out of World War Two as the world's largest creditor, and remained so for over three decades. By the mid-1980s, however, it had become the world's largest net debtor.[35] By the end of 1999, its net foreign debt was one and a half trillion dollars, six times as big as that of the next largest foreign debtor.[36] This at first glance might seem to suggest a serious erosion of American financial capabilities. While there has certainly been some decline, however, U.S. capabilities remain much greater than its net debtor status would suggest. As shown in figure 2, the U.S. remains by far the world's largest foreign direct investor, with a total more than four times as large as its

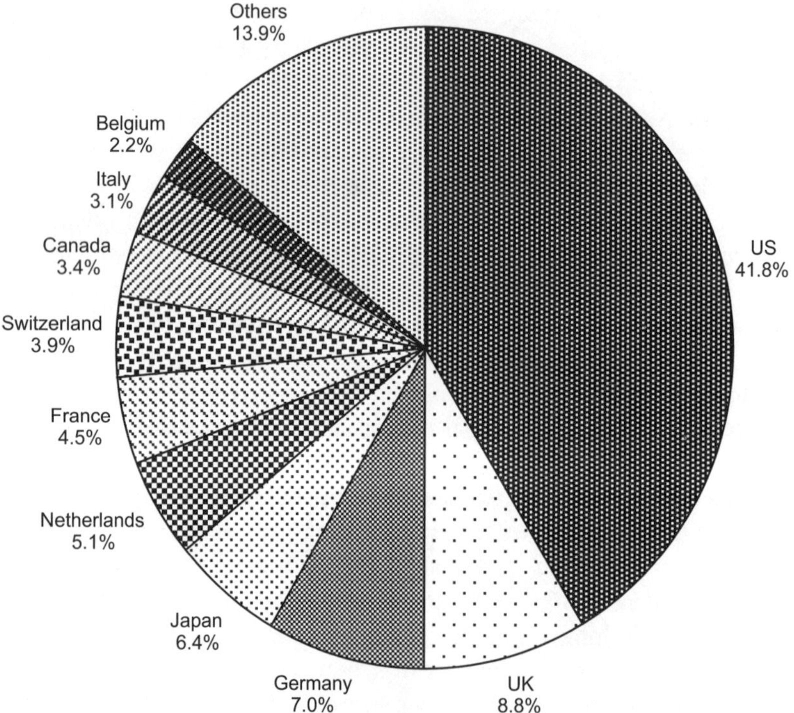

Figure 7.2: Foreign Direct Investment, 1997, as a percentage of the global total.

Source: International Monetary Fund, *Balance of Payments Statistics Yearbook, 2000* (Washington: IMF, 2000). 1997 is the most recent year for which figures for all of the listed countries are available.

next closest rival. Second place goes to the United Kingdom, with the Germany and Japan not far behind.

Interestingly, American relative capabilities grew in the last half of this period even as its net foreign debt has soared. There have been some changes of position among the other large investors, but the list remains the same, and the second-place country has always remained far behind the United States.[37] This discussion of capabilities is, however, complicated by the growing international economic presence of the European Union as an institution. Given the prominence of the United Kingdom as an investor, it is even further complicated by the distinction between the fifteen members of the European Union (EU) and the twelve participants in European Monetary Union. But, since much of the foreign investment of member countries is in other member countries, the EU as a whole, and even less so the Euro 12, does not displace the United States as the world's largest foreign investor, nor is it likely to in the foreseeable future.[38]

In all, the United States retains the greatest capabilities of international financial predominance of any country, but these capabilities are far below what they were at mid-century. They are also far below those of either Great Britain or the Netherlands in their respective eras of leadership. It is interesting to note more broadly that current levels of foreign direct investment are not particularly high by historical standards. On the eve of World War One British foreign investment totaled some $20 billion, from a GDP of roughly half that size. Britain remains the most motivated among major foreign investors, and its current stock of foreign direct investment totaled some $375 billion as of 1997, equal to just under 30% of GDP.[39] The stock of the largest current foreign direct investor, the United States, is some $1.8 trillion.[40] This is equivalent to some one-fifth of current U.S. GDP. In other words, levels of long-term foreign investment among the world's financial leaders at the end of the twentieth century seem substantially less, relative to the size of their economies, than they were at the end of the nineteenth. Aggregate international investment levels, as a percentage of GDP, have in fact only recently reached the levels of the *early* 1800s.[41]

In terms of the logic of motivations of financial predominance, the United States is among the lowest of the major industrialized countries. Income earned abroad as a proportion of GDP over the course of the past decade and a half has fluctuated between 2% and 3%. Allowing for the effects of the business cycle, the ratio seems quite stable over the medium term. This is more than double the figure of the immediate postwar era; the United States should have a stronger financial motivation to lead the international economy than it did in the 1940s and 1950s. It is, however, far from being sufficiently motivated to be financially predominant. The equivalent figure for the United Kingdom is some five times as high, not quite as high as in the heyday of British leadership in the late nineteenth century, but of the same order of magnitude. France, Japan, and Germany seem to be at roughly double the American level, although the Japanese figure has shown a consistent upward trend in the past decade and a half.[42] It is interesting to note, however, that it is only really the Japanese figures that show this upward trend. Despite all of the discussion of globalization in the past decade, the proportion of national income earned abroad in the world's largest industrialized economies has remained relatively static overall. Figure 3 shows this trend.

In short, to the extent that the logic of financial predominance is associated with international economic and monetary leadership, the figures are mixed but on the whole not promising. The country with the greatest international financial capabilities has among the lowest financial motivation to lead. The countries with the highest motiva-

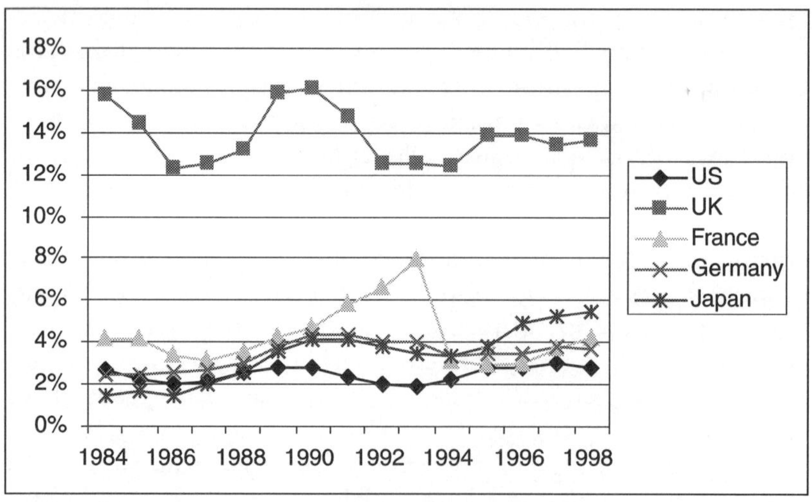

Figure 7.3: Income Earned Abroad as a percentage of gross domestic product.

Source: International Monetary Fund, *International Financial Statistics Yearbook 1999* (Washington: IMF, 1999).

tions tend to have relatively low capabilities. The only country where both capabilities and motivations are growing consistently is Japan, but it has a long way to go before either measure approached financial predominance. The countries of the European Union taken together have considerable international financial capabilities. One of the most capable and motivated, the United Kingdom is, however, one of the few EU members that is not participation in EMU, and the financial motivations of the Euro 12 are lower than those in Japan.

Furthermore, the domestic political structures and processes in these countries do not bode particularly well for leadership. The United States certainly has some of the habits of leadership, and tends in crises to have a willing followership, in that it tends to be looked to by other countries for leadership, and the dollar tends to be looked to as a safe haven. And, as was suggested earlier, its international financial motivations are considerably stronger than they were in the Bretton Woods era. But the elements of its domestic political structure that interfered with attempts to lead then are still there, as is the isolationist streak of a large and relatively geographically isolated country. And the end of the Cold War has removed one of the focal points of American internationalism. This did not prove too great an obstacle to U.S. internationalism, particularly on economic issues, through much of the 1990s. Even then, however, there seemed to be increasing domestic opposition to aspects of globalization, such as the trading regime. And many of the functions of leadership fulfilled by the United States in this period were predicated on good economic times, and on a massive and growing current accounts deficit, and on the ability of the United States to use the central position of the dollar to externalize adjustment costs.[43] The United States was only able to act as the import market that pulled the rest of the world's economies along in the latter half of the decade, for example, by running current accounts deficits that by the end of the decade equaled 1% of total global economic output.[44] It is unlikely that the rest of the world will continue to fund a deficit of that magnitude in perpetuity. In general, then, the United States fulfilled many of the functions of leadership in the 1990s, but did not seem willing to bear great costs to do so.

The Japanese domestic political process seems, if anything, even less well suited to leadership than the American. Western political science tended prior to the 1990s to characterize the Japanese policy-making process as one of strong, centralized, independent bureaucracies making coordinated decisions based on a vision of the long-term national good, the view expressed by such terms as "Japan, Inc."[45] This would suggest a government capable of adopting leadership policies whenever it came to view such policies as being in the national economic interest. More recent work, though, suggests that the Japanese bureaucracy is in fact far more open to parochial interests and less powerful than was previously believed.[46] This new view of the Japanese policy-making process would seem to be supported by inability of the Japanese government to act as a domestic economic leader capable of pulling the country out of its decade-long economic crisis. This would suggest that the Japanese government is not likely to play an aggressive role in adopting the mantle of international economic leadership.

Finally, the European Union is a problematic source for leadership because of the complexity of the EU's political structure, and because in the end it is not entirely clear whether ultimate sovereignty on economic issues lies at the national or the Union level, and if the latter whether with the EU 15 or the Euro 12. In other words, the countries within the EU lack the capabilities to lead on their own, and the EU as a whole shows few signs of being able to coordinate policy sufficiently to lead. The ability to coordinate extra-European policy more effectively is, to be sure, one of the lead items on the EU's agenda. But the difficulty that the European Central Bank has had in getting the level of international credibility in its youth enjoyed by some of its national predecessors suggests that credible leadership from the EU as a polity is, at best, a ways into the future.

Multilateralism and Regionalism

The picture we are left with at this point is of an international system in which the norm of multilateral cooperation is highly institutionalized, and in which multilateral institutions are looked to for the provision of the functions of international economic and monetary leadership. Multilateral institutions are not, however, the best providers of these functions, particularly of crisis leadership. But none of the world's current major economic powers has the capabilities and motivations of financial predominance. How, then, can we best ensure leadership in future international economic and monetary crises?

One answer to this question is multilateralist regionalism. Multilateralism and regionalism are generally seen as divergent trends in international economic governance. Regionalism is in fact seen by some analysts as antithetical to multilateralism. But the contemporary practice of regionalism, as exemplified by such organizations as the EU, NAFTA, Mercosur, or APEC, is itself based on multilateral practices. Regional security forums have long been an accepted part of the multilateral system, and seen as complementary to, rather than in competition with, global forums. As a social construction and a core element of the normative structure of the contemporary international system, multilateralism need not be global. There is certainly an economic argument to be made in favor of global, rather than regional, international institutions. The broader the geographical coverage of a market-perfecting agreement, the greater the efficiency gains realized. In other words, the more international scope given to the mechanism of comparative advantage, the more wealth it should create.

The argument that global economic institutions should be more efficient than regional ones is about exchange, however, not about leadership. The more parties to a system of free trade, the more efficient production should be. But this does not necessarily mean that more followers to a system of leadership will make the system more stable in crises. The process of recovery from the Great Depression suggests that there are circumstances in which a devolution from global to regional patterns of leadership can radically improve the ability of international systems to recover from economic shocks. The problem with regional leadership in the interwar system was that it came along with regionalism in other economic institutions as well. The regions were exclusive, not inclusive, and there were few mechanisms for economic interchange among them.

In this context, contemporary regional economic institutions can be seen as being more akin to contemporary regional security organizations that to the interwar economic blocs. They do not replace global multilateralism, they augment it. It needs augmentation because, in the absence of real and committed economic leadership, the global institutions risk becoming expressions of the lowest common denominator of state preferences, and this denominator may in fact be too low to guarantee cooperation in the long run. This risk of deadlock beyond the lowest common denominator expressed itself repeatedly in the last decade of the twentieth century, from the ultimately unsuccessful Structural Impediment Initiative negotiations between the United States and Japan at the beginning of the decade to the failure of the WTO meeting in Seattle at the end. This risk affects all of the functions of leadership. With respect to the provision of a currency for international exchange, it is apparent in the sometimes explicit goal of those in charge of the Euro to challenge the dollar for the benefits of seigneurage. With respect to liquidity, it is apparent in failed discussions about the "international financial architecture,"[47] and in the willingness of countries to flout rulings of the WTO's Dispute Settlement Mechanism. And with respect to property rights, it can be seen in the increasing tensions to be heard among the American, European, and Asian models of capitalism.

Regional economic multilateralism can raise this lowest common denominator significantly, in two ways. The first is by grouping countries with more compatible economic outlooks. But, perhaps more important, regionalism can make leadership easier. The primary reason that leadership worked within regional economic blocs in the 1930s, where it had not globally, is that countries that were not financially predominant internationally were regionally. In some cases capabilities that could not support leadership internationally could do so regionally. In other cases, motivations that were insufficient to reliably bear the cost of leadership internationally were sufficient to bear the much lower costs of regional leadership. An analogous situation exists in the contemporary international political economy.

The United States, the European Union, and Japan are each viable potential regional economic leaders. The United States has the greatest capabilities and a history of international leadership, but low financial motivation. The European Union has weaker capabilities and, on the whole, only modest motivation, and its capacity for decisive leadership is hampered by its internal structure. Japan has the weakest capabilities of the three, and a history in the second half of the twentieth century of international passivity. It does, however, have stronger financial motivation than the United States, and arguably than the EU, and is the only one of the three to be consistently growing on both measures. It has also, since the end of the Cold War, been gradually increasing the degree to which it is willing to make its voice heard in international politics.

Furthermore, each of the three is already engaged regionally. The United States has special arrangements with the countries of North America and the Caribbean, and has traditionally had strong regional interests in South America. The EU has special economic agreements with many European nonmembers, and with much of Africa and South Asia through the Lomé Accords, as well as through the vestiges of the British and French empires. Although it is true that U.S. and European financial motivations to lead in South America and Africa, respectively, are weak, it is also true that the costs, given the relative economic size of the potential leader, are low. It is also true that the United States and Europe have institutional contacts and traditions of leadership in these regions. Japan has weaker institutional contacts, and little tradition of leadership, with respect to the Asia-Pacific region,[48] and its relative size is much smaller. But its financial motivations are stronger.

In short, regionalism, the norm of multilateralism, and the logic of money interact well. The normative structure of multilateralism should allow for regional economic and monetary leadership in an inclusive rather than exclusive way. In other words, the hegemony of multilateralist ideas in contemporary international politics means that regional arrangements are likely to be thought of as complements to, rather than replacements for, a broader international pattern of coordination. A purely rationalist approach to the study of international economic leadership is unlikely to spot the fundamental difference in normative structure between the contemporary world and that of the 1930s, when regionalism became exclusive. A pure constructivist approach is unlikely to spot the underlying demand for leadership that drives the regionalism. It is only by combining the two methodological approaches that the contemporary potential for inclusive regionalism can be seen.

Notes

NOTES TO CHAPTER 1

1. For example, Robert Gilpin, *War and Change in World Politics* (Cambridge: Cambridge University Press, 1981).

2. These functions are based loosely on those suggested by David Lake in "Leadership, Hegemony, and the International Economy: Naked Emperor or Tattered Monarch With Potential?" *International Studies Quarterly* vol. 37 (1993), pp. 459–489.

3. On the role of economic centers in the evolution of capitalism, see Fernand Braudel, *Civilization and Capitalism*, vol. II, *The Wheels of Commerce* (New York: Harper and Row, 1982), and vol. III, *The Perspective of the World* (New York: Harper and Row, 1984), and Randall Germain, *The International Organization of Credit: States and Global Finance in the World-Economy* (Cambridge: Cambridge University Press, 1997).

4. On institutional competition among various forms of political organization and the eventual triumph of the state over such forms as city-states and mercantile leagues, see Hendrik Spruyt, *The Sovereign State and its Competitors: An Analysis of Systems Change* (Princeton: Princeton University Press, 1994).

5. Most notably, there was a first wave in the mid-1970s, of which the seminal examples are Charles Kindleberger, *The World in Depression, 1929–1939* (Berkeley: The University of California Press, 1973), and Stephen Krasner, "State Power and the Structure of International Trade," *World Politics* vol. 28 (1976), pp. 317–347. There was a second wave lasting roughly from John Conybeare's "Public Goods, Prisoners' Dilemmas, and the International Political Economy," *International Studies Quarterly* vol. 28 (1984), pp. 5–22, to Joanne Gowa's "Rational Hegemons, Excludable Goods, and Small Groups: An Epitaph for Hegemonic Stability Theory?" *World Politics* vol. 41 (1989), pp. 307–324. Finally, there was a brief resurgence in the mid-1990s, marked by David Lake's "Leadership, Hegemony, and the International Economy."

6. An example of this is Krasner, "State Power and the Structure of International Trade."

7. For example, see Kindleberger, *The World in Depression*. For a critical example, see Fred Block, *The Origins of International Economic Disorder: A Study of United States International Monetary Policy from World War II to the Present* (Berkeley: The University of California Press, 1977). An exception to the generalization that studies focus either on the nonspecific or the nongeneralizable is David Lake, *Power, Protection, and Free Trade: International Sources of U.S. Commercial Strategy, 1887–1939* (Ithaca: Cornell University Press, 1988), which draws broad conclusions about patterns of foreign economic policy from the case of the United States.

8. The basic idea of economics as a separate field of knowledge, in fact, only arises in the middle of the time period covered in the case studies in Chapters 3–6.

9. An example of the former approach is Bruce Russett, "The Mysterious Case of Vanishing Hegemony: Or, Is Mark Twain Really Dead," *International Organization* vol. 39 (1985), pp. 207–231. Examples of the latter include Conybeare, "Public Goods, Prisoners' Dilemmas, and the International Political Economy," and Gowa, "Rational Hegemons, Excludable Goods, and Small Groups," both of which begin with assumptions of rational state utility maximization.

10. On the effects of information and communication technologies on international relations, see Ronald Deibert, *Parchment, Printing, and Hypermedia: Communication in World Order Transformation* (New York: Columbia University Press, 1997). On the relationship between polarity and patterns of international economic interaction, see Joanne Gowa, *Allies, Adversaries, and International Trade* (Princeton: Princeton University Press, 1994).

11. The epistemological basis of this assumption will be discussed in the next chapter.

12. This follows Kindleberger's analysis in *The World in Depression*.

13. For example, Krasner, in "State Power and the Structure of International Trade," uses share of world trade as one of four indicators for his independent variable, while Duncan Snidal, in "The Limits of Hegemonic Stability Theory," *International Organization* vol. 39 (1985), pp. 579–614, uses an unspecified indicator of generic size.

14. See, respectively, Vladimir Lenin, *Imperialism: The Highest Stage of Capitalism*, in Lenin, *Selected Works* (Moscow: Progress Publishers, 1968 [1917]), and Karl Kautsky, *Nationalstaat, Imperialistischer Staat und Staatenbund* (Nurnberg: Frankische Verlagsanstalt, 1915).

15. A good review of this literature can be found in Lake, "Leadership, Hegemony, and the International Economy."

16. On this note compare Krasner, "State Power and the Structure of International Trade," with Robert Gilpin, *U.S. Power and the Multinational Corporation: The Political Economy of Foreign Direct Investment* (New York: Basic Books, 1975).

17. See, for example, Snidal, "The Limits of Hegemonic Stability Theory."

18. Kindleberger, *The World in Depression.*

19. P. J. Cain and A. G. Hopkins, "Gentlemanly Capitalism and British Expansion Overseas: I. The Old Colonial System, 1688–1850," *Economic History Review*, 2nd series, vol. 39 (1986), pp. 501–525, and "Gentlemanly Capitalism and British Expansion Overseas: II. New Imperialism, 1850–1945," *Economic History Review*, 2nd series, vol. 40 (1987), pp. 1–26.

20. This usage follows that of Alexander Wendt in *Social Theory of International Politics* (Cambridge: Cambridge University Press, 1999).

21. This definition closely follows Wendt's in *Social Theory*, p. 1.

22. On post-positivism see Yosef Lapid, "The Third Debate: On the Prospects of International Theory in a Post-Positivist Era," *International Studies Quarterly* vol. 33 (1989), pp. 235–254.

23. See, for example, Richard Ashley, "The Geopolitics of Geopolitical Space: Toward a Critical Social Theory of International Politics," *Alternatives* vol. 12 (1987), pp. 403–434, and R. B. J. Walker, *Inside/Outside: International Relations as Critical Theory* (Cambridge: Cambridge University Press, 1993).

24. See, for example, Wendt, *Social Theory*, Chapter 3.

25. The epistemological assumptions underlying this statement will be discussed in the next chapter.

NOTES TO CHAPTER 2

1. Predatory hegemony refers to a situation in which a hegemonic country imposes an order on the international system that clearly favors the hegemon. On the distinction between "leadership theory" and "hegemony theory," see David A. Lake, "Leadership, Hegemony, and the International Economy: Naked Emperor or Tattered Monarch with Potential?" in *International Studies Quarterly* vol. 37 (1993), pp. 459–489.

2. See, for example, Giulio Gallarotti, *The Anatomy of an International Monetary Regime: The Classical Gold Standard, 1880–1914* (Oxford: Oxford University Press, 1995).

3. For discussions of the idea of structural goods in the international political economy and of why they are needed, see David Lake, *Power, Protection, and Free Trade: The International Sources of American Commercial Strategy, 1887–1939* (Ithaca: Cornell University Press, 1988), pp. 33–35, and Jeffry Frieden, "Capital Politics: Creditors and the International Political Economy," in *Journal of Public Policy* vol. 8 (1988), pp. 271–276.

4. Robert O. Keohane, "The Demand for International Regimes," in *International Organization* vol. 36 (1982), pp. 325–356.

5. Charles Kindleberger, *The World in Depression, 1929–1939* (Berkeley: University of California Press, 1973), pp. 288–295.

6. Lake, "Leadership, Hegemony, and the International Economy?", pp. 462–463.

7. Charles Kindleberger, "The Benefits of International Money," in *Journal of International Economics* vol. 2 (1972), pp. 425–442.

8. Robert O. Keohane, *After Hegemony: Cooperation and Discord in the World Political Economy* (Princeton: Princeton University Press, 1984), pp. 85–93.

9. Eric Helleiner, "National Currencies and National Identities," in *American Behavioral Sciences* vol. 41 (1998), pp. 1409–1436. See also Benjamin J. Cohen, *The Geography of Money* (Ithaca: Cornell University Press, 1998).

10. Details of these relationships can be found in any basic textbook on international economics and payments.

11. Although the willingness of users to accept a currency as a store of value is in turn somewhat dependent on their expectations of government policy. For example, the preference of Russians for dollars rather than roubles as a store of value in the mid-1990s, even when the rouble was relatively stable, had much to do with a widespread lack of faith in future government policy.

12. For a discussion of the concept of an international lender of last resort, see Charles Kindleberger, *Manias, Panics, and Crashes: A History of Financial Crises* (New York: Basic Books, 1978), pp. 182–209.

13. The details of this process can differ substantially from case to case however. The relationship between leaders' liquidity and international liquidity in discussed in historical context in all four case study chapters.

14. For a fuller discussion of, as he refers to them, international "property rules," see Charles Lipson, *Standing Guard: Protecting Foreign Capital in the Nineteenth and Twentieth Centuries* (Berkeley: University of California Press, 1985).

15. Douglass C. North and Robert Paul Thomas, *The Rise of the Western World: A New Economic History* (Cambridge: Cambridge University Press, 1973). See Also Douglass C. North, *Structure and Change in Economic History* (New York: Norton, 1981).

16. This element of leadership, enforcing a county's preferred norms on others, is the primary focus of realist versions of hegemonic stability theory. See, for example, Stephen Krasner, "State Power and the Structure of International Trade," in *World Politics* vol. 28 (1976), pp. 317–347, and Robert Gilpin, *War and Change in World Politics* (Cambridge: Cambridge University Press, 1981).

17. See, for example, Kurt Burch, *"Property" and the Making of the International System* (Boulder: Lynne Rienner, 1998), p. 13.

18. Deutche Bundesbank, *The Deutche Bundesbank: Its Monetary Policy Instruments and Functions*, 3rd ed. (Frankfurt am Main: Deutche Bundesbank, 1989).

19. Federal Reserve Board, *The Federal Reserve System: Purposes & Functions* (Washington: Board of Governors of the Federal Reserve System, 1994).

20. For example, Milton Friedman and Anna Jacobson Schwartz, *A Monetary History of the United States, 1867–1960* (Princeton: Princeton University Press, 1963), pp. 395–399, 627–632.

21. It is interesting to note that this sort of intersubjective knowledge can take some time to develop. For example, the Reichsbank's tight-money policy in 1924–1926, less than half a decade after the hyperinflation, faced significant domestic opposition; the social consensus on anti-inflationary rigor seen after the war had not yet developed. See William McNeil, *American Money and the Weimar Republic: Economics and Politics on the Eve of the Great Depression* (New York: Columbia University Press, 1986), pp. 112–114.

22. Antonio Gramsci, *Selections from the Prison Notebooks of Antonio Gramsci*, edited and translated by Quintin Hoare and Geoffrey Nowell Smith (New York: International Publishers, 1971), pp. 348, 419. There is a considerable literature applying Gramscian concepts to international relations theory. This literature tends to focus on different aspects of Gramscian thought, but is not dissonant with the use to which Gramsci is being put here. See, for example, Robert Cox, *Production, Power, and World Order: Social Forces and the Making of History* (New York : Columbia University Press, 1987), and Stephen Gill, ed., *Gramsci, Historical Materialism and International Relations* (Cambridge: Cambridge University Press, 1993).

23. This is the core theme of the constructivist literature in international relations, a number of examples of which are discussed, and cited, in the next

section. For the same observation from a realist perspective, see Edward Hallett Carr, *The Twenty Years' Crisis, 1919–1939* (London: Macmillan, 1939).

24. Burch, *"Property" and the Making of the International System.*

25. See, for example, Kenneth N. Waltz, *Theory of International Politics* (Reading, MA: Addison-Wesley, 1979), and Keohane, *After Hegemony.*

26. See, inter alia, Alexander E. Wendt, "Anarchy Is What States Make of It," in *International Organization* vol. 46 (1992), pp. 391–425.

27. Wendt, "Anarchy Is What States Make of It," and *Social Theory of International Politics* (Cambridge: Cambridge University Press, 1999), pp. 246–312, respectively.

28. This position is shared across the constructivist research community, broadly defined. For example, despite the title, Barry Buzan, Charles Jones, and Richard Little argue in *The Logic of Anarchy: Neorealism to Structural Realism* (New York: Columbia University Press, 1993) that there is no single logic inherent in anarchical systems.

29. For a more nuanced discussion of MAD, see Robert Jervis, *The Meaning of the Nuclear Revolution: Statecraft and the Prospect of Armageddon* (Ithaca: Cornell University Press, 1989), pp. 74–106.

30. The term "common" is used here to indicate not only that actors faced the same circumstances and shared the same goals, but that they held them in common; in other words, that they recognized the mutuality of the situation. For either superpower to expect MAD to work, for example, they each had not only to have a desire to prevent their use, but also to recognize that the other shared the desire.

31. Robert Jervis, *Systems Effects: Complexity in Political and Social Life* (Princeton: Princeton University Press, 1997), pp. 275–279.

32. At a more basic level of definition, money is being referred to here as something that represents value in other goods, rather than something that has a use value of its own (in the latter case one is really engaged in a form of barter, rather than a form of monetary exchange). On this distinction, see George Simmel, *The Philosophy of Money*, trans. Tom Bottomore and David Frisby (London: Routledge, 1978).

33. For example, in many traditional agrarian societies one looked to one's children, rather than one's monetary savings, to provide for one's old age. This suggests an economic system in which money is not viewed as the most reliable store of value.

34. "Th[e] function of money is served by anything that is generally (not necessarily universally, but very commonly) accepted by people in exchange

for goods and services. The 'thing' may be porpoise teeth, bits of gold, copper coins, pieces of paper, or credits on the books of a bank; the only essential requirement of an object to be used as money is that people in general be willing to accept it in exchange for goods and services." Lester V. Chandler, *The Economics of Money and Banking*, 6th ed. (New York: Harper & Row, 1973), p. 8.

35. See, for example, Helleiner, "National Currencies and National Identities."

36. For both a thorough and a seminal discussion of this argument, see Simmel, *The Philosophy of Money*. For a more recent treatment, see Nigel Dodd, *The Sociology of Money: Economics, Reason & Contemporary Society* (New York: Continuum, 1994).

37. For an indicator of this process of change, see Robert Triffin, *The Evolution of the International Monetary System* (Princeton, NJ: International Finance Section, Dept. of Economics Princeton University, 1964).

38. See, for example, Robert Mundell, *Monetary Theory: Inflation, Interest, and Growth in the World Economy* (Pacific Palisades, CA: Goodyear Publishing, 1971).

39. On the development of the basic allocative mechanisms of the Soviet economy, see Alec Nove, *An Economic History of the U.S.S.R.*, 2nd ed. (London: Penguin, 1989), and Nina Halpern, "Creating Socialist Economies: Stalinist Political Economy and the Impact of Ideas," in Judith Goldstien and Robert Keohane, eds., *Ideas and Foreign Policy: Beliefs, Institutions, and Political Change* (Ithaca, NY: Cornell University Press, 1993).

40. In Gramscian language, common sense.

41. Cf. Chapter 1, notes 5–7, 9, 13, and 15.

42. On optimal tariffs, see Robert Gilpin, *The Political Economy of International Relations*(Princeton: Princeton University Press, 1987), p. 179. On the use of trade concessions to influence other states' foreign and defense policies, see Albert Hirschman, *National Power and the Structure of Foreign Trade* (Berkeley: University of California Press, 1980 [1945]).

43. For example, Kindleberger, in *The World in Depression*, discusses one case only, and Krasner, in "State Power and the Structure of International Trade," admits that his argument only explains the timing of open trade systems in three of six cases.

44. The link between leadership and finance has been suggested by Arthur Stein, "The Hegemon's Dilemma: Great Britain, the United States, and the International Economic Order," in *International Organization* vol. 38 (1984),

pp. 355–86, and Richard Rosecrance and Jennifer Taw, "Japan and the Theory of International Leadership," in *World Politics* vol. 42 (1990), pp. 184–209. Neither of these arguments, however, fully spells out the associated logic.

45. These logics are discussed, inter alia, by Charles Kindleberger in *Balance of Payments Deficits and the International Market for Liquidity* (Princeton: International Finance Section, Department of Economics, Princeton University, 1965).

46. This distinction is similar to the one drawn by Charles Lipson in *Standing Guard*, pp. 4–5. It is not precisely the same, however, inasmuch as illiquid portfolio investment can functionally be long-term capital.

47. For a discussion of the concept of the national interest, see Stephen Krasner, *Defending the National Interest: Raw Materials Investments and U.S. Foreign Policy* (Princeton: Princeton University Press, 1978).

48. This is a standard practice of game theoretical approaches to international relations theory, in which states are simply assigned a hypothetical preference. See, for example, Helen Milner, *Interests, Institutions, and Information: Domestic Politics and International Relations* (Princeton: Princeton University Press, 1997), p. 33.

49. Wendt, *Social Theory*, Chapter 5.

50. For this argument from a rational choice perspective, see Milner, *Interests, Institutions, and Information;* from an interpretivist perspective, see Audie Klotz, *Norms in International Relations: The Struggle Against Apartheid* (Ithaca: Cornell University Press, 1995).

51. International financial interests and manufacturing exporters will generally prefer an open international trading system as it expands the potential for international commerce. Industries that focus on the domestic market are more likely to favor tariffs, because they help to keep foreign competition out.

52. This is less true of those policies that are expressions of the Gramscian "common sense" at that place and time, however.

53. This kind of international economic role is often referred to as entrepôt trade, and is best exemplified in the contemporary world by Hong Kong and Singapore, the international trade of both of which is greater than their GDP.

54. An increased risk of violence means that investors should demand a higher return (a risk premium) than would otherwise be the case, reducing the number of viable investment opportunities. And the need for more insurance adds directly to the cost of international commerce.

55. Lipson, *Standing Guard.*

56. See Charles Kindleberger, "Dominance and Leadership in the International Economy: Exploitation, Public Goods, and Free Rides," in *International Studies Quarterly* vol. 25 (1981), p. 248.

57. Kindleberger, *Manias, Panics, and Crashes.*

58. On the subject of relative gains, see inter alia Joseph Grieco, *Cooperation Among Nations: Europe, America, and Non-Tariff Barriers to Trade* (Ithaca: Cornell University Press, 1990).

59. A topical example of such an argument is provided by strategic trade theory, which argues that dominant countries are best placed to impose optimal tariffs rather than free trade. See, for example, John Conybeare, "Public Goods, Prisoners' Dilemmas, and the International Political Economy," in *International Studies Quarterly* vol. 28 (1984), pp. 5–22.

60. Vladimir Lennin, *Imperialism: The Highest Stage of Capitalism* (Moscow: Progress Publishers, 1968 [1917]), and John Hobson, *Imperialism, A Study* (Anne Arbor: University of Michigan Press, 1965 [1902]).

61. This has arguably, however, been changing rapidly recently, as financial instruments such as mutual funds make international investors of many middle-class savers. This should have the effect of magnifying motivations for leadership. But, as mutual funds invest mostly in liquid assets such as foreign equities, the magnifying effect may be quite muted.

62. This follows from Mancur Olson's argument in *The Logic of Collective Action: Public Goods and the Theory of Groups* (Cambridge, MA: Harvard University Press, 1965). In any society in which money can, through whatever mechanism, improve access to government, concentrated money will be able to do so more effectively by reducing collective action problems.

63. Olson, *The Logic of Collective Action.*

64. This argument is based on the idea that increased exposure to international economic activity will have the effect of empowering the owners of a country's best-endowed factors of production in the domestic political arena. See Ronald Rogowski, *Commerce and Coalitions: How Trade Affects Domestic Political Alignments* (Princeton: Princeton University Press, 1989), and Paul Midford, "International Trade and Domestic Politics: Improving on Rogowski's Model of Political Alignments," in *International Organization* vol. 47 (1993), pp. 535–564.

65. Eric Helleiner, in *States and the Reemergence of Global Finance: From Bretton Woods to the 1990s* (Ithaca, NY: Cornell University Press, 1994) makes a similar set of arguments, although he categorizes them somewhat differently.

66. See, for example, Janet Kelly, "International Monetary Systems and National Security," in Knorr and Trager, eds., *Economic Issues and National*

Security (Lawrence: Regents Press of Kansas, 1077), Stephen Krasner, "U.S. Commercial and Monetary Policy," in Peter Katzenstein, ed., *Between Power and Plenty: Foreign Economic Policies of Advanced Industrialized States* (Madison: University of Wisconsin Press, 1978), and G. John Ikenberry, "A World Economy Restored: Expert Consensus and the Anglo-American Postwar Settlement," in *International Organization* vol. 46 (1992), pp. 289–322.

67. For example, Joanne Gowa, "Public Goods and Political Institutions: Trade and Monetary Policy Processes in the United States," in *International Organization* vol. 42 (1988).

68. Ibid.

69. Gramsci defines this as "the 'spontaneous' consent given by the great masses of the population to the general direction imposed on social life by the dominant fundamental group." *Selections from the Prison Notebooks*, p. 12.

70. The concept of intersubjectivity is used here in a fairly standard sense. See, for example, Wendt, *Social Theory of International Politics*, pp. 160–161. For a constructivist account of the role of identity in international politics, see Bruce Cronin, *Community Under Anarchy: Transnational Identity and the Evolution of Cooperation* (New York: Columbia University Press, 1999).

71. Nineteenth-century British ideas of financial orthodoxy will be discussed in Chapter 4. For a discussion of the evolution of ideas of financial orthodoxy in the postwar period, from "embedded liberalism" to "competitive liberalism," see Kathleen McNamara, *The Currency of Ideas: Monetary Politics in the European Union* (Ithaca, NY: Cornell University Press, 1998).

72. Donald Moggridge, *The Return to Gold, 1925: The Formulation of Economic Policy and Its Critics* (Cambridge: Cambridge University Press, 1969), and Charles Kindleberger, *A Financial History of Western Europe* (London: George Allen and Unwin, 1984), p. 332.

73. For three competing structural theories of how the balance of power affects international economic relations, see Waltz, *Theory of International Politics*, Gilpin, *War and Change*, and Joanne Gowa, *Allies, Adversaries, and International Trade* (Princeton: Princeton University Press, 1994).

74. In the words of R.B.J. Walker, "Theories of international relations . . . may be read as a characteristic discourse of the modern state and as a constitutive practice." Walker, *Inside/Outside: International Relations as Political Theory* (Cambridge: Cambridge University Press, 1993), p. 6.

75. For versions of this orthodoxy from a variety of analytic perspectives, see McNamara, *The Currency of Ideas*; Steven Bernstein, *The Compromise of Liberal Environmentalism* (New York: Columbia University Press, 2001), and

the World Bank, *World Development Report 1997: The State in a Changing World* (New York: Oxford University Press, 1997).

76. Arthur Stinchcombe refers to this sort of causality structure as "historicist" explanation, a description that fits well with the methodology of this book. Stinchcombe, *Constructing Social Theories* (Chicago: The University of Chicago Press, 1968), p. 59. For a discussion of feedback loops, see Jervis, *Systems Effects*, Chapter 4.

NOTES TO CHAPTER 3

1. See, for example, Fernand Braudel, *The Perspective of the World: Civilization and Capitalism, 15th–18th Century,* Vol. III (New York: Harper and Row, 1984), p. 75

2. For example, Mark Brawley, *Liberal Leadership: Great Powers and their Challengers in Peace and War* (Ithaca, NY: Cornell University Press, 1993).

3. This refers to the literatures on hegemony both within the international political economy and the international security literatures. For an example of various ways of measuring hegemony, see Bruce Russett, "The Mysterious Case of Vanishing Hegemony: Or, Is Mark Twain Really Dead?" in *International Organization* vol. 39 (1985), pp. 207–231.

4. Derek McKay and H.M. Scott, *The Rise of the Great Powers 1648–1815* (London: Longman, 1983), p. 36. There were periods at the very beginning of the seventeenth century when, due to the ongoing war with Spain, the Dutch did in fact have more men under arms than the French, but never enough to give them any real superiority, and only for a short period.

5. Orest Ranum, *The Century of Louis XIV* (New York: Harper and Row, 1972). See also H. G. Koenigsberger, *Early Modern Europe 1500–1789* (London: Longman, 1987), Ch. 4, and Peter Gay and R. K. Webb, *Modern Europe to 1815* (New York: Haper and Row, 1973), Chapters 6 and 7.

6. Exports here refer to exports of domestically-produced goods, and does not include re-exports. "France . . . led the world in the volume industrial production, foreign and domestic trade to a date late in the 18th century." C. H. Wilson, "Trade, Society, and the State," in Rich and Wilson, eds., *The Cambridge Economic History of Europe*, Vol. IV: *The Economy of Expanding Europe in the Sixteenth and Seventeenth Centuries* (Cambridge: Cambridge University Press, 1967), p. 529

7. J. H. Parry, "Transportation and Trade Routes," Chapter 3 in *The Cambridge Economic History of Europe*, Vol. IV.

8. Braudel, *The Perspective of the World*, pp. 143–154.

9. Violet Barbour, *Capitalism in Amsterdam in the Seventeenth Century* (Baltimore: Johns Hopkins Press, 1950), p. 17.

10. Ibid., p. 16, Charles Wilson, *The Dutch Republic and the Civilization of the Seventeenth Century* (New York: McGraw-Hill, 1968), p. 21 and Chapter 9, and Braudel, *The Perspective of the World*, p. 185.

11. Braudel, pp. 185–187, Barbour, *Capitalism in Amsterdam*, pp. 15–19.

12. Charles Kindleberger, *A Financial History of Western Europe*, 2nd ed. (Oxford: Oxford University Press, 1993), pp. 208–210.

13. Parry, "Transportation and Trade Routes," pp. 210–211.

14. Ralph Davis, *English Merchant Shipping and Anglo-Dutch Rivalry in the Seventeenth Century* (London: Her Majesty's Stationary Office, 1975), pp. 10–17, and Parry, "Transport and Trade Routes," pp. 210–214.

15. "Colbert estimated in 1669 that 'the maritime trade of all Europe is carried out by twenty thousand ships, of which fifteen to sixteen thousand are Dutch . . . and five to six hundred are French.'" Carlo Cipolla, *Before the Industrial Revolution: European Society and Economy, 1000–1700* (New York: W.W. Norton, 1976), p. 250.

16. On the organization of trade, see Fernand Braudel, *The Identity of France,* Vol. II: *People and Production* (London: Collins, 1988), pp. 557–559.

17. For a description of the development of French absolutism, see David Parker, *The Makings of French Absolutism* (London: Edward Arnold, 1983).

18. Eli Heckscher, *Mercantilism*, Vol. 1 (New York: Garland Publishers, 1983 [1935]), pp. 178–84.

19. Herman Van Der Wee, "Monetary, Credit, and Banking Systems," in *The Cambridge Economic History of Europe*, Vol. V, pp. 358–362. Offices here means governmental positions: The monarchy would, for example, sell the right to collect taxes in a certain area to an individual, who would buy it as an investment.

20. William Beik, *Absolutism and Society in 17th Century France: State Power and Provincial Aristocracy in Languedoc* (Cambridge: Cambridge University Press, 1985), Chapter 11.

21. The two inland provinces, Gelderland and Overijsel, retained notably feudal political structures. Holland and Zeeland, the richest and most commercial of the five coastal provinces, were predominantly republican in their governmental systems. The other three coastal provinces, Groningen, Friesland, and Utrecht, retained aspects of both forms of government, although they

leaned more toward republicanism. The boundaries of these provinces resemble those of present-day Dutch internal political divisions.

22. Charles Wilson, *Profit and Power: A Study of England and the Dutch Wars* (London: Longman, Green and Co., 1957), pp. 12–14. The real control of the *Stadtholder* over national policy varied substantially over time, as will be discussed.

23. Although as the trend among regents to withdraw from active trading and become rentièrs progressed, there was an increasing tendency to abuse and profiteer from public office, as will be discussed. Wilson, *The Dutch Republic*, p. 44.

24. See Ralph Davis, *The Rise of the Atlantic Economies* (London: Weidenfeld and Nicholson, 1973), pp. 110–113. On the decline of the landed nobility, see J. H. Huizinga, *Dutch Civilization in the Seventeenth Century* (New York: Frederick Unger, 1968), pp. 9–46.

25. I refer here to the Prince of Orange as an office, rather than as a person. Over the course of the seventeenth century four individuals held the office: Maurice, Frederick Henry, William II, and William III.

26. The Prince from 1618–1650 and 1672–1702, the Grand Pensionary of Holland at other times. A. J. Barnouw, *The Making of Modern Holland: A Short History* (New York: W.W. Norton, 1944), Chapters V–VII

27. C. R. Boxer, *The Anglo-Dutch Wars of the Seventeenth Century, 1652–74* (London: Her Majesty's Stationary Office 1974), p. 7.

28. This was a relatively minor concern because the geography of the Netherlands (a swamp on the southern borders and shallow river estuaries surrounding many major cities) made it very difficult to invade successfully.

29. Wilson, *The Dutch Republic*, pp. 48–49.

30. Davis, *The Rise of the Atlantic Economies*, p. 187.

31. Wilson, "Trade, Society and the State," p. 531.

32. Ibid., p. 532.

33. This is true of a political national interest. The United Provinces, and particularly Holland, did engage in very large-scale and long-term urban planning and public works.

34. Robert Ekelund and Robert Tollison, *Mercantilism as a Rent-Seeking Society: Economic Regulation in Historical Perspective* (College Station: Texas A&M University Press, 1981).

35. See ibid., Chapter 1, for a discussion of how mercantilism is generally seen in the economic history literature.

36. Wilson, "Trade, Society, and the State," pp. 506–515.

37. For a review of French economic policy in this period, see Ekelund and Tollison, *Mercantilism as a Rent-Seeking Society*, Chapter 4, and Heckscher, *Mercantilism*, vol. 1, part 1, Chapter 5.

38. For a discussion of the profitability of the Dutch East India Company, see Femme Gaastra, "The Shifting Balance of Trade of the Dutch East India Company," pp. 47–70.

39. Van Loon, *The Fall of the Dutch Republic*, pp. 61–62.

40. See Niels Steensgaard, *The Asian Trade Revolution of the Seventeenth Century: The East India Companies and the Decline of the Caravan Trade* (Chicago: The University of Chicago Press, 1973), pp. 131–133, and Braudel, *The Perspective of the World*, pp. 218–220.

41. Here, as is the case throughout this chapter, "United Provinces" or "The Netherlands" is used to refer to the whole country or its government, "Holland" is used to refer specifically to the province or its government, and "Amsterdam" is used to refer specifically to the city and to civic government.

42. F. P. Braudel and F. Spooner, "Prices in Europe from 1450 to 1750," in *The Cambridge Economic History of Europe*, Vol. IV, p. 458.

43. Some estimates are as much as 50% higher than this figure. Ibid., p. 463.

44. For a detailed discussion of the history and role of the Bank of Amsterdam see J. G. van Dillen, "The Bank of Amsterdam," in van Dillen, ed., *History of the Principle Public Banks* (New York: Augustus M. Kelley, 1965 [1934]).

45. Banknotes are promises to pay that sum when redeemed sometime in the future. If the currency of account is devalued, the bank would have to pay out less in specie than it originally received in exchange for the note.

46. Charles P. Kindleberger, *Manias, Panics, and Crashes: A History of Financial Crises* (New York: Basic Books, 1978).

47. Braudel, *The Perspective of the World*, pp. 207–219 and 235–265. The term "factors" refers to trade and commercial representatives permanently stationed abroad.

48. See Barbour, *Capitalism in Amsterdam*, Chapter V, for a discussion.

49. See Barbour, Chapter VI.

50. Many historians argue that the tax rates were so high that they were a major contributing factor to Dutch decline in the eighteenth century. By taxing consumption, the Dutch drove up the domestic costs of labor, and thus undermined their industrial competitiveness. Wilson, *The Dutch Republic*, pp. 232–223.

51. Braudel, *The Perspective of the World*, pp. 200–201, and Boxer, *The Dutch Seaborne Empire*, p. 317.

52. The physical expansion of the city of Amsterdam was in fact carefully planned around the needs of the entrepôt trade. See, for example, A.E.J. Morris, *Histoty of Urban Form: Prehistory to the Rennaissance* (New York: Wiley, 1974), pp. 163–166, and Robert E. Dickinson, *The Western European City: A Geographical Interpretation* (London: Routledge, 1968), p. 162.

53. For example, see Barbour, *Capitalism in Amsterdam*, pp. 33–34.

54. Although this innovation might seem from a contemporary political perspective to be of questionable value at best, it did coordinate property rights in a way that significantly increased the profitablity of European commerce.

55. The organizational reason has already been alluded to—the fact that the Dutch navy was a collection of the provincial navies without any effective central coordination. This led to considerable inefficiencies in the use of available resources. Dutch ships also tended to be shallower than other naval ships, particularly English. This was necessitated by the shallowness of some Dutch harbors, but decreased their military effectiveness. See Boxer, *The Anglo-Dutch Wars*.

56. This is true of the seventeenth century. In the eighteenth century an increase in the cost of borrowing for the Admiralty played a significant role in the decline of Dutch military and political power. Boxer, *The Dutch Seaborne Empire*, p. 118.

57. Kristoff Glamann, "The Changing Pattern of Trade," in E. E. Rich and C. H. Wilson, eds., *The Cambridge Economic History of Europe*, Vol. V: *The Economic Organization of Early Modern Europe* (Cambridge: Cambridge University Press, 1977), pp. 218–222, and Braudel, *The Perspective of the World*, p. 207.

58. Braudel, *The Perspective of the World*, p. 267. See also Barbour, *Capitalism in Amsterdam*, pp. 125–127.

59. Hendrick Van Loon, *Fall of the Dutch Republic* (Boston: Haughton Mifflin, 1913), pp. 44–45.

60. Charles Kindleberger, *A Financial History of Western Europe* (London: George Allen and Unwin, 1984), pp. 215–217, and Braudel, *The Perspective of the World*, pp. 267–273.

61. Ibid.

62. Braudel, *The Perspective of the World*, pp. 273–276. For a detailed description of these events, see Van Loon, *Fall of the Dutch Republic*, Chapter VIII.

63. Pieter Geyl, *The Netherlands in the Seventeenth Century* (London: Ernest Benn Ltd., 1964), Chapter VII.

64. C. R. Boxer, *The Dutch Seaborne Empire, 1600–1800* (London: Penguin, 1965), pp. 118–210.

65. Wilson, *The Dutch Republic*, pp. 55–56.

66. Compare note 20. See also Boxer, *The Dutch Seaborne Empire*, pp. 328–330, and Wilson, *The Dutch Republic*, pp. 236–237.

67. See Van Loon, *Fall of the Dutch Republic*, for details.

NOTES TO CHAPTER 4

1. This is, for example, the essence of the argument that Robert Gilpin makes in *U.S. Power and the Multinational Corporation: The Political Economy of Foreign Direct Investment* (New York: Basic Books, 1975), Chapter 3. See also Stephen Krasner, "State Power and the Structure of Foreign Trade," in *World Politics* vol. 28 (1976), pp. 335–337.

2. Measuring comparative wealth for this time period is very difficult due to inadequate data. The wealthiest country in aggregate in Europe at the time was probably Russia, due to sheer size, with England and France not far behind. For a comparison of English and French national wealth throughout the eighteenth century see Peter Mathias and Patrick O'Brien, "Taxation in Britain and France, 1715–1810: A Comparison of the Social and Economic Incidence of Taxes Collected for the Central Government," in *Journal of European Economic History* vol. 5 (1976), pp. 601–650.

3. See Paul Bairoch, "Europe's Gross National Product, 1800–1975," in *Journal of European Economic History* vol. 5 (1976), pp. 273–340.

4. Ralph Davis, *The Rise of the English Shipping Industry in the 17th and 18th Centuries* (London: Macmillan, 1962), Chapters II and XVII.

5. Ibid., p. 43. The dating of the beginning of the industrial revolution is a matter of historical dispute, but is usually put somewhere in the 1740–1780 range.

6. Ibid., pp. 518–519, and Ralph Davis, *The Rise of the Atlantic Economies* (London: Weidenfeld and Nicholson, 1973), Chapters 15 and 16. For a general overview of mercantilism, see Eli Heckscher, *Mercantilism* (New York: Garland Publishers, 1983 [1935]).

7. The main difference being that the Dutch company operated primarily in what is now Indonesia, whereas its English counterpart concentrated on the Indian subcontinent.

8. Peter Mathias, *The First Industrial Nation: An Economic History of Britain, 1700–1914*, 2nd ed. (London: Methuen, 1983), pp. 76–84, Ralph Davis, "English Foreign Trade, 1700–1774," in W. E. Michinton, *The Growth of English Overseas Trade in the Seventeenth and Eighteenth Centuries* (London: Methuen, 1969), pp. 114–117, Leonard Blussé and Femme Gaastra, "Companies and Trade: Some Reflections on a Workshop and a Concept," Chapters 1, and K. N. Chaudhuri, "The English East India Company in the 17th and 18th Centuries: A Pre-Modern Multinational Organization," Chapters 3 in Blussé and Gaastra, eds., *Companies and Trade: Essays on Overseas Trading Companies During the Ancien Regime* (The Hague: Leiden University Press, 1981), and Robert Ekelund and Robert Tollison, *Mercantilism as a Rent-Seeking Society: Economic Regulation in Historical Perspective* (College Station: Texas A&M University Press, 1981).

9. See P. J. Cain and A. G. Hopkins, "Gentlemanly Capitalism and British Expansion Overseas: I. The Old Colonial System, 1688–1850," in *Economic History Review*, 2nd ser., vol. 39 (1986), pp. 522–523.

10. Sir John Clapham, *The Bank of England: A History* (Cambridge: Cambridge University Press, 1944), and John Giuseppi, *The Bank of England: A History from its Foundation in 1694* (London: Evans Brothers, 1966).

11. For a general history of the British financial sector, see Michael Collins, *Money and Banking in the UK: A History* (London: Croom Helm, 1988).

12. Cain and Hopkins, "Gentlemanly Capitalism: I," p. 517.

13. Ibid., pp. 514–516.

14. Cain and Hopkins, "Gentlemanly Capitalism and British Expansion Overseas: II. New Imperialism, 1850–1945," in *Economic History Review*, 2nd ser., vol. 40 (1987), p. 3. You may recall from the previous chapter that this was true of Dutch as well as British investors.

15. Mathias, *The First Industrial Nation*, p. 39.

16. Paul Kennedy, *The Rise and Fall of the Great Powers: Economic Change and Military Conflict from 1500 to 2000* (New York: Random House, 1987), pp. 122–125.

17. For a discussion of the development of what came to be known as financial or monetary orthodoxy, both as a set of policies and as an economic dogma, see Frank Whitson Fetter, *Development of British Monetary Orthodoxy, 1797–1875* (Cambridge, MA: Harvard University Press, 1965).

18. Except for two brief periods during the Crimean and Boer wars, when deficits were run to pay for the war efforts. These were relatively small, though, and quite short-lived, and therefore had little impact on overall investment patterns. For details of British public finance in this period, see B. R. Mitchell and Phyllis Deane, *Abstract of British Historical Statistics* (Cambridge: Cambridge University Press, 1962), pp. 393–410.

19. Mathias, *The First Industrial Nation*, pp. 293–305. Some analysts argue that the flow of investment capital overseas crippled the ability of British industry to modernize and stay competitive as the Continent and the United States industrialized. They do not adequately make the case, though, that there was a domestic demand for this capital, that it would have been used efficiently or effectively if it had been retained within the country. See, for example, Gilpin, *U.S. Power and the Multinational Corporation*, Chapter 3.

20. Albert Imlah, *Economic Elements in the Pax Britannica: Studies in British Foreign Trade in the Nineteenth Century* (Cambridge, MA: Harvard University Press, 1958), pp. 72–74, and Phyllis Deane and W. A. Cole, *British Economic Growth, 1688–1959*, 2nd ed. (Cambridge: Cambridge University Press, 1967), p. 166.

21. Mathias, *The First Industrial Nation*, p. 279.

22. Foreign investment figures from Harvey Fisk, *The Inter-Ally Debts: An Analysis of War and Post-War Public Finances, 1914–23* (New York: Bankers Trust Company, 1924), Chapters XVI–XXII. Shipping figures from S. G. Sturmey, *British Shipping and World Competition* (London: The Athlone Press, 1962), Chapter 2. National and per capita income figures from Bairoch, "Europe's Gross National Product," pp. 273–340. Trade figures from Simon Kuznets, *Modern Economic Growth: Rate, Structure, and Spread* (New Haven: Yale University Press, 1966), pp. 306–308.

23. Ibid. An intermediate category that fits neither into trade services nor foreign investment but is equally a part of financial predominance, is international financial services. See Lance Davis and Robert Huttenback, "The Export of British Finance, 1865–1914," in *The Journal of Imperial and Commonwealth History* vol. 13 (1985), and Stanley Chapman, *The Rise of Merchant Banking* (London: George Allen & Unwin, 1984).

24. The pound sterling equalled 240 pence (or 20 shillings at 12 pence per shilling). The medieval penny coins from which these terms originated

were sterling silver, and wieghed 1/240th of a pound—hence the name of the currency.

25. See Collins, *Money and Banking in the U.K.*, Chapter 6, and Giuseppi, *The Bank of England*, pp. 91, 95. Privately owned is used here to mean not government-owned. The Bank was in fact publicly traded rather than being privately held.

26. See Collins, pp. 191–192, Clapham, *The Bank of England: A History*, p. 419, and Youssef Cassis, "Bankers and English Society in the Late 19th Century," in *Economic History Review*, ser. 2 vol. 38 (1985), p. 215, and *Les Banquiers de la City à l'Epoque Edouardienne* (Geneva: Librairie Droz, 1984), p. 118.

27. The term English*men* is used intentionally here. Women could not vote until after World War One.

28. See Gordon Craig, *Europe Since 1815* (New York: Holt, Rinehart and Winston, 1974), Chapters 4, 10, and 13.

29. A good example of the use of foreign economic policy to serve security goals is the French use of loans to the Russian government as a form of diplomatic leverage to encourage an alliance. France and, to a lesser extent, Germany were quite prone to channeling foreign investment for political ends in this manner. See Herbert Feis, *Europe, The World's Banker, 1870–1914: An Account of European Foreign Investment and the Connection of World Finance with Diplomacy Before the War* (Clifton, NJ: Augustus Kelley Publishers, 1964), pp. 133–142, 169–176, 212–229, and 318–320.

30. See Nicholas Rogers, "Money, Land, and Lineage: The Big Bourgeoisie of Hanoverian London," in *Social History* vol. 4 (1979), pp. 438–444.

31. See, for example, Boyd Hilton, *Corn, Cash, Commerce: The Economic Policies of Tory Governments, 1815–1830* (Oxford: Oxford University Press, 1977), p. 179.

32. Technically the gold standard dates from 1774, at which time silver was officially demonitized (that is, the government ceased fixing the price)—between 1717 and 1774 there was a bimetallic standard. Although it was not a "true" gold standard until this date, the effect from 1717 was that desired of a gold standard, currency stability. See Charles Kindleberger, *A Financial History of Western Europe* (London: George Allen and Unwin, 1984), pp. 57–60.

33. Although a stable currency did serve the government's interest in social stability, as the inflationary devaluations of the sixteenth century had generated popular discontent.

34. See Hilton, *Corn, Cash, Commerce,* Chapter VI.

35. Imlah, *Economic Elements in the Pax Britannica,* p. 118.

36. The British at the time had a relatively mobile class system, in that people of lower birth could join the nobility, through such routes as great wealth or public service. The "old" landed interests referred to here are those of the nobility for whom land served as the primary source, rather than the primary expression, of wealth. See Michael McCahill, "Peerage Creation and the Changing Character of the British Nobility, 1750–1850," in Clyve Jones and David Lewis Jones, eds., *Peers, Politics, and Power: The House of Lords, 1603–1911* (London, The Hambledon Press, 1986).

37. Hilton, *Corn, Cash, Commerce,* Chapter VI.

38. See, for example, Jack Snyder, *Myths of Empire: Domestic Politics and International Ambition* (Ithaca, NY: Cornell University Press, 1991), p. 191.

39. Mathias, *The First Industrial Nation,* pp. 270–271.

40. For a discussion of the debate surrounding this later form of protectionism, see Aaron Friedberg, *The Weary Titan: Britain and the Experience of Relative Decline, 1895–1905* (Princeton: Princeton University Press, 1988), Chapter 2.

41. No pun intended.

42. B. R. Mitchell, *European Historical Statistics, 1750–1975,* p. 171.

43. Ibid.

44. See W. D. Rubinstein, *Men of Property: The Very Wealthy in Britain Since the Industrial Revolution* (London: Croom Helm, 1981), especially pp. 108–110, and "Wealth, Elites, and the Class Structure of Modern Britain," in *Past & Present* vol. 76 (1977), especially pp. 99–112, and C. H. Lee, "Regional Growth and Structural Change in Victorian Britain," in *Economic History Review,* 2nd ser., vol. 34 (1981), pp. 438–452.

45. Cain and Hopkins, "Gentlemanly Capitalism: I," especially pp. 501–510, and "II," especially p. 1.

46. Chapman, *The Rise of Merchant Banking,* Chapter 10. Sir Clinton Dawkins, on moving into merchant banking from the civil service in 1900, commented that it "does not involve long hours or much fatigue. . . . I am happy enough in the City, but there is *not* enough to do there." In Chapman, p. 169.

47. Hilton, *Corn, Cash, Commerce,* pp. vii–viii, 179–180.

48. Financiers were elevated either through the purchase of substantial estates or public service. The former route was open to industrialists, but the

location and workload of merchant banks allowed them much more time for the latter. See McCahill, "Peerage Creation and the Changing Character of the British Nobility." See also Cain and Hopkins, "Gentlemanly Capitalism: II," pp. 2–3.

49. See Craig, *Europe Since 1815*, p. 80.

50. Adam Smith, *An Inquiry into the Nature and Causes of the Wealth of Nations.*

51. See Timothy McKeown, "Hegemonic Stability Theory and 19th Century Tariff Levels in Europe," in *International Organization* vol. 37 (1983), pp. 73–91.

52. See Peter Gourevitch, *Politics in Hard Times: Comparative Responses to International Economic Crises* (Ithaca, NY: Cornell University Press, 1986), especially Chapter 3. There were some industrial and agricultural groups that clearly saw that their interests lay with higher tariffs, and they attempted to act accordingly. However, pro-free trade groups, among whom the London financial community was prominent, prevailed. See D.C.M. Platt, *Finance, Trade, and Politics in British Foreign Policy, 1815–1914* (Oxford: Oxford University Press, 1968), pp. 105–107.

53. Smith, *An Inquiry into the Nature and Causes of the Wealth of Nations*, vol. II, bk. IV, Chapter VII, p. 145.

54. See Hilton, *Corn, Cash, Commerce*, pp. 32–33.

55. Cain and Hopkins, "Gentlemanly Capitalism: I," p. 517.

56. See Irwin Unger, *The Greenback Era: A Social and Political History of American Finance, 1865–1879* (Princeton: Princeton University Press, 1964), Chapter IV, pp. 120–131.

57. The principle exception to orthodoxy in the United States was the period of the Civil War and its immediate aftermath. For a discussion of American tariff policies in this period, see David Lake, *Power, Protection, and Free Trade: International Sources of U.S. Commercial Strategy, 1887–1939* (Ithaca, NY: Cornell University Press, 1988), especially p. 101. The debate in the United States over resumption of the gold standard is an interesting example of the reception abroad of British ideas of monetary orthodoxy, and is discussed in detail by Unger.

58. In the period from 1854 to 1856, for example, 94% of British imports were raw materials, and 70% were agricultural products. Of this latter category, 49% were industrial raw materials, such as cotton, and 51% were foodstuffs, of which corn constituted 34%. Figures from Ralph Davis, *The Industrial Revolution and British Overseas Trade* (Leicester: Leicester University Press, 1979), pp. 124–125.

59. See Mitchell and Deane, *Abstract of British Historical Statistics*, pp. 386–395.

60. Mathias, *The First Industrial Nation*, pp. 272–273.

61. Although this power was on the decline anyway, and may well not have lasted long even had agricultural protection been retained. See Cain and Hopkins, "Gentlemanly Capitalism: I," fn. 83.

62. It is debatable whether Paris was, up to that point, a bona fide international financial centre. See Kindleberger, *A Financial History of Western Europe*, pp. 265–268. By 1890, it was an "absolute certainty" that the City of London was the financial center of the world. Cassis, *Les Banquiers de la City*, p. 169.

63. Mistakes in this case would be either intervening in international crises when it was not necessary, or failing to intervene when it would have been prudent to do so. Mathias argues that failings on the part of the Bank of England in dealing with international crises by the end of the century were not attributable to its Court of Directors, but rather were caused by a failure of Bank assets, due to institutional constraints, to keep up with the growth of money markets. Mathias, *The First Industrial Nation*, p. 327.

64. With an ounce of gold equaling three pounds sterling, seventeen shillings, and ten and a half pence, to be specific.

65. Imlah, *Economic Elements of the Pax Britannica*, pp. 70–75.

66. Ibid., pp. 154–155.

67. For a comprehensive list of these tariffs, see Joanne Gowa, *Allies, Adversaries, and International Trade* (Princeton: Princeton University Press, 1994), Appendix B.

68. W. W. Rostow, *The World Economy: History and Prospects* (Austin: The University of Texas Press, 1978), pp. 70–73.

69. Mathias, *The First Industrial Nation*, p. 279.

70. With the possible exception of 1876–1878. Imlah, *Economic Elements of the Pax Britannica*, pp. 70–75.

71. See Feis, *Europe, The World's Banker*, pp. 113–117. This ability to act by themselves left the British government to maintain policy stability by getting involved in foreign investment disputes relatively rarely.

72. In fact, by the second half of this depression, the relative decline in imports caused by constrained domestic consumption allowed for a marked increase in the capital sent abroad. Mathias, *The First Industrial Nation*, p. 279.

73. Kindleberger, *A Financial History of Western Europe*, pp. 90–92, 277–283. There were a handful of occasions on which the Bank of England itself ran into liquidity problems and needed help, the most notable of which was the Baring crisis of 1890. This help was generally provided by the Bank of France, and on one particular occasion help was forthcoming from the Russian State Bank. This reciprocal aid represented less a sense of international responsibility than an expectation of need of a healthy and friendly Bank of England in the future.

74. Bruce Russett, "The Mysterious Case of Vanishing Hegemony: Or, Is Mark Twain Really Dead," in *International Organization* vol. 39 (1985), p. 217.

75. As late as the beginning of the twentieth century, a member of the Committee of Imperial Defense, Lord Fisher, could reasonably suggest that the British Army be administered as a mere "annex of the Navy." Barbara Tuchman, *The Guns of August* (New York: Macmillan, 1962), p. 66, quoting from Admiral Sir Reginald Bacon, *Life of Lord Fisher*, vol. 2, pp. 182–183.

76. See Paul Kennedy, *The Rise and Fall of British Naval Mastery* (Malabar, FL: Krieger, 1976), Chapters 6–8.

77. Ibid.

78. For a good example, see A.J.P. Taylor, *The Struggle for Mastery in Europe, 1848–1914* (Oxford: Oxford University Press, 1954), pp. 288–290.

79. Two seminal works making this argument are John Hobson, *Imperialism, A Study* (Ann Arbor: University of Michigan Press, 1965 [1902]), and Vladimir Lenin, *Imperialism: The Highest Stage of Capitalism,* in Lenin, *Selected Works* (Moscow: Progress Publishers, 1968 [1917]).

80. See, for example, Lance Davis and Robert Huttenback, *Mammon and the Pursuit of Empire: The Political Economy of British Imperial Expansion, 1860–1912* (Cambridge: Cambridge University Press, 1986). For a general discussion of the issue, see Benjamin Cohen, *The Question of Imperialism: The Political Economy of Dominance and Dependence* (New York: Basic Books, 1973).

81. Cassis, *Les Banquiers de la City à l'Epoque Edouardienne*, p. 118.

82. See Friedberg, *The Weary Titan*, Chapter 2 for a discussion of imperial preference, and S. G. Checkland, "The Mind of the City, 1870–1914," in *Oxford Economic Papers,* new ser., vol. 9 (1957), pp. 262 and 276 concerning bimetalism.

83. For example, it has been estimated that France relied on foreign borrowing to cover 16.1% of the costs of its war effort, Russia 18.3%, Rumania 37.8%, and Serbia a full 100%. Of this borrowing, the proportion borrowed

from Britain was 54.3% in the case of France, 84.3% for Russia, 27.8% for Rumania, and 30.0% for Serbia. Most of the remainder came from France, except for French loans which came from the United States. All figures are net of reciprocal loans. French loans to the smaller allies were financed largely out of the loans the French received from the British. Roughly 39.9% of all inter-allied war loans were made by Britain, 42.0% by the United States, 12.3% by France, and the remaining 5.8% by all other allies combined. Figures derived from Fisk, *The Inter-Ally Debts,* pp. 330–331 and 348–439.

84. William Woodruff, *The Impact of Western Man: A Study of Europe's Role in the World Economy, 1750–1960* (New York: St. Martin's Press, 1966), pp. 154–156.

85. U.S. Department of Commerce, *Historical Statistics of the United States* (Washington, DC: Bureau of the Census 1960), p. 565.

86. Fisk, *The Inter-Ally Debts*, pp. 274–275.

87. See Stephen Schuker, *The End of French Predominance in Europe: The Financial Crisis of 1924 and the Adoption of the Dawes Plan* (Chapel Hill: University of North Carolina Press, 1976), pp. 9–11, and *American "Reparations" to Germany, 1919–33: Implications for the Third World Debt Crisis* (Princeton: Princeton University Department of Economics, 1988), p. 15.

88. The figures are actually from 1851 and 1861. Imlah, *Economic Elements in the Pax Britannica*, pp. 72–74, Deane Cole, *British Economic Growth*, p. 166.

89. Mathias, *The First Industrial Nation*, p. 279.

90. Giulio Gallarotti, *The Anatomy of an International Monetary Regime: The Classical Gold Standard, 1880–1914* (New York: Oxford University Press, 1995).

91. See, for example, Paul Cain, "Capitalism, War and Internationalism in the Thought of Richard Cobden," *British Journal of International Studies* 1979, pp. 229–247.

NOTES TO CHAPTER 5

1. Comparisons with the Great Depression have been made since the 1980s. These include Charles Kindleberger, *The 1930s and the 1980s: Parallels and Differences* (Singapore: ASEAN Economic Research Unit, Institute of Southeast Asian Studies, 1989), and Kenneth Oye, *Economic Discrimination and Political Exchange: World Political Economy in the 1930s and 1980s* (Princeton: Princeton University Press, 1992). Many of the international structural issues that generated this literature in the first place remain unresolved.

2. Charles P. Kindleberger, *The World in Depression, 1929–1939*, rev. ed. (Berkeley: The University of California Press, 1986), p. 289.

3. David Lake, *Power, Protection, and Free Trade: International Sources of U.S. Commercial Strategy, 1887–1939* (Ithaca, NY: Cornell University Press, 1988), p. 62.

4. Harvey Fisk, *The Inter-Ally Debts: An Analysis of War and Post-War Public Finances* (New York: Bankers Trust Company, 1924), p. 330.

5. Monetary values are presented primarily in American dollars in this chapter. Sterling was worth $4.86 at the prewar par, which was reestablished in 1925. Some references are also made in this chapter to gold marks, which were worth .238 of a gold dollar (a dollar convertible to one-twentieth of an ounce of gold). Thus the figure of just over £4 billion given in the last chapter as total British foreign investment by 1914 is equal to the $20 billion given below.

6. See Fisk, *The Inter-Ally Debts,* pp. 314–316.

7. See The League of Nations, *Memorandum on International Trade and Balances of Payments, 1912–1926* (Geneva: League of Nations, 1927), pp. 183–186.

8. See William McNeil, *American Money and the Weimar Republic: Economics and Politics on the Eve of the Great Depression* (New York: Columbia University Press, 1986), for example, p. 10. The book in general provides an excellent review of German foreign economic policy in the 1920s.

9. League of Nations, *Memorandum on International Trade and Balances of Payments,* pp. 183–186. This is based on returns to foreign investment, and assumes that these rates were roughly similar across states.

10. Ibid.

11. See Albert Hirschman, *National Power and the Structure of Foreign Trade* (Berkeley: University of California Press, 1980 [1945]), for a discussion of the political effects of the German trading system.

12. Kindleberger, *The World in Depression*, p. 159.

13. Among the explanations for the Great Depression are monetarist arguments, as in Milton Friedman and Anna Jacobson Schwartz, *A Monetary History of the United States, 1867–1960* (Princeton: Princeton University Press, 1963), Keynesian arguments, for example Peter Temin, *Did Monetary Forces Cause the Great Depression?* (New York: W.W. Norton, 1976), cyclical arguments, such as found in Joseph Schumpeter, *Business Cycles: A Theoretical, Historical, and Statistical Analysis of the Capitalist Process* (New York: McGraw-Hill, 1939), eclectic or "fortuitous" arguments, like Paul Samuelson's "Myths

and Realities about the Crash and Depression," in *Journal of Portfolio Management* vol. 6 (1979), pp. 7–10, and arguments centering on the failure of international economic leadership, such as Charles Kindleberger, *The World in Depression, 1929–1939* (Berkeley: University of California Press, 1973). This list is far from exhaustive; it is merely suggestive. The economic and historical literature on the subject is enormous.

14. Kindleberger, *The World in Depression.*

15. Barry Eichengreen, *Golden Fetters: The Gold Standard and the Great Depression, 1919–1939* (Oxford: Oxford University Press, 1992).

16. This use of the term "international regime" is from Stephen Krasner, "Structural Causes and Regime Consequences: Regimes as Intervening variables," in Krasner, ed., *International Regimes* (Ithaca, NY: Cornell University Press, 1983), especially p. 1.

17. Kindleberger, *The World in Depression*, esp. pp. 290–291 and 296–298.

18. Both Eichengreen's theory of the obsolescence of the gold standard, and Friedman and Schwartz's monetarism take this approach, although they identify different theories as misguided.

19. This is what Stephen Krasner suggests to explain both the continuation of British hegemonic policies after their decline in capabilities according to his measures, and the American failure to adopt these policies until World War Two, despite having the capabilities from the 1920s. Krasner, "State Power and the Structure of International Trade," in *World Politics* vol. 28 (1976), pp. 341–343.

20. Fisk, *The Inter-Ally Debts*, p. 275.

21. Fisk, *The Inter-Ally Debts*, pp. 275, 284–288, 310, 314–316, 348–349, and the League of Nations, *International Trade and Balances of Payments, 1912–26*, pp. 183–186.

22. S. G. Sturmey, *British Shipping and World Competition* (London: The Athlone Press, 1962), p. 37.

23. Fisk, *The Inter-Ally Debts*, pp. 348–349.

24. B. R. Mitchell and Phyllis Deane, *Abstract of British Historical Statistics* (Cambridge: Cambridge University Press, 1962), pp. 334–335, and Kindleberger, *The World in Depression*, p. 40.

25. Peter Mathias, *The First Industrial Nation: An Economic History of Britain, 1700–1914*, 2nd ed. (London: Methuen, 1983), pp. 300 and 436–437.

26. League of Nations, *Balance of Payments, 1930*, p. 30.

27. B. R. Mitchell, *British Historical Statistics* (Cambridge: Cambridge University Press, 1988), pp. 871–872, and Mathias, *The First Industrial Nation*, pp. 279 and 423.

28. Mitchell and Deane, *Abstract of British Historical Statistics,* pp. 355 and 368.

29. Donald Moggridge, *The Return to Gold, 1925: The Formulation of Economic Policy and Its Critics* (Cambridge: Cambridge University Press, 1969).

30. Charles Kindleberger, *A Financial History of Western Europe* (London: George Allen and Unwin, 1984), p. 332.

31. See, inter alia, Rodney Lowe, *Adjusting to Democracy: The Role of the Ministry of Labour in British Politics, 1916–1939* (New York: Oxford University Press, 1986). One indication of this expansion is the gradual replacement by the Labour Party of the Liberal Party as the more left anchor of Britain's two-party political system. Labour remained committed to financial orthodoxy, but tariff policy was not a part of this commitment.

32. For a discussion of the development of British tariffs during and immediately after the war, see O. Delle Donne, *European Tariff Policies Since the World War* (New York: Adelphi, 1928), part II, Chapter II.

33. Primary products tend to need a market for distressed goods most for two reasons. The first is that the factors of production used are usually less mobile than those used in manufactures. For example, a mine can only be used to produce a specific ore, and farmland is often suitable to only a few kinds of crops. The means that the loss of markets will be more difficult to compensate for. The second is that primary product exports on average come from less developed countries than exports of manufactures. Being less developed, these countries are likely less able to cope with economic dislocation.

34. David Calleo suggests that it was the change from a primarily self-equilibrating system prior to World War One to a much more consciously managed system after the war that was the primary source of monetary instability in the 1920s. Calleo, "The Historiography of the Interwar Period," pp. 247–249.

35. See, for example, Schuker, *The End of French Predominance*, part II.

36. This argument is consonant with Eichengreen's in *Golden Fetters.*

37. For a somewhat different interpretation that focuses specifically on institutional design rather than international finance and national identity, see Mark Brawley, *Afterglow or Adjustment? Domestic Institutions and Responses to Overstretch* (New York: Columbia University Press, 1999).

38. In the late spring of 1931 the Bank of England, acting unilaterally, lent $7 million to Austria's Creditanstalt, which was in the midst of a run. By mid-summer, the Bank of England itself was under such pressure that it was forced to request repayment of the loan and seek emergency credits in Paris and New York. This effectively ended its role as the lender of last resort. Kindleberger, *The World in Depression*, pp. 144–158.

39. For a description of the process by which the Bank of England came to request of the government that convertibility be suspended, see Stephen Clarke, *Central Bank Cooperation 1924–31* (New York: Federal Reserve Bank of New York, 1967), Chapter 8.

40. Abel, *A History of British Tariffs*, Chapter 5.

41. Abel, *A History of British Tariffs*, Chapter 4.

42. In fact, there was even some pressure to the contrary. "In his annual speech [for 1932] the chairman of the Midlands Bank . . . opposed Britain returning to gold, claiming that it had been off the gold standard for sixteen months, and nothing catastrophic had happened." Kindleberger, *The World in Depression*, p. 201.

43. The term "regionalism" as used here refers to any subglobal international grouping that represents a viable international economic system on its own. It need not be geographically contiguous.

44. Eichengreen, *Golden Fetters*, p. 338.

45. Fisk, *The Inter-Ally Debts*, pp. 284–288.

46. Kuisel, *Capitalism and the State in Modern France*, Chapter 1.

47. Fisk, *The Inter-Ally Debts*, pp. 284–228.

48. Ibid., p. 247.

49. David Calleo, "The Historiography of the Interwar Period," p. 231.

50. Schuker, *The End of French Predominance in Europe*, p. 5.

51. The original reparations plan called for Germany to pay annually 2 billion gold marks plus a sum equal to 26% of the value of German exports, for thirty-six years. Of this, France would get on average 52%. The German government adhered to this schedule for only half a year, but it did provide the original baseline for French expectations. Schuker, *The End of French Predominance*, pp. 14–15.

52. For an account of the background to and development of these crises, see Schuker, *The End of French Predominance*.

53. Richard Kuisel, *Capitalism and the State in Modern France: Renovation and Economic Management in the Twentieth Century* (Cambridge: Cambridge University Press, 1981), pp. 73–75. The effects of these crises on exchange rates can be found in Alfred Sauvy, *Histoire Économique de la France Entre les Deux Guerres* (Paris: Economica, 1984), vol. III, pp. 395–397. Sauvy also discusses the crises in Vol. I, Chapters III and IV.

54. See, for example, Judith Kooker, "French Financial Diplomacy: The Interwar Years," in Benjamin Rowlands, ed., *Balance of Power or Hegemony: The Interwar Monetary System* (New York: NYU Press, 1976), pp. 92–95.

55. Kuisel, *Capitalism and the State in Modern France*, p. 73.

56. Sauvy, *Histoire Économique de la France*, Vol. I, pp. 60–61.

57. Quoted in Kuisel, *Capitalism and the State in Modern France*, p. 75.

58. Ibid., p. 74.

59. Sauvy, *Histoire Économique de la France*, vol. III, pp. 396–397, gives exchange rates for the Franc in this period, and Lake, *Power, Protection, and Free Trade*, p. 165, provides an index of its instability.

60. This is the essence of Schuker's argument in *The End of French Predominance*.

61. Eichengreen, *Golden Fetters*, p. 192.

62. Delle Donne, *European Tariff Policies*, pp. 144–145 and 156–158.

63. For discussions of this crisis, see, *inter alia*, Kindleberger, *The World in Depression*, pp. 144–164, Clarke, *Central Bank Cooperation*, pp. 182–218, Fritz Weber, "From Imperial to Regional Banking: The Austrian Banking System, 1918–1938," in *Banking, Currency, and Finance in Europe Between the Wars*, ed. Charles H. Feinstein (Oxford: Carendon Press, 1995), and Eichengreen, *Golden Fetters*.

64. Bilateralist, managed approaches to international trade, because they mute the role of the market, also lessen the need for a currency for international exchange.

65. Sauvy, *Histoire Économique de la France*, Vol. II, Chapter VI.

66. See Stephen Clarke, "Exchange-Rate Stabilization in the Mid-1930s: Negotiating the Tripartite Agreement," in *Studies in International Finance*, International Finance Section, Princeton University, #41 (1979).

67. Eichengreen, *Golden Fetters*, pp. 70–71.

68. Leffler, *The Elusive Quest*, p. 56.

69. Lake, *Power, Protection, and Free Trade*, pp. 101, 126, 155.

70. See, for example, Robert Ferrell, *Woodrow Wilson and World War One: 1917–1921* (New York: Harper & Row, 1985), and Charles Mee, *The End of Order* (New York: E.P. Dutton, 1980).

71. Although, as suggested in Chapter 2, it is the gross rather than net position that is the more important measure for our purposes here.

72. Figures taken from Fisk, *The Inter-Ally Debts*, p. 310.

73. More specifically, in the six-year period from 1924 to 1929 Americans invested a total of $6,429 million, or an annual average of $1,072 million, abroad while the British invested a total of $3,301 million, or an annual average of $550 million. League of Nations, *Memorandum on International Trade and Balance of Payments, 1927–29* (Geneva: League of Nations, 1930), p. 30.

74. Ibid.

75. Fisk, *The Inter-Ally Debts*, p. 265.

76. League of Nations, *Balance of Payments 1931 and 1932, Including an Analysis of Capital Movements up to September 1933* (Geneva: League of Nations, 1933), p. 9.

77. This was exactly the way the American government was designed to work. See, for example, *The Federalist*, ed. Henry Cabot Lodge (New York: Modern Library, 1941), esp. #10.

78. For a seminal discussion of logrolling in American foreign economic policy, see Theodore Lowi, "American Business, Public Policy, Case-Studies, and Political Theory," in *World Politics* vol. 16 (1964), pp. 677–715.

79. See Lake, *Power, Protection, and Free Trade*, pp. 82–87.

80. This explanation of the motivations underlying American tariff policy follows that of Lake in *Power, Protection, and Free Trade.*

81. For a discussion of the creation of the Federal Reserve System, see Robert Owen, *The Federal Reserve Act* (New York: The Century Company, 1919). For discussion of its operation, see Marshall McMahon, *Federal Reserve Behavior, 1923–1931* (New York: Garland Publishers, 1993), and Carl Moore, *The Federal Reserve System: A History of the First 75 Years* (Jefferson, NC: McFarland & Co., 1990).

82. See, for example, Melvin Leffler, *The Elusive Quest: America's Pursuit of European Stability and French Security, 1919–1933* (Chapel Hill: The University of North Carolina Press, 1979), pp. 59–60.

83. To the extent that they are never mentioned at all in international economic histories of the time. For example, Stephen Clarke, in *Central Bank Cooperation*, refers to the Federal Reserve Bank of New York as the central bank of the country for international purposes, and to Benjamin Strong, its chairman, as America's central banker.

84. Examples of this latter activity include emergency loans to the United Kingdom in 1925 and Italy in 1926. Kindleberger, *A Financial History of Western Europe*, pp. 339 and 362. For a comprehensive history of Morgan & Co., see Ron Chernow, *The House of Morgan: An American Banking Dynasty and the Rise of Modern Finance* (New York: Atlantic Monthly Press, 1990).

85. Leffler, *The Elusive Quest*, p. 188. For examples of Morgan's role, see Kindleberger, *A Financial History of Western Europe*, pp. 352, 362, and 375, *The World in Depression*, pp. 22, 33, 39, 143–144, McNeil, *American Money and the Weimar Republic*, pp. 28–29 and 38, and Stephen Schuker, *The End of French Predominance in Europe*, pp. 141–253.

86. Eichengreen, *Golden Fetters*, pp. 70–71.

87. Fred Block, *The Origins of International Economic Disorder: A Study of United States International Monetary Policy from World War II to the Present* (Berkeley: University of California Press, 1977), pp. 20–21 and 30–31.

88. Moore's *The Federal Reserve System.*

89. At the International Financial Conference in Brussels in 1920, for example, the American representative was quoted as saying "that Americans will find it difficult to convince themselves in large numbers and to great amounts that Europe under present conditions is a good business risk. . . . We have always found opportunities for investment at home and have never grown into the habit of sending our money abroad." In other words, countercyclical lending could not be counted on and the government would not interfere in the market to promote it. Kindleberger, *A Financial History of Western Europe*, p. 334.

90. League of Nations, *Balance of Payments 1931 and 1932*, p. 9.

91. "American experience with international loans has not been sufficiently happy to encourage it to enter into additional ventures." Herbert Feis, quoted in Kindleberger, *The World in Depression*, p. 208.

92. Lake, *Power, Protection, and Free Trade*, pp. 163–173.

93. Ibid., pp. 199–200.

94. This interpretation of these tariffs follows Lake, in *Power, Protection, and Free Trade*, Chapter 6.

95. The logic behind these devaluations was sometimes questionable. For example, "Morgenthau [the Secretary of the Treasury] reported that Roosevelt once proposed raising the price [of gold] 21 cents because it was three times 7 cents and seven was a lucky number." Kindleberger, *The World in Depression*, p. 223.

96. See Beth Simmons, "Why Innovate? Founding the Bank for International Settlements," in *World Politics* vol. 45 (1993), p. 374.

97. See, for example, Leffler, *The Elusive Quest*, pp. 205–210.

98. For example, the World Economic Conference was convened in 1933, in part to address the issue of exchange rate stability. During this conference, Roosevelt stated that "when the world works out concerted policies in the majority of nations to produce balanced budgets and living within their means, then we can properly discuss a better distribution of the world's gold." This implies that the United States would only cooperate in taking action to end the crisis after the crisis was over. Needless to say, this effectively killed the conference. Kindleberger, *The World in Depression*, p. 216.

99. For a discussion of whether the choice of a different design expedient might have led to a more robust system, see Eichengreen, *Golden Fetters.*

100. See, for example, the quotation in note 98.

NOTES TO CHAPTER 6

1. International Monetary Fund, *International Financial Statistics*, January 1948. Based on official holdings of monetary gold.

2. The IBRD has become part of the World Bank and the GATT has been incorporated into the WTO, but both still exist and function.

3. Stephen Krasner, "State Power and the Structure of International Trade," in *World Politics* vol. 28 (1976), appendix, and Bruce Russett, "The Mysterious Case of Vanishing Hegemony: Or, Is Mark Twain Really Dead?" in *International Organization* vol. 39 (1985), p. 114.

4. Krasner, "State Power," and Russett, "Vanishing Hegemony." For a more general political statement of American postwar hegemony, see Robert Gilpin, *War and Change in World Politics* (Cambridge: Cambridge University Press, 1981), especially p. 231.

5. On the Soviet international economic system see, inter alia, Paul Marer, "The Political Economy of Soviet Relations with Eastern Europe," in Sarah Meiklejohn Terry, ed., *Soviet Policy in Eastern Europe* (New Haven: Yale University Press, 1984), especially pp. 163–165 and 169–171.

6. International Monetary Fund, *Balance of Payments Yearbook, 1947* (Washington: International Monetary Fund, 1948), p. 362.

7. Ibid., pp. 337 and 348.

8. Ibid., p. 348.

9. U.S. Department of Commerce, *Survey of Current Business*, February 1946, p. 26.

10. IMF, *Balance of Payments Yearbook, 1947*, p. 362.

11. Ibid., pp. 348–349, and Department of Commerce, *Survey of Current Business*, February 1953, Statistical Summary.

12. IMF, *Balance of Payments Yearbook, 1948* (Washington: International Monetary Fund, 1949). This does not include figures for Switzerland, which did not calculate balance-of-payments statistics at that time. This should not, however, affect the result.

13. These were not war debts in the traditional sense. Rather, the British government had spent this sum abroad, primarily in countries such as India and Egypt, in prosecuting the war. The governments of the recipient countries had agreed that this money, in sterling, would not be spent during the war. After the war, though, they remained as a constant and potentially immediate threat to the British balance of payments, unless the various governments involved agreed to some way of either writing off or postponing the use of these sterling balances.

14. IMF, *Balance of Payments Yearbook, 1950* (Washington: International Monetary Fund, 1951), p. 402.

15. Ibid., pp. 402–403.

16. IMF, *Balance of Payments Yearbook, 1950*, pp. 402–403, and Department of Commerce, *Survey of Current Business*, February 1953, statistical summary.

17. Department of Commerce, *Survey of Current Business*, December 1953, pp. 12–13.

18. IMF, *Balance of Payments Yearbook, 1950*, p. 402.

19. IMF, *Balance of Payments Yearbook, 1947*, pp. 362–365.

20. IMF, *International Financial Statistics*, January 1948.

21. Walter LaFeber, *America, Russia, and the Cold War, 1945–1980*, 4th ed. (New York: John Wiley & Sons, 1980), pp. 60–63, and Block, *Origins of International Economic Disorder*, p. 35.

22. For a brief discussion of the context of these programs, see Peter Gourevitch, *Politics in Hard Times: Comparative Responses to International Economic Crises* (Ithaca, NY: Cornell University Press, 1986), pp. 147–153.

23. Richard Gardner, *Sterling-Dollar Diplomacy in Current Perspective: The Origins and the Prospects of our International Economic Order* (New York: Columbia University Press, 1980), pp. 129–133.

24. Quoted in Gardner, *Sterling-Dollar Diplomacy*, p. 76.

25. IMF, *International Financial Statistics*, 1948.

26. See Roy Harrod, *The Life of John Maynard Keynes* (London: Macmillan, 1951), pp. 629–635.

27. See, for example, Fred Block, *The Origins of International Economic Disorder: A Study of United States International Monetary Policy from World War II to the Present* (Berkeley: University of California Press, 1977), pp. 38–40.

28. Although by the late 1940s this situation had in a way reversed itself, as Treasury (and Morgenthau as well, although he was no longer in charge) showed a commitment to the existing institutions, the IMF and World Bank, that they felt conflicted with the Marshall Plan. See Alan Milward, "Was the Marshall Plan Necessary," in *Diplomatic History* vol. 13 (1989), p. 235.

29. See Block, *Origins of International Economic Disorder*, for a discussion.

30. Gardner, *Sterling-Dollar Diplomacy*, pp. 193–194.

31. This discussion largely follows Gardner's in *Sterling-Dollar Diplomacy*.

32. John Ikenberry, however, argues that underlying these differences of opinion was a more fundamental epistemic community based on Keynes' ideas. G. John Ikenberry, "A World Economy Restored: Expert Consensus and the Anglo-American Postwar Settlement," *International Organization* vol. 46 (1992) pp. 289–321.

33. Quoted in Gardner, *Sterling–Dollar Diplomacy*, p. 130. See also Block, *Origins of International Economic Disorder*, pp. 46–47.

34. On the use of economic policy for political ends, see Albert Hirschman, *National Power and the Structure of Foreign Trade* (Berkeley: University of California Press, 1980[1945]).

35. Armand Van Dormael, *Bretton Woods: Birth of a Monetary System* (New York: Holmes & Meier, 1978), Chapter 9.

36. The New York banking community did, however, have some effect in toning down some of the more interventionist proposals for the IMF introduced at Bretton Woods and its preparatory conferences. See Eric

Helleiner, *States and the Reemergence of Global Finance: From Bretton Woods to the 1990s* (Ithaca, NY: Cornell University Press, 1994).

37. For a more general and conceptual discussion of multilateralism, see John Ruggie, "Multilateralism: The Anatomy of an Institution," in *International Organization* vol. 46 (1992), pp. 561–598. This specific understanding is reviewed there as well, p. 586.

38. See for example, Gardner, *Sterling-Dollar Diplomacy*, p. 109.

39. Once again, this reflects the government's negotiating position. Gardner, *Sterling-Dollar Diplomacy*, pp. 154–156.

40. Quoted in ibid., p. 196.

41. This view was most strongly held at the Department of State. There were some at the Department of Commerce who allowed that American employment levels did have an independent effect on American imports and foreign investment, and hence on international trade and investment levels. Gardner, *Sterling-Dollar Diplomacy*, p. 105.

42. Department of Commerce, *Survey of Current Business*, February 1946, p. 24. There is some question, though, as to how accurate this figure is, given wartime price distortions and particularly the difficulty of national accounting in an allied war effort.

43. See Winston Churchill, *The Second World War: The Grand Alliance* (Boston: Houghton Mifflin, 1950), pp. 683–684.

44. Department of Commerce, *Survey of Current Business*, February 1946, pp. 24–25, shows the dramatic and sudden increase in the magnitude and proportion of American exports requiring payment.

45. Harrod, *Life of Keynes*, p. 597.

46. Gardner, *Sterling-Dollar Diplomacy*, pp. 193–194.

47. Ibid., pp. 196–199.

48. Walter LaFeber, *America, Russia, and the Cold War*, Chapter 3.

49. For a discussion of the specific workings of this system, see van Dormael, *Bretton Woods*.

50. On the use of its monetary position to externalize adjustment, see Helleiner, *States and the Reemergence of Global Finance*.

51. Block, *Origins of International Economic Disorder*, Chapter 7.

52. John Gerard Ruggie argues that this domestic flexibility was designed to allow room for Keynesian demand management domestically in

all participant countries while preserving a liberal international order. To a certain extent this is true, but the structural position of the dollar nonetheless allowed the United States to externalize the effects of its domestic policies in a way that other countries could not. Ruggie, "International Regimes, Transactions, and Change: Embedded Liberalism in the Postwar Economic Order," in *International Organization* vol. 36 (1982).

53. Department of Commerce, *Survey of Current Business*, October 1972.

54. See E. F. Penrose, *Economic Planning for the Peace* (Princeton: Princeton University Press, 1953), pp. 106–107. It has been suggested that the United States purposefully manipulated British reserve levels to force them into the position of having to accept such a quid pro quo. See Gabriel Kolko, *The Politics of War* (New York: Random House, 1968), pp. 283–287.

55. See Gardner, *Sterling-Dollar Diplomacy*, Chapter XVII.

56. Ibid.

57. There were significant exceptions to and loopholes in this rule, but it nonetheless stood as the basic principle.

58. Gardner, *Sterling-Dollar Diplomacy*, pp. 374–378.

59. Political and Economic Planning Organization, *Atlantic Tariffs and Trade: A Report* (London: Allen and Unwin, 1962), part 1.

60. There is little evidence to suggest that exporters themselves were motivated to support the more generous American aid programs in the late 1940s. Rather, it was the government that was concerned with maintaining aggregate export levels to avoid recession. Robert Gilpin argues that aspects of the American provision of liquidity internationally, particularly the national foreign investment policy, were in fact deleterious to the American ability to export in the long run. And, in any case, the ability of the United States to export in the long term is not necessarily the primary interest of individual exporters. He does not argue, though, that this was true for the period in question here. Gilpin, *U.S. Power and the Multinational Corporation: The Political Economy of Foreign Direct Investment* (New York: Basic Books, 1975).

61. Ibid.

62. There are some histories that suggest that most of these economies were by that time fairly stable anyway, and that Marshall Plan aid was unnecessary for reconstruction. See Alan Milward, *The Reconstruction of Western Europe, 1945–51* (Berkeley: University of California Press, 1984). Even if it was not strictly necessary, however, the aid was nevertheless a significant boost to international liquidity.

63. What is said here of Europe is also mostly true of Japan as well.

64. The Marshall Plan was intended to increase American security with respect to the Soviet Union by creating an economically productive, market-oriented, and socially stable Europe as a buffer against communist expansion. See Michael Hogan, *The Marshall Plan: America, Britain, and the Reconstruction of Europe, 1947–1952* (Cambridge: Cambridge University Press, 1987), Alan Milward, *The Reconstruction of Western Europe, 1945–51*, and Charles Maier, "The Politics of Productivity: Foundations of American International Economic Policy After World War II," in Maier, ed., *The Cold War in Europe: Era of a Divided Continent* (New York: Marcus Weiner, 1991).

65. Robert Gilpin, *U.S. Power and the Multinational Corporation*, pp. 113–115.

66. For a discussion of their effectiveness see Bradford DeLong and Barry Eichengreen, "The Marshall Plan: History's Most Successful Structural Adjustment Program," *Working Paper # 91–184* (Berkeley: Department of Economics, University of California at Berkeley, 1991).

67. Neither the IMF nor the World Bank use the one country, one vote system common to many international organizations. They both allocate votes to members based on subscriptions—that is, the proportion of their capital historically contributed by the member. The relative size of American subscriptions gave the United States an effective veto over decisions in both bodies.

68. See, for example, John Lewis Gaddis, *Strategies of Containment: A Critical Appraisal of Postwar American National Security Policy* (Oxford: Oxford University Press, 1982), Chapters 5 and 6.

69. The process of development of the American balance-of-payments deficit is discussed in Fred Block, *The Origins of International Economic Disorder*, Chapter 6. Although his interpretation of this history is contentious, his description of the development of the deficit itself is relatively straightforward.

70. See Randall Hinshaw, *The European Community and American Trade: A Study in Atlantic Economics and Policy* (New York: Praeger Press, 1964), pp. 23–25, 47.

71. Robert Triffin, *Gold and the Dollar Crisis: The Future of Convertibility* (New Haven: Yale University Press, 1960).

72. Not everyone agreed that the deficit was necessarily a problem. Some proponents of an American leadership role argued that it was a legitimate method for providing international liquidity. See, for example, Charles

Kindleberger, *Balance of Payments Deficits and the International Market for Liquidity* (Princeton: Princeton Essays in International Finance, 1965).

73. For a detailed discussion of this decision, see Joanne Gowa, *Closing the Gold Window: Domestic Politics and the End of Bretton Woods* (Ithaca, NY: Cornell University Press, 1983).

74. For a review of this debate, see Howard Jones and Randall Woods, "Origins of the Cold War in Europe and the Near East: Recent Historiography and the National Security Imperative," in *Diplomatic History* vol. 18 (1993), pp. 251–276.

75. This logic does not necessarily favor the traditional security argument for American postwar policy over the revisionist export-driven argument, as Europe was also the United States' most threatened export market. The key point here is the disjuncture between American foreign economic policy and American foreign investment.

76. This is the essence of Ruggie's reading of the history in "International Regimes, Transactions, and Change."

NOTES TO CHAPTER 7

1. This is so because on the one hand it is difficult to speak of a country being predominant in investment in the international economy if another country has more investment, and on the other, with more than half of the total, a country would have more than everyone else combined.

2. Income earned abroad as a percentage of Swiss GDP has been well over 10% for over two decades. International Monetary Fund, *International Financial Statistics Yearbook, 1999* (Washington, IMF, 1999), pp. 862–867. Earlier data on Switzerland is less reliable, but a similar level of motivation is likely.

3. David Lake, *Power, Protection, and Free Trade: International Sources of U.S. Commercial Strategy, 1887–1939* (Ithaca, NY: Cornell University Press, 1988), pp. 30, 52–54.

4. This is discussed in some detail in Chapters 4 and 5.

5. Charles Kindleberger, *The World in Depression, 1929–1939* (Berkeley: University of California Press, 1973).

6. Stephen Krasner, "State Power and the Structure of International Trade," *World Politics* vol. 28 (1976), pp. 317–347.

7. John Conybeare, "Public Goods, Prisoners' Dilemmas, and the International Political Economy," *International Studies Quarterly* vol. 28 (1984), pp. 5–22.

8. On the political thought of Cobden, see Paul Cain, "Capitalism, War and Internationalism in the Thought of Richard Cobden," *British Journal of International Studies* 1979, pp. 229–247.

9. For a discussion of state identity in international relations, see Bruce Cronin, *Community Under Anarchy: Transnational Identity and the Evolution of Cooperation* (New York: Columbia University Press, 1999).

10. Krasner, "State Power and the Structure of International Trade."

11. Stephen Krasner uses the phrase "brittle stalks" to describe international systems that are highly institutionalized but of low durability and/or resilience. Krasner, *Sovereignty: Organized Hypocrisy* (Princeton: Princeton University Press, 1999), pp. 56–58.

12. John Gerrard Ruggie, "Multilateralism: The Anatomy of an Institution," *International Organization* vol. 46 (1992), pp. 561–598.

13. See, for example, Lipsey, Purvis, Sparks, and Steiner, *Economics* (New York: Harper and Row, 1982), pp. 706–710. If more than one source can issue a currency, it becomes a common pool resource, which creates the most difficult kind of collective action problem to solve. As such, currencies that can be issued by more than one source are very unlikely to command the confidence of a market that has access to sovereign currencies. On common pool resources in international politics, see J. Samuel Barkin and George E. Shambaugh, eds., *Anarchy and the Environment: The International Relations of Common Pool Resources* (Albany: The State University of New York Press, 1999).

14. National central banks hold a substantial majority of the voting power in the ECB, however. See the "Protocol on the European System of Central Banks and on the European Central Bank," Protocol 18 of the *Treaty on European Union* (Luxembourg: Office for Official Publications of the European Communities, 1992), especially articles VII and X.

15. One of the arguments against the need for a leader is the contention that leadership goods can be provided collectively. But models of this sort of collective provision usually assume constant benefits from leadership: See, for example, Duncan Snidal, "The Limits of Hegemonic Stability Theory," in *International Organization* vol. 39 (1985). The argument here is that the benefits can in some cases actually decrease as the size of the group providing it increases.

16. See Mancur Olson, *The Logic of Collective Action: Public Goods and the Theory of Groups* (Cambridge, MA: Harvard University Press, 1965).

17. On the effect of shadows of the future on international cooperation, see Kenneth A. Oye, "Explaining Cooperation under Anarchy: Hypotheses

and Strategies," in Oye, ed., *Cooperation Under Anarchy* (Princeton: Princeton University Press, 1986), pp. 1–23, and James D. Fearon, "Bargaining, Enforcement, and International Cooepration," *International Organization* vol. 52 (1998), pp. 269–306.

18. On the distinction between embedded liberalism and competitive liberalism, see Kathleen R. McNamara, *The Currency of Ideas: Monetary Politics in the European Union* (Ithaca, NY: Cornell University Press, 1998).

19. This can be understood either in terms of transparency, as per the institutionalist literature, or in terms of hegemony, as per the Gramscian literature.

20. Of official foreign exchange reserves, over two-thirds of the total are in dollars. Bank for International Settlements, *68th Annual Report* (Basle: BIS, 1998), p. 105. All figures are as of the end of 1997.

21. These quantities may be becoming too great, however, as will be discussed. For historical context, see the discussion of the Triffin dilemma in the previous chapter.

22. See, inter alia, C. Fred Bergsten and C. Randall Henning, *Global Economic Leadership and the Group of Seven* (Washington, DC: Institute for International Economics, 1996).

23. The EU hopes to capture some of the benefits of seignurage currently accruing to the United States as a result of the international role of the dollar. Whether or not the Euro will have any success at displacing the dollar is another question. On the benefits of seignurage, see Benjamin J. Cohen, *The Geography of Money* (Ithaca: Cornell University Press, 1998), pp. 123–125.

24. See, for example, Jagdish Bhagwati, *Protectionism* (Cambridge, MA: MIT Press, 1988), especially Chapter 1.

25. See, for example, Jeffrey L. Dunoff, "The Death of the Trade Regime," *European Journal of International Law* vol. 10 (1999), pp. 733–762.

26. GATT rules both allow for retaliation against dumping and, in article XVIII (B), for infant industry protection and protective action in cases of foreign exchange scarcity. All three of these releases from the demands of free trade hamper the market-for-distressed-goods function. World Trade Organization, *General Agreement on Tariffs and Trade 1994* (Geneva: WTO, 1994).

27. The most notable example of this role in the post-Bretton Woods era was the IMF's role in brokering settlements of the Latin American debt crises in the early to mid-1980s.

28. Organization for Economic Cooperation and Development, "Informal Consultations on International Investment," OECD News Release, 3 December, 1998.

29. Although estimates of daily international financial flows are in the trillions of dollars, total net international financing for the entire *year* of 1997, the highest to that date, was $865 billion. This suggests that a large majority of these daily flows are short term and do not represent new commitments. Bank for International Settlements, *68th Annual Report* (Basle: Bank for International Settlements, 1998), p. 143.

30. For a discussion of American policy toward foreign investment, see Robert Gilpin, *U.S. Power and the Multinational Corporation: The Political Economy of Foreign Direct Investment* (New York: Basic Books, 1975), esp. Chapters IV–VI.

31. See, for example, Martin Feldstein, "Domestic Savings and International Capital Movements in the Long Run and the Short Run," in *European Economic Review* vol. 21 (1983), especially pp. 132–133.

32. See, for example, Mervyn King, Mario Draghi, David Lipton, Andrew Sheng, Pablo Guidoff, and Martin Werner, "Reports on the International Financial Architecture," G-22, October 1998.

33. This usage follows that of the Universal Declaration of Human Rights and the International Covenant on Civil and Political Rights, as discussed in R. J. Vincent, *Human Rights and International Relations* (Cambridge: Cambridge University Press, 1986).

34. At its peak in 1994, Japanese GDP was over 69% of its U.S. equivalent in currency terms. By 1997, this ratio had fallen to less than half. International Monetary Fund, *International Financial Statistics Yearbook 1999* (Washington: IMF, 1999), pp. 547, 551, 931.

35. IMF, *Balance of Payments Statistics Yearbook*, various years.

36. The precise figure was $1,474 billion. The runner-up was Australia, at $250 billion. International Monetary Fund, *Balance of Payments Statistics Yearbook 2000* (Washington: IMF, 2000), Part 1.

37. IMF, *Balance of Payments Statistics Yearbook*, various years.

38. IMF, *Balance of Payments Statistics Yearbook 1998, Part 1.*

39. IMF, *Balance of Payments Statistics Yearbook 1998.*

40. This is also a 1997 figure. Ibid., p. 857.

41. Janice Thomson and Stephen Krasner, "Global Transactions and the Consolidation of Sovereignty," in Ernst-Otto Czempiel and James Rosenau, eds., *Global Changes and Theoretical Challenges: Approaches to World Politics for the 1990s* (Lexington, MA: Lexington Books, 1989), p. 201.

42. All data in this paragraph are from IMF, *International Financial Statistics Yearbook 1999.*

43. Eric Helleiner, *States and the Reemergence of Global Finance: From Bretton Woods to the 1990s* (Ithaca, NY: Cornell University Press, 1994), pp. 201–202.

44. IMF, *International Financial Statistics Yearbook 1999.*

45. The seminal expression of this view can be found in Chalmers Johnson, *MITI and the Japanese Miracle: The Growth of Industrial Policy, 1925–1975* (Stanford: Stanford University Press, 1982). This characterization was generally made in reference primarily to Japanese industrial policy, and not monetary policy.

46. See, for example, Robert M. Uriu, *Troubled Industries: Confronting Economic Change in Japan* (Ithaca, NY: Cornell University Press, 1996), Samuel Kernell, "The Primacy of Politics in Economic Policy," in Samuel Kernel, ed., *Parallel Politics: Economic Policymaking in Japan and the United States* (Washington: Brookings Institute, 1991), pp. 325–378, Daniel Okimoto, "Political Inclusivity: The Domestic Structure of Trade," in Takashi Inoguchi and Daniel Okimoto, eds., *The Political Economy of Japan, Volume 2: The Changing International Context* (Stanford: Stanford University Press, 1988), pp. 305–344, and Peter Cowhey, "Elect Locally—Order Globally: Domestic Politics and Multilateral Cooperation," in John Ruggie, ed., *Multilateralism Matters: The Theory and Praxis of an Institutional Form* (New York: Columbia University Press, 1993), pp. 157–200.

47. Compare note 25.

48. Japanese leadership in the creation of new regional economic institutions is expanding, however. See, for example, "Swapping Notes," *The Economist*, May 13, 2000, pp. 76–77.

References

Ashley, Richard, "The Geopolitics of Geopolitical Space: Toward a Critical Social Theory of International Politics," *Alternatives* vol. 12 (1987), pp. 403–434.

Bairoch, Paul, "Europe's Gross National Product, 1800–1975," *Journal of European Economic History*, vol. 5 (1976), pp. 273–340.

Bank for International Settlements, *68th Annual Report* (Basel: Bank for International Settlements, 1998).

Barbour, Violet, *Capitalism in Amsterdam in the Seventeenth Century* (Baltimore: Johns Hopkins Press, 1950).

Barkin, J. Samuel, and George E. Shambaugh, eds., *Anarchy and the Environment: The International Relations of Common Pool Resources* (Albany: The State University of New York Press, 1999).

Barnouw, A. J., *The Making of Modern Holland: A Short History* (New York: W.W. Norton, 1944).

Beik, William, *Absolutism and Society in 17th Century France: State Power and Provincial Aristocracy in Languedoc* (Cambridge: Cambridge University Press, 1985).

Bergsten, C. Fred, and C. Randall Henning, *Global Economic Leadership and the Group of Seven* (Washington, DC: Institute for International Economics, 1996).

Bernstein, Steven, *The Compromise of Liberal Environmentalism* (New York: Columbia University Press, 2001).

Bhagwati, Jagdish, *Protectionism* (Cambridge, MA: MIT Press, 1988).

Block, Fred, *The Origins of International Economic Disorder: A Study of United States International Monetary Policy from World War II to the Present* (Berkeley: The University of California Press, 1977).

Blussé, Leonard, and Femme Gaastra, "Companies and Trade: Some Reflections on a Workshop and a Concept," in Blussé and Gaastra, eds., *Companies and Trade: Essays on Overseas Trading Companies During the Ancien Regime* (The Hague: Leiden University Press, 1981).

Boxer, C. R., *The Dutch Seaborne Empire, 1600–1800* (London: Penguin, 1965), pp. 118–120.

———, *The Anglo-Dutch Wars of the Seventeenth Century, 1652–74* (London: Her Majesty's Stationary Office, 1974).

Braudel, Fernand, *The Wheels of Commerce: Civilization and Capitalism, 15th–18th Century, Vol. II* (New York: Harper and Row, 1982).

———, *The Perspective of the World: Civilization and Capitalism, 15th–18th Century, Vol. III* (New York: Harper and Row, 1984).

———, *The Identity of France, Vol. II: People and Production* (London: Collins, 1988).

Braudel, F. P., and F. Spooner, "Prices in Europe from 1450 to 1750," in Rich and Wilson, eds., *The Cambridge Economic History of Europe, Vol. IV: The Economy of Expanding Europe in the Sixteenth and Seventeenth Centuries* (Cambridge: Cambridge University Press, 1967) p. 458.

Brawley, Mark, *Liberal Leadership: Great Powers and their Challengers in Peace and War* (Ithaca: Cornell University Press, 1993).

———, *Afterglow or Adjustment? Domestic Institutions and Responses to Overstretch* (New York: Columbia University Press, 1999).

Burch, Kurt, *"Property" and the Making of the International System* (Boulder: Lynne Rienner, 1998).

Buzan, Barry, Charles Jones, and Richard Little, *The Logic of Anarchy: Neorealism to Structural Realism* (New York: Columbia University Press, 1993).

Cain, Paul, "Capitalism, War and Internationalism in the Thought of Richard Cobden," *British Journal of International Studies* vol. 5 (1979), pp. 229–247.

Cain, P. J., and A. G. Hopkins, "Gentlemanly Capitalism and British Expansion Overseas: I. The Old Colonial System, 1688–1850," *Economic History Review* 2nd ser., vol. 39 (1986), pp. 522–523.

———, "Gentlemanly Capitalism and British Expansion Overseas: II. New Imperialism, 1850–1945," *Economic History Review*, 2nd ser., vol. 40 (1987).

Carr, Edward Hallett, *The Twenty Years' Crisis, 1919–1939* (London: Macmillan, 1939).

Cassis, Youssef, *Les Banquiers de la City à l'Epoque Edouardienne* (Geneva: Librairie Droz, 1984).

———, "Bankers and English Society in the Late 19th Century," *Economic History Review*, ser. 2 vol. 38 (1985), p. 215.

Chandler, Lester V., *The Economics of Money and Banking*, 6th ed. (New York: Harper and Row, 1973).

Chapman, Stanley, *The Rise of Merchant Banking* (London: George Allen & Unwin, 1984).

Chaudhuri, K. N., "The English East India Company in the 17th and 18th Centuries: A Pre-Modern Multinational Organization," in Blussé and Gaastra, eds., *Companies and Trade: Essays on Overseas Trading Companies During the Ancien Regime* (The Hague: Leiden University Press, 1981).

Checkland, S. G., "The Mind of the City, 1870–1914," *Oxford Economic Papers,* new ser., vol. 9 (1957).

Chernow, Ron, *The House of Morgan: An American Banking Dynasty and the Rise of Modern Finance* (New York: Atlantic Monthly Press, 1990).

Churchill, Winston, *The Second World War: The Grand Alliance* (Boston: Houghton Mifflin, 1950).

Cipolla, Carlo, *Before the Industrial Revolution: European Society and Economy, 1000–1700* (New York: W.W. Norton, 1976).

Clapham, Sir John, *The Bank of England: A History* (Cambridge: Cambridge University Press, 1944).

Clarke, Stephen, *Central Bank Cooperation 1924–31* (New York: Federal Reserve Bank of New York, 1967).

———, "Exchange-Rate Stabilization in the Mid-1930s: Negotiating the Tripartite Agreement," in *Studies in International Finance*, International Finance Section, Princeton University, #41 (1979).

Cohen, Benjamin, *The Question of Imperialism: The Political Economy of Dominance and Dependence* (New York: Basic Books, 1973).

———, *The Geography of Money* (Ithaca: Cornell University Press, 1998).

Collins, Michael, *Money and Banking in the UK: A History* (London: Croom Helm, 1988).

Conybeare, John, "Public Goods, Prisoners' Dilemmas, and the International Political Economy," *International Studies Quarterly* vol. 28 (1984), pp. 5–22.

Cowhey, Peter, "Elect Locally—Order Globally: Domestic Politics and Multilateral Cooperation," in John Ruggie, ed., *Multilateralism Matters: The Theory and Praxis of an Institutional Form* (New York: Columbia University Press, 1993), pp. 157–200.

Cox, Robert, *Production, Power, and World Order: Social Forces and the Making of History* (New York : Columbia University Press, 1987).

Craig, Gordon, *Europe Since 1815* (New York: Holt, Rinehart and Winston, 1974).

Cronin, Bruce, *Community Under Anarchy: Transnational Identity and the Evolution of Cooperation* (New York: Columbia University Press, 1999).

Davis, Lance, and Robert Huttenback, "The Export of British Finance, 1865–1914," *The Journal of Imperial and Commonwealth History* vol. 13 (1985).

————, *Mammon and the Pursuit of Empire: The Political Economy of British Imperial Expansion, 1860–1912* (Cambridge: Cambridge University Press, 1986).

Davis, Ralph, *The Rise of the English Shipping Industry in the 17th and 18th Centuries* (London: Macmillan, 1962).

————, "English Foreign Trade, 1700–1774," in W. E. Michinton, *The Growth of English Overseas Trade in the Seventeenth and Eighteenth Centuries* (London: Methuen, 1969).

————, *The Rise of the Atlantic Economies* (London: Weidenfeld and Nicholson, 1973).

————, *English Merchant Shipping and Anglo-Dutch Rivalry in the Seventeenth Century* (London: Her Majesty's Stationary Office, 1975).

————, *The Industrial Revolution and British Overseas Trade* (Leicester: Leicester University Press, 1979).

Deane, Phyllis, and W. A. Cole, *British Economic Growth, 1688–1959*, 2nd ed. (Cambridge: Cambridge University Press, 1967).

Deibert, Ronald, *Parchment, Printing, and Hypermedia: Communication in World Order Transformation* (New York: Columbia University Press, 1997).

DeLong, Bradford, and Barry Eichengreen, "The Marshall Plan: History's Most Successful Structural Adjustment Program," *Working Paper #91–184* (Berkeley: Department of Economics, University of California at Berkeley, 1991).

Dodd, Nigel, *The Sociology of Money: Economics, Reason & Contemporary Society* (New York: Continuum, 1994).

Delle Donne, O., *European Tariff Policies Since the World War* (New York: Adelphi, 1928).

Deutche Bundesbank, *The Deutche Bundesbank: Its Monetary Policy Instruments and Functions*, 3rd ed. (Frankfurt am Main: Deutche Bundesbank, 1989).

Dickinson, Robert E., *The Western European City: A Geographical Interpretation* (London: Routledge, 1968).

Dunoff, Jeffrey L., "The Death of the Trade Regime," *European Journal of International Law* vol. 10 (1999), pp. 733–762.

Eichengreen, Barry, *Golden Fetters: The Gold Standard and the Great Depression, 1919–1939* (Oxford: Oxford University Press, 1992).

Ekelund, Robert, and Robert Tollison, *Mercantilism as a Rent-Seeking Society: Economic Regulation in Historical Perspective* (College Station: Texas A&M University Press, 1981).

European Communities, "Protocol on the European System of Central Banks and on the European Central Bank," Protocol 18 of the *Treaty on European Union* (Luxembourg: Office for Official Publications of the European Communities, 1992).

Fearon, James D., "Bargaining, Enforcement, and International Cooepration," *International Organization* vol. 52 (1998), pp. 269–306.

Federal Reserve Board, *The Federal Reserve System: Purposes & Functions* (Washington: Board of Governors of the Federal Reserve System, 1994).

Feis, Herbert, *Europe, The World's Banker, 1870–1914: An Account of European Foreign Investment and the Connection of World Finance with Diplomacy Before the War* (Clifton, NJ: Augustus Kelley Publishers, 1964).

Feldstein, Martin, "Domestic Savings and International Capital Movements in the Long Run and the Short Run," in *European Economic Review* vol. 21 (1983), pp. 129–151.

Ferrell, Robert, *Woodrow Wilson and World War One: 1917–1921* (New York: Harper and Row, 1985).

Fetter, Frank Whitson, *Development of British Monetary Orthodoxy, 1797–1875* (Cambridge, MA: Harvard University Press, 1965).

Fisk, Harvey, *The Inter-Ally Debts: An Analysis of War and Post-War Public Finances, 1914–23* (New York: Bankers Trust Company, 1924).

Friedberg, Aaron, *The Weary Titan: Britain and the Experience of Relative Decline, 1895–1905* (Princeton: Princeton University Press, 1988).

Frieden, Jeffry, "Capital Politics: Creditors and the International Political Economy," *Journal of Public Policy* vol. 8 (1988), pp. 271–276.

Friedman, Milton, and Anna Jacobson Schwartz, *A Monetary History of the United States, 1867–1960* (Princeton: Princeton University Press, 1963).

Gaastra, Femme, "The Shifting Balance of Trade of the Dutch East India Company," in Blossé and Gaastra, eds., *Companies and Trade: Essays on Overseas Trading Companies During the Ancien Regime* (The Hague: Leiden University Press, 1981), pp. 47–70.

Gaddis, John Lewis, *Strategies of Containment: A Critical Appraisal of Postwar American National Security Policy* (Oxford: Oxford University Press, 1982).

Gallarotti, Giulio, *The Anatomy of an International Monetary Regime: The Classical Gold Standard, 1880–1914* (Oxford: Oxford University Press, 1995).

Gardner, Richard, *Sterling-Dollar Diplomacy in Current Perspective: The Origins and the Prospects of our International Economic Order* (New York: Columbia University Press, 1980).

Gay, Peter, and R. K. Webb, *Modern Europe to 1815* (New York: Haper and Row, 1973).

Germain, Randall D., *The International Organization of Credit: States and Global Finance in the World-Economy* (Cambridge: Cambridge University Press, 1997).

Geyl, Pieter, *The Netherlands in the Seventeenth Century* (London: Ernest Benn Ltd., 1964).

Gill, Stephen, ed., *Gramsci, Historical Materialism and International Relations* (Cambridge: Cambridge University Press, 1993).

Gilpin, Robert, *U.S. Power and the Multinational Corporation: The Political Economy of Foreign Direct Investment* (New York: Basic Books, 1975).

———, *War and Change in World Politics* (Cambridge: Cambridge University Press, 1981).

———, *The Political Economy of International Relations* (Princeton: Princeton University Press, 1987).

Giuseppi, John, *The Bank of England: A History from its Foundation in 1694* (London: Evans Brothers, 1966).

Glamann, Kristoff, "The Changing Pattern of Trade," in E. E. Rich and C. H. Wilson, eds., *The Cambridge Economic History of Europe, Vol. V: The Economic Organization of Early Modern Europe* (Cambridge: Cambridge University Press, 1977).

Gourevitch, Peter, *Politics in Hard Times: Comparative Responses to International Economic Crises* (Ithaca: Cornell University Press, 1986).

Gowa, Joanne, *Closing the Gold Window: Domestic Politics and the End of Bretton Woods* (Ithaca: Cornell University Press, 1983).

———, "Public Goods and Political Institutions: Trade and Monetary Policy Processes in the United States," *International Organization* vol. 42 (1988), pp. 15–32.

———, "Rational Hegemons, Excludable Goods, and Small Groups: An Epitaph for Hegemonic Stability Theory?" *World Politics* vol. 41 (1989), pp. 307–324.

———, *Allies, Adversaries, and International Trade* (Princeton: Princeton University Press, 1994).

Gramsci, Antonio, *Selections from the Prison Notebooks of Antonio Gramsci*, edited and translated by Quintin Hoare and Geoffrey Nowell Smith (New York: International Publishers, 1971).

Grieco, Joseph, *Cooperation Among Nations: Europe, America, and Non-Tariff Barriers to Trade* (Ithaca: Cornell University Press, 1990).

Halpern, Nina, "Creating Socialist Economies: Stalinist Political Economy and the Impact of Ideas," in Judith Goldstien and Robert Keohane, eds., *Ideas and Foreign Policy: Beliefs, Institutions, and Political Change* (Ithaca, NY: Cornell University Press, 1993).

Harrod, Roy, *The Life of John Maynard Keynes* (London: Macmillan, 1951).

Heckscher, Eli, *Mercantilism* (New York: Garland Publishers, 1983 [1935]).

Helleiner, Eric, *States and the Reemergence of Global Finance: From Bretton Woods to the 1990s* (Ithaca, NY: Cornell University Press, 1994).

———, "National Currencies and National Identities," *American Behavioral Sciences* vol. 41 (1998).

Hilton, Boyd, *Corn, Cash, Commerce: The Economic Policies of Tory Governments, 1815–1830* (Oxford: Oxford University Press, 1977).

Hinshaw, Randall, *The European Community and American Trade: A Study in Atlantic Economics and Policy* (New York: Praeger Press, 1964).

Hirschman, Albert, *National Power and the Structure of Foreign Trade* (Berkeley: University of California Press, 1980 [1945]).

Hobson, John, *Imperialism, A Study* (Anne Arbor: University of Michigan Press, 1965 [1902]).

Hogan, Michael, *The Marshall Plan: America, Britain, and the Reconstruction of Europe, 1947–1952* (Cambridge: Cambridge University Press, 1987).

Huizinga, J. H., *Dutch Civilization in the Seventeenth Century* (New York: Frederick Unger, 1968).

Ikenberry, G. John, "A World Economy Restored: Expert Consensus and the Anglo-American Postwar Settlement," *International Organization* vol. 46 (1992), pp. 289–322.

Imlah, Albert, *Economic Elements in the Pax Britannica: Studies in British Foreign Trade in the Nineteenth Century* (Cambridge, MA: Harvard University Press, 1958).

International Monetary Fund, *Balance of Payments Yearbook, 1947* (Washington: IMF, 1948).

———, *International Financial Statistics*, January 1948.

———, *Balance of Payments Yearbook, 1948* (Washington: IMF, 1949).

———, *Balance of Payments Yearbook, 1950* (Washington: IMF, 1951).

———, *Balance of Payments Statistics Yearbook 1998* (Washington: IMF, 1998).

———, *International Financial Statistics Yearbook 1999* (Washington: IMF, 1999).

Jervis, Robert, *The Meaning of the Nuclear Revolution: Statecraft and the Prospect of Armageddon* (Ithaca, NY: Cornell University Press, 1989).

———, *Systems Effects: Complexity in Political and Social Life* (Princeton: Princeton University Press, 1997).

Johnson, Chalmers, *MITI and the Japanese Miracle: The Growth of Industrial Policy, 1925–1975* (Stanford: Stanford University Press, 1982).

Jones, Howard, and Randall Woods, "Origins of the Cold War in Europe and the Near East: Recent Historiography and the National Security Imperative," *Diplomatic History* vol. 18 (1993), pp. 251–276.

Kautsky, Karl, *Nationalstaat, Imperialistischer Staat und Staatenbund* (Nurnberg: Frankische Verlagsanstalt, 1915).

Kelly, Janet, "International Monetary Systems and National Security," in Knorr and Trager, eds., *Economic Issues and National Security* (Lawrence: Regents Press of Kansas, 1977).

Kennedy, Paul, *The Rise and Fall of British Naval Mastery* (Malabar, FL: Krieger, 1976).

———, *The Rise and Fall of the Great Powers: Economic Change and Military Conflict from 1500 to 2000* (New York: Random House, 1987).

Keohane, Robert O., "The Demand for International Regimes," *International Organization* vol. 36 (1982), pp. 325–356.

———, *After Hegemony: Cooperation and Discord in the World Political Economy* (Princeton: Princeton University Press, 1984).

Kernell, Samuel, "The Primacy of Politics in Economic Policy," in Samuel Kernell, ed., *Parallel Politics: Economic Policymaking in Japan and the United States* (Washington: Brookings Institute, 1991).

Kindleberger, Charles P., *Balance of Payments Deficits and the International Market for Liquidity* (Princeton: International Finance Section, Department of Economics, Princeton University, 1965).

———, "The Benefits of International Money," *Journal of International Economics* vol. 2 (1972), pp. 425–442.

———, *The World in Depression, 1929–1939* (Berkeley: University of California Press, 1973).

———, *Manias, Panics, and Crashes: A History of Financial Crises* (New York: Basic Books, 1978).

———, "Dominance and Leadership in the International Economy: Exploitation, Public Goods, and Free Rides," *International Studies Quarterly* vol. 25 (1981), pp. 242–254.

———, *A Financial History of Western Europe* (London: George Allen and Unwin, 1984).

———, *The World in Depression, 1929–1939*, rev. ed. (Berkeley: The University of California Press, 1986).

———, *The 1930s and the 1980s: Parallels and Differences* (Singapore: ASEAN Economic Research Unit, Institute of Southeast Asian Studies, 1989).

———, *A Financial History of Western Europe*, 2nd ed. (Oxford: Oxford University Press, 1993).

King, Mervyn, Mario Draghi, David Lipton, Andrew Sheng, Pablo Guidoff, and Martin Werner, "Reports on the International Financial Architecture," G–22, October 1998.

Klotz, Audie, *Norms in International Relations: The Struggle Against Apartheid* (Ithaca: Cornell University Press, 1995).

Koenigsberger, H.G., *Early Modern Europe 1500–1789* (London: Longman, 1987).

Kolko, Gabriel, *The Politics of War* (New York: Random House, 1968).

Kooker, Judith, "French Financial Diplomacy: The Interwar Years," in Benjamin Rowlands, ed., *Balance of Power or Hegemony: The Interwar Monetary System* (New York: NYU Press, 1976) pp. 92–95.

Krasner, Stephen, "State Power and the Structure of International Trade," *World Politics* vol. 28 (1976), pp. 317–347.

————, "U.S. Commercial and Monetary Policy," in Peter Katzenstein, ed., *Between Power and Plenty: Foreign Economic Policies of Advanced Industrialized States* (Madison: University of Wisconsin Press, 1978).

————, *Defending the National Interest: Raw Materials Investments and U.S. Foreign Policy* (Princeton: Princeton University Press, 1978).

————, "Structural Causes and Regime Consequences: Regimes as Intervening Variables," in Krasner, ed., *International Regimes* (Ithaca, Cornell University Press, 1983).

————, *Sovereignty: Organized Hypocrisy* (Princeton: Princeton University Press, 1999),

Kuisel, Richard, *Capitalism and the State in Modern France: Renovation and Economic Management in the Twentieth Century* (Cambridge: Cambridge University Press, 1981).

Kuznets, Simon, *Modern Economic Growth: Rate, Structure, and Spread* (New Haven: Yale University Press, 1966).

LaFeber, Walter, *America, Russia, and the Cold War, 1945–1980*, 4th ed. (New York: John Wiley & Sons, 1980).

Lake, David, *Power, Protection, and Free Trade: The International Sources of American Commercial Strategy, 1887–1939* (Ithaca: Cornell University Press, 1988).

————, "Leadership, Hegemony, and the International Economy: Naked Emperor or Tattered Monarch With Potential?" *International Studies Quarterly* vol. 37 (1993), pp. 459–489.

Lapid, Yosef, "The Third Debate: On the Prospects of International Theory in a Post-Positivist Era," *International Studies Quarterly* vol. 33 (1989), pp. 235–254.

The League of Nations, *Memorandum on International Trade and Balances of Payments, 1912–1926* (Geneva: League of Nations, 1927).

———, *Memorandum on International Trade and Balance of Payments, 1927–29* (Geneva: League of Nations, 1930).

———, *Balance of Payments 1931 and 1932, Including an Analysis of Capital Movements up to September 1933* (Geneva: League of Nations, 1933).

Lee, C. H., "Regional Growth and Structural Change in Victorian Britain," *Economic History Review*, 2nd ser., vol. 34 (1981), pp. 438–452.

Leffler, Melvin, *The Elusive Quest: America's Pursuit of European Stability and French Security, 1919–1933* (Chapel Hill: The University of North Carolina Press, 1979).

Lenin, Vladimir, *Imperialism: The Highest Stage of Capitalism,* in Lenin, *Selected Works* (Moscow: Progress Publishers, 1968 [1917]).

Lipsey, Purvis, Sparks, and Steiner, *Economics* (New York: Harper and Row, 1982).

Lipson, Charles, *Standing Guard: Protecting Foreign Capital in the Nineteenth and Twentieth Centuries* (Berkeley: University of California Press, 1985).

Lodge, Henry Cabot, ed., *The Federalist* (New York: Modern Library, 1941).

Lowe, Rodney, *Adjusting to Democracy: The Role of the Ministry of Labour in British Politics, 1916–1939* (New York: Oxford University Press, 1986).

Lowi, Theodore, "American Business, Public Policy, Case-Studies, and Political Theory," in *World Politics* vol. 16 (1964), pp. 677–715.

Maier, Charles, "The Politics of Productivity: Foundations of American International Economic Policy After World War II," in Maier, ed., *The Cold War in Europe: Era of a Divided Continent* (New York: Marcus Weiner, 1991).

Marer, Paul, "The Political Economy of Soviet Relations with Eastern Europe," in Sarah Meiklejohn Terry, ed., *Soviet Policy in Eastern Europe* (New Haven: Yale University Press, 1984).

Mathias, Peter, *The First Industrial Nation: An Economic History of Britain, 1700–1914*, 2nd ed. (London: Methuen, 1983).

Mathias, Peter, and Patrick O'Brien, "Taxation in Britain and France, 1715–1810: A Comparison of the Social and Economic Incidence of Taxes Collected for the Central Government," *Journal of European Economic History* vol. 5 (1976), pp. 601–650.

McCahill, Michael, "Peerage Creation and the Changing Character of the British Nobility, 1750–1850," in Clyve Jones and David Lewis Jones, eds., *Peers, Politics, and Power: The House of Lords, 1603–1911* (London: The Hambledon Press, 1986).

McKay, Derek, and H. M. Scott, *The Rise of the Great Powers 1648–1815* (London: Longman, 1983).

McKeown, Timothy, "Hegemonic Stability Theory and 19th century Tariff Levels in Europe," *International Organization* vol. 37 (1983), pp. 73–91.

McMahon, Marshall, *Federal Reserve Behavior, 1923–1931* (New York: Garland Publishers, 1993).

McNamara, Kathleen, *The Currency of Ideas: Monetary Politics in the European Union* (Ithaca, NY: Cornell University Press, 1998).

McNeil, William, *American Money and the Weimar Republic: Economics and Politics on the Eve of the Great Depression* (New York: Columbia University Press, 1986).

Mee, Charles, *The End of Order* (New York: E.P. Dutton, 1980).

Midford, Paul, "International Trade and Domestic Politics: Improving on Rogowski's Model of Political Alignments," *International Organization* vol. 47 (1993), pp. 535–564.

Milner, Helen, *Interests, Institutions, and Information: Domestic Politics and International Relations* (Princeton: Princeton University Press, 1997).

Milward, Alan, *The Reconstruction of Western Europe, 1945–51* (Berkeley: University of California Press, 1984).

———, "Was the Marshall Plan Necessary," *Diplomatic History* vol. 13 (1989), pp. 231–253.

Mitchell, B. R., *British Historical Statistics* (Cambridge: Cambridge University Press, 1988).

Mitchell, B. R., and Phyllis Deane, *Abstract of British Historical Statistics* (Cambridge: Cambridge University Press, 1962).

Moggridge, Donald, *The Return to Gold, 1925: The Formulation of Economic Policy and Its Critics* (Cambridge: Cambridge University Press, 1969).

Moore, Carl, *The Federal Reserve System: A History of the First 75 Years* (Jefferson, NC: McFarland & Co., 1990).

Morris, A.E.J., *History of Urban Form: Prehistory to the Rennaissance* (New York: Wiley, 1974).

Mundell, Robert, *Monetary Theory: Inflation, Interest, and Growth in the World Economy* (Pacific Palisades, CA: Goodyear Publishing, 1971).

North, Douglass C., *Structure and Change in Economic History* (New York: Norton, 1981).

North, Douglass C., and Robert Paul Thomas, *The Rise of the Western World: A New Economic History* (Cambridge: Cambridge University Press, 1973).

Nove, Alec, *An Economic History of the U.S.S.R.*, 2nd ed. (London: Penguin, 1989).

Okimoto, Daniel, "Political Inclusivity: The Domestic Structure of Trade," in Takashi Inoguchi and Daniel Okimoto, eds., *The Political Economy of Japan, Volume 2: The Changing International Context* (Stanford: Stanford University Press, 1988).

Olson, Mancur, *The Logic of Collective Action: Public Goods and the Theory of Groups* (Cambridge, MA: Harvard University Press, 1965).

Organization for Economic Cooperation and Development, "Informal Consultations on International Investment," OECD News Release, 3 December, 1998.

Owen, Robert, *The Federal Reserve Act* (New York: The Century Company, 1919).

Oye, Kenneth, "Explaining Cooperation under Anarchy: Hypotheses and Strategies," in Oye, ed., *Cooperation Under Anarchy* (Princeton: Princeton University Press, 1986).

————, *Economic Discrimination and Political Exchange: World Political Economy in the 1930s and 1980s* (Princeton: Princeton University Press, 1992).

Parker, David, *The Makings of French Absolutism* (London: Edward Arnold, 1983).

Parry, J. H., "Transportation and Trade Routes," in Rich and Wilson, eds., *The Cambridge Economic History of Europe, Vol. IV: The Economy of Expanding Europe in the Sixteenth and Seventeenth Centuries* (Cambridge: Cambridge University Press, 1967).

Penrose, E. F., *Economic Planning for the Peace* (Princeton: Princeton University Press, 1953).

Platt, D.C.M., *Finance, Trade, and Politics in British Foreign Policy, 1815–1914* (Oxford: Oxford University Press, 1968).

Political and Economic Planning Organization, *Atlantic Tariffs and Trade: A Report* (London: Allen and Unwin, 1962).

Ranum, Orest, *The Century of Louis XIV* (New York: Harper & Row, 1972).

Rogers, Nicholas, "Money, Land, and Lineage: The Big Bourgeoisie of Hanoverian London," *Social History* vol. 4 (1979), pp. 437–454.

Rogowski, Ronald, *Commerce and Coalitions: How Trade Affects Domestic Political Alignments* (Princeton: Princeton University Press, 1989).

Rosecrance, Richard, and Jennifer Taw, "Japan and the Theory of International Leadership," *World Politics* vol. 42 (1990), pp. 184–209.

Rostow, W. W., *The World Economy: History and Prospects* (Austin: The University of Texas Press, 1978).

Rubinstein, W. D., "Wealth, Elites, and the Class Structure of Modern Britain," *Past & Present* vol. 76 (1977), pp. 99–126.

———, *Men of Property: The Very Wealthy in Britain Since the Industrial Revolution* (London: Croom Helm, 1981).

Ruggie, John Gerard, "International Regimes, Transactions, and Change: Embedded Liberalism in the Postwar Economic Order," *International Organization* vol. 36 (1982), pp. 379–415.

———, "Multilateralism: The Anatomy of an Institution," *International Organization* vol. 46 (1992), pp. 561–598.

Russett, Bruce, "The Mysterious Case of Vanishing Hegemony: Or, Is Mark Twain Really Dead," *International Organization* vol. 39 (1985), pp. 207–231.

Samuelson, Paul, "Myths and Realities about the Crash and Depression," *Journal of Portfolio Management* vol. 6 (1979).

Sauvy, Alfred, *Histoire Économique de la France Entre les Deux Guerres* (Paris: Economica, 1984).

Schuker, Stephen, *The End of French Predominance in Europe: The Financial Crisis of 1924 and the Adoption of the Dawes Plan* (Chapel Hill: The University of North Carolina Press, 1976).

———, *American "Reparations" to Germany, 1919–33: Implications for the Third World Debt Crisis* (Princeton: Princeton University Department of Economics, 1988).

Schumpeter, Joseph, *Business Cycles: A Theoretical, Historical, and Statistical Analysis of the Capitalist Process* (New York: McGraw-Hill, 1939).

Simmel, George, *The Philosophy of Money*, trans. Tom Bottomore and David Frisby (London: Routledge, 1978).

Simmons, Beth, "Why Innovate? Founding the Bank for International Settlements," *World Politics* vol. 45 (1993), pp. 361–405.

Smith, Adam, *An Inquiry into the Nature and Causes of the Wealth of Nations* (Oxford : Clarendon Press, 1976 [1776]).

Snidal, Duncan, "The Limits of Hegemonic Stability Theory," *International Organization* vol. 39 (1985), pp. 579–614.

Snyder, Jack, *Myths of Empire: Domestic Politics and International Ambition* (Ithaca, NY: Cornell University Press, 1991).

Spruyt, Hendrik, *The Sovereign State and Its Competitors: An Analysis of Systems Change* (Princeton: Princeton University Press, 1994).

Steensgaard, Niels, *The Asian Trade Revolution of the Seventeenth Century: The East India Companies and the Decline of the Caravan Trade* (Chicago: The University of Chicago Press, 1973).

Stein, Arthur, "The Hegemon's Dilemma: Great Britain, the United States, and the International Economic Order," *International Organization* vol. 38 (1984), pp. 355–386.

Stinchcombe, Arthur, *Constructing Social Theories* (Chicago: The University of Chicago Press, 1968).

Sturmey, S. G., *British Shipping and World Competition* (London: The Athlone Press, 1962).

Taylor, A.J.P., *The Struggle for Mastery in Europe, 1848–1914* (Oxford: Oxford University Press, 1954).

Temin, Peter, *Did Monetary Forces Cause the Great Depression?* (New York: W.W. Norton, 1976).

Thomson, Janice, and Stephen Krasner, "Global Transactions and the Consolidation of Sovereignty," in Ernst-Otto Czempiel and James Rosenau, eds., *Global Changes and Theoretical Challenges: Approaches to World Politics for the 1990s* (Lexington, MA: Lexington Books, 1989).

Triffin, Robert, *Gold and the Dollar Crisis: The Future of Convertibility* (New Haven: Yale University Press, 1960).

———, *The Evolution of the International Monetary System* (Princeton, NJ: International Finance Section, Dept. of Economics Princeton University, 1964).

Tuchman, Barbara, *The Guns of August* (New York: Macmillan, 1962).

Unger, Irwin, *The Greenback Era: A Social and Political History of American Finance, 1865–1879* (Princeton: Princeton University Press, 1964).

United States Department of Commerce, *Historical Statistics of the United States* (Washington, DC: Bureau of the Census 1960).

———, *Survey of Current Business*, various issues.

Uriu, Robert M., *Troubled Industries: Confronting Economic Change in Japan* (Ithaca, NY: Cornell University Press, 1996)

Van Der Wee, Herman, "Monetary, Credit, and Banking Systems," in E. E. Rich and C. H. Wilson, eds., *The Cambridge Economic History of Europe, Vol. V: The Economic Organization of Early Modern Europe* (Cambridge: Cambridge University Press, 1977), pp. 358–362.

van Dillen, J. G., "The Bank of Amsterdam," in van Dillen, ed., *History of the Principle Public Banks* (New York: Augustus M. Kelley, 1965 [1934]).

van Dormael, Armand, *Bretton Woods: Birth of a Monetary System* (New York: Holmes & Meier, 1978).

Van Loon, Hendrick, *Fall of the Dutch Republic* (Boston: Haughton Mifflin, 1913).

Vincent, R. J., *Human Rights and International Relations* (Cambridge: Cambridge University Press, 1986).

Walker, R. B. J., *Inside/Outside: International Relations as Critical Theory* (Cambridge: Cambridge University Press, 1993).

Waltz, Kenneth N., *Theory of International Politics* (Reading, MA: Addison-Wesley, 1979).

Weber, Fritz, "From Imperial to Regional Banking: The Austrian Banking System, 1918–1938," in *Banking, Currency, and Finance in Europe Between the Wars*, ed. Charles H. Feinstein (Oxford: Clarendon Press, 1995).

Wendt, Alexander E., "Anarchy Is What States Make of It," *International Organization* vol. 46 (1992), pp. 391–425.

———, *Social Theory of International Politics* (Cambridge: Cambridge University Press, 1999).

Wilson, Charles H., *Profit and Power: A Study of England and the Dutch Wars* (London: Longman, Green and Co., 1957).

———, "Trade, Society, and the State," in Rich and Wilson, eds., *The Cambridge Economic History of Europe, Vol. IV: The Economy of Expanding Europe in the Sixteenth and Seventeenth Centuries* (Cambridge: Cambridge University Press, 1967).

———, *The Dutch Republic and the Civilization of the Seventeenth Century* (New York: McGraw-Hill, 1968).

Woodruff, William, *The Impact of Western Man: A Study of Europe's Role in the World Economy, 1750–1960* (New York: St. Martin's Press, 1966).

World Bank, *World Development Report 1997: The State in a Changing World* (New York: Oxford University Press, 1997).

World Trade Organization, *General Agreement on Tariffs and Trade 1994* (Geneva: WTO, 1994).

Index

SUNY series in Global Politics

James N. Rosenau, Editor

LIST OF TITLES

American Patriotism in a Global Society—Betty Jean Craige

The Political Discourse of Anarchy: A Disciplinary History of International Relations—Brian C. Schmidt

From Pirates to Drug Lords: The Post—Cold War Caribbean Security Environment—Michael C. Desch, Jorge I. Dominguez, and Andres Serbin (eds.)

Collective Conflict Management and Changing World Politics—Joseph Lepgold and Thomas G. Weiss (eds.)

Zones of Peace in the Third World: South America and West Africa in Comparative Perspective—Arie M. Kacowicz

Private Authority and International Affairs—A. Claire Cutler, Virginia Haufler, and Tony Porter (eds.)

Harmonizing Europe: Nation-States within the Common Market—Francesco G. Duina

Economic Interdependence in Ukrainian-Russian Relations—Paul J. D'Anieri

Leapfrogging Development? The Political Economy of Telecommunications Restructuring—J. P. Singh

States, Firms, and Power: Successful Sanctions in United States Foreign Policy—George E. Shambaugh

Approaches to Global Governance Theory—Martin Hewson and Timothy J. Sinclair (eds.)

After Authority: War, Peace, and Global Politics in the Twenty-First Century—Ronnie D. Lipschutz

Pondering Postinternationalism: A Paradigm for the Twenty-First Century—Heidi H. Hobbs (ed.)

Beyond Boundaries? Disciplines, Paradigms, and Theoretical Integration in International Studies—Rudra Sil and Eileen M. Doherty (eds.)

Why Movements Matter: The West German Peace Movement and U.S. Arms Control Policy—Steve Breyman

International Relations—Still an American Social Science? Toward Diversity in International Thought—Robert M. A. Crawford and Darryl S. L. Jarvis (eds.)

Which Lessons Matter? American Foreign Policy Decision Making in the Middle East, 1979–1987—Christopher Hemmer (ed.)

Hierarchy Amidst Anarchy: Transaction Costs and Institutional Choice—Katja Weber

Counter-Hegemony and Foreign Policy: The Dialectics of Marginalized and Global Forces in Jamaica—Randolph B. Persaud

Global Limits: Immanuel Kant, International Relations, and Critique of World Politics—Mark F. N. Franke

Power and Ideas: North-South Politics of Intellectual Property and Antitrust—Susan K. Sell

Money and Power in Europe: The Political Economy of European Monetary Cooperation—Matthias Kaelberer

Agency and Ethics: The Politics of Military Intervention—Anthony F. Lang, Jr.

Life After the Soviet Union: The Newly Independent Republics of the Transcaucasus and Central Asia—Nozar Alaolmolki

Theories of International Cooperation and the Primacy of Anarchy: Explaining U.S. International Monetary Policy-Making After Bretton Woods—Jennifer Sterling-Folker

Information Technologies and Global Politics: The Changing Scope of Power and Governance—James N. Rosenau and J. P. Singh (eds.)

Technology, Democracy, and Development: International Conflict and Cooperation in the Information Age—Juliann Emmons Allison (ed.)

The Arab-Israeli Conflict Transformed: Fifty Years of Interstate and Ethnic Crises—Hemda Ben-Yehuda and Shmuel Sandler

Systems of Violence: The Political Economy of War and Peace in Colombia—Nazih Richani

Debating the Global Financial Architecture—Leslie Elliot Armijo

Political Space: Frontiers of Change and Governance in a Globalizing World—Yale Ferguson and R. J. Barry Jones (eds.)

Crisis Theory and World Order: Heideggerian Reflections—Norman K. Swazo

Political Identity and Social Change: The Remaking of the South African Social Order—Jamie Frueh

What Moves Man: The Realist Theory of International Relations and Its Judgment of Human Nature—Annette Freyberg-Inan.